Everyone Can Win

A Real-World Guide to Competitive Athletics

Coach Tony Hardin

Copyright © 2019 Tony Hardin
All rights reserved.

**Published By
Publishing Advantage Group**

www.publishingadvantagegroup.com

Dedication

Jesus Christ, My Lord and savior

Linda, my loving and supportive wife

My sons Steve, TJ, and Ben – being your dad is the highest honor and greatest joy of my life.

Testimonials

"Coach Hardin was a tremendous coach and will always hold a special spot in my life, He had a unique way of reaching young men like very few I have ever been around. On the court, he taught me so many great qualities that I still use today, such as a strong work ethic and deep understanding of mental toughness and how to have discipline in every phase of your life."

- **Jason Witten** | Current Tight End for the Dallas Cowboys & Former Basketball star for Coach Hardin.

"Tony Hardin has won on and off the court as one of the most successful basketball coaches in Tennessee. He understands how athletics can prepare young people for a successful life whether we win or lose. Athletics is a great teacher of life lessons, read and learn from a coach that understands."

- **John Shulman** | Current President & CEO of the 720 Sports Group, 2nd winningest coach in University of Tennessee at Chattanooga history, 24 years of college coaching experience.

"Tony brought his love for high school athletics, commitment to helping students succeed and his winning attitude to Planet HS. He made the transition from coach and educator to the business world look easy through his personal commitment to the same values that he taught his players. Tony's sincerity and understanding of the challenges facing today's school athletic departments allowed him to succeed in dealing with schools from a businessman's perspective."

-Joe Hawkins | CEO and Founder of PlanetHS, LLC - Leading provider of software to High School athletic departments and state athletic associations

"I had the pleasure to coach with Tony Hardin at Elizabethton High School in the late 90's and early 2000's. I also had the unenvious task of coaching against Tony while we both served in middle school coaching positions years prior. In both situations, I observed Tony's patience, belief in every kid and the ability to control the tempo in a basketball game. Tony's ability to observe the situation and adjust a game plan accordingly was one of his greatest strength's. His easygoing demeanor has served him well and his ability to see the best in every person is something everyone could learn.

The ability to relate with people and kids from all walks of life and across multiple decades is indeed a unique trait. Tony's the type person who wants the best for everyone. When I applied for an administrative position, he was the first to support me, provide advice and want the best for my family and me. Tony's a real person who makes those around him feel better every time they interact."

-Rick Wilson | Director of HR/Support Services - Former Assistant Director of Schools, Maryville City Schools.

Contents

Introduction 1

Chapter 1 – Parents 5
The Most Important Support 5
Types of Robbing Parents 7
Vicarious Parents: 7
Helicopter or Lawnmower Parents: 11
Non-Involved Parents: 13
Overprotective Parents: 14
Meddling Parents: 16
Pragmatic Parents: 18
Parenting Lessons 20
Modeling: 20
Evaluating: 22
Create Teaching Moments: 24
Maintain Correct Perspective: 26
Allow Failure: 28
Allow Coaches to Coach: 28
Parameters & Expectations: 30
Counseling/Teaching: 31
Empowering: 34
Make Listening an Art: 34
Practicing Good Parent Posture 35
Poem - **TO MY ATHLETE** 40

Chapter 2 – Coaches 43
The Most Important Model 43
Ego 44
Chemistry 45

The Connection 46
    Make Listening an Art 48
    Speak in Different Tongues 50
    Giving and Gaining Trust 52
    Celebration 54
    Empowering Players 55
    Peer Pressure 57
    Criticism..58
    Overcoaching 62
    Be a Player Advocate 62
    Create Gateway Moments...........................63
    Motivation 66
    Teamwork 68
    Support Staff..68
A Coach's Prayer 69
Programing Success 70
Choose Your Legacy 72
The Best Teacher – Quotes 74
Practicing Good Coaching Posture.....................................77
Poem – **A Coach** **79**

Chapter 3 Players 81
The Approach is Key 81
Trophies 81
Triple Check..82
Earn It 83
Embrace Competition 85
Building Confidence..86
Seize the Day 88
Desire Coaching...89
Intense Listening 89
Defining Moments 90
Time Management..94
Honesty 94

Practicing Good Player Posture 96

Chapter 4 Teachers, Administrators, Extended Family 99
The Safety Net 99
Common Sense Approach 100
Encourage Leadership 101
The Critic 101
Practicing Good Support Posture 104

Chapter 5 Why Competitive Athletics 105
The Great Life-Skills Platform 105
Job Readiness 109
Interpersonal Skills 110
Help for Today 112
First Hand 114
Perspectives 114

Chapter 6 Conclusion 119
Everyone Can Win 119

Introduction

There are players, coaches, parents, and communities that may not currently deserve to win. But in this collection of reflections, I will explain how everyone can win. Yes, everyone can truly win and isn't that what society praises, isn't that the stuff a hero is made of, isn't that the goal of every player, coach, teacher, parent, and community to simply win?

In this book I will use real-world experiences to discuss the right and wrong way to approach athletics from the standpoint of each of the stakeholders and techniques to help you develop into the best version of the role that you play in a child's life. Whether or not you fit into one of the specific categories of parent, coach, administrator, or player, I believe you can find value in the attitudes and techniques that I will discuss. To those who do belong in one of these categories, the future of our country is in your hands because if we do not approach athletics with the correct frame of mind, then we are destroying the absolute best vehicle toward the mature development of our youth that we have at our disposal. It is my great contention that if the stakeholders' approach is correct, then everyone can win.

Competitive athletics is at an all-time high. More people are involved in athletic competition than ever before. According to the NYU Child Study Center, sports participation is a major factor in the development of most American children. About 20 million American children ages six through 16 play organized out-of-school sports, and about 25 million youth play competitive school sports. It is estimated that 30 to 45 million children ages six through 18 participate in at least one school or community-based athletic program.

The benefits of being involved in competitive athletics are almost infinite. Research from the NYU Child Study Center has shown that sports contribute to psychological well-being by reducing anxiety and depression and enhancing self-esteem. In sports, kids find a social milieu that can promote a spirit of social interaction, cooperation and friendship. Sports help kids think critically and solve problems, build self-discipline, trust, respect for others, leadership and coping skills, all of which form the foundation of character building. Sports have also been shown to improve academic and occupational outcomes, lower school dropout and deter delinquency and, of course, sports develop the mind/body connection by strengthening the body and training.

It is my strong belief that athletics is the last great classroom for life skills. Participants must learn to cope with the ups and downs of a season. They must also learn

Introduction

to have a work ethic if they are to improve the skills necessary to be successful in the sport of their choice. Character is developed during these seasons while dealing with both the winning and the losing. These athletes mature during competition as they learn to deal with emotions in a proper manner. What more could we desire out of an activity than for it to help develop – coping skills, work ethic, character, maturity, leadership, and self-esteem?

So, what could be the problem with competitive athletics? Athletics is very much like a good drug – there is a right and a wrong way to use it. Although I have coached numerous sports, the majority of the stories that I will share are based on my time as a basketball coach. In some of the stories I will be using fictitious names, but the experiences are true and written to the best of my recollection. It is my hope that these reflections will make the concepts within this manuscript come to life and, not to mention, a more enjoyable read. My dream would be that reading this collect will somehow help many stakeholders across the board to examine how we approach youth sports.

Everyone Can Win

Chapter I. The Parents
The Most Important Support

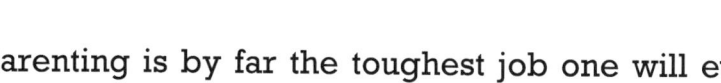

Parenting is by far the toughest job one will ever love. It is the greatest responsibility that a person embraces in their life and comes with both great challenges and great rewards.

I have been very blessed in my coaching career to have many parents who were very supportive of their child and the program in which they participated. These parents have a good grasp of the value of athletics within the maturing process of their child. Bottom line – they see the big picture along with the lifelong value in the total experience and do not focus on one specific situation. They allow their child to learn the values and life lessons that the ups and downs of being on a team present. These parents allow their personal expectations for their child to be set by his or her progression in the sport.

One of the best teams that I had the privilege of coaching had a group of parents who understood their role. Some of the players on this team did not have supportive parents, and the good parents just took up the slack as encouragers to each member of the team. Through all the pearls of the season these parents could always be heard saying positive things about the guys on the team. I believe that this group got it. They saw the value of the team and modeled correct behaviors for this young group of athletes. Because of such a positive experience, almost every member of that team has gone on to do great things in their chosen vocation. This type of atmosphere helps to build youth with an attitude of appreciation which I think is a huge key to success. I have seen this attitude of gratitude develop and watched many of these former players go on to be successful in their adult life because they go about their business with a vigor that is unmatched.

Supportive parents can be seen at almost every event, and they will quickly put to bed any negative conversations about the team, individuals on the team, or the coaching staff. This is a huge help to their child because it helps to build a positive atmosphere in which they can embrace the experience and grow. Supportive parents value the maturing process more than **any one moment**; and, therefore, they help to council their child and their teammates during the tough times that every season presents.

If a parent or parental figure is to teach his child how to grow into a mature adult, then the art of modeling correct behavior must be developed. Many of the reasons that an athlete does not have a positive experience in the sport that they participate in is rooted in the attitude of the parent. If the parent presents the incorrect attitude, then the athlete will have a very difficult time getting true value out of the experience. The best attitude for a parent is to be supportive, encouraging, and allow the child to <u>succeed</u> and <u>fail</u> without any pressure from the parent. This attitude will allow the child to experience the entire scope of what a competitive sport has to offer. Parents who do not exhibit this attitude become thieves because they are robbing their children of valuable learning experiences. Most of these parents do love their child, but they do not understand that the goal of parenting is to teach a child to make good decisions that they are happy with for years to come. In order to teach a child to make decisions, he or she must be allowed to practice making decisions. Most coaches would agree with me that correct practice does improve the result, so I pose this question: HOW is a child to learn the art of making decisions if they do not practice this endeavor. In the next section I will discuss diverse types of parents who steal from their children the vital experience that comes from living in the moment and coping with the short term and long-term effects of the entire situation.

Types of Robbing Parents

Vicarious Parents

Webster's definition of Vicarious – (experienced or realized through imaginative or <u>sympathetic</u> participation in the experience of another)

These are the parents who live through their children and live and die with each play. They push their children to the brink of collapse and will do anything in their power to make their child the star of the team. They feel and display major disappointment if the child fails in any way.

Let me put this in a real-life perspective with some real-life stories. The stories that I will share throughout this narrative are drawn from firsthand experiences, but I will use fictional names for each character to make sure that each person can keep their personal anonymity.

Vicky and Paul believe that their son is the best player to ever pick up a basketball, and they are convinced that anyone who even suggests that he should work to improve has lost their mind. As their son, Terry, develops, he becomes a very egotistical person and a selfish player. When Terry was a freshman, my coaching staff tried to get him to improve his skill and fix his very unorthodox shot; but because of the parents' attitude, he would never work to change his shot and improve his skill. He also felt like the school owed him something because he played basketball which lead to his lack of effort in the classroom. Terry had a decent high school career on the floor, but not a college coach in the country would give a smell of a scholarship because of his lack of fundamental skill development and his low academic record.

The Parents

By putting their son on a pedestal and supporting the idea that he was already great, they chose not to support an attitude that would encourage the youth to work. These parents sabotaged any value from playing – he did not transfer the experiences into life skills and did not play at all after high school. Their attitude robbed their son of a very valuable life-learning experience.

These vicarious parents cannot accept that their child might get value out of a smaller role on a team. I once had a player who went through our tryouts and our coaching staff just loved his effort but realized that he was limited with ability. We met with this player, Joe, and asked him if he would like to be a part of our team with the understanding that he would not see much playing time. Joe was thrilled and said that getting to wear the uniform was one of his proudest moments. Enter the mother who could not stand that HER son sat the bench. This mother walked out onto the floor during a game and took a picture of Joe sitting on the bench. Joe asked her why she chose to do that and then said that she wanted to save it to show it to her younger son so that he would not want to play team sports. Joe was so embarrassed by his mother's actions that he quit the team. What a shame because she tarnished something that Joe was very proud of, he understood the value of being a good teammate and took pride in just being on the team and being a part of something bigger than himself.

There are a lot of these types of parents in the youth

leagues around the world. One situation that still bothers me to this day happened because the parents of this child convinced him that he should be playing shortstop and batting in the leadoff position. He was at this time starting at second base and batting 5th which best suited our team and his skill level. The player and I had developed a great relationship, and he was a leader on our team.

The parents continually complained about this situation until they built a wedge between the two of us which caused friction on our team and robbed him of some valuable lessons about work ethic, accepting roles, appreciation, and becoming unselfish instead of selfish. What a great lesson he could have absorbed. Consider this: Selflessness is an essential key to happiness and fulfillment because it is very difficult to be happy if you are a selfish person. Once you get the one thing that you think will make you happy, it quickly becomes old, and on the horizon, there appears a new shiny thing that somehow the selfish person believes is happiness. If a person truly values giving, then they will feel a great sense of satisfaction from being on the giving instead of the receiving side. This approach will also yield a major growth in self-worth when this unselfish person is able to help someone. An unselfish person will have a much better shot at happiness than the person who frames everything around themselves.

*"Happiness is spiritual, born of truth and love.
It is unselfish; therefore, it cannot exist alone,
But requires all mankind to share it."*
Mary Baker Eddy

I also believe that even if a child initially feels that they have not been given a fair shot, but they make a choice to embrace the role given to them on the team, this athlete will soon grow proud of their contribution and feel good about the part that they play on the squad. This decision to embrace the role rather than reject it will in turn help build a more positive self-image. An athlete in this scenario can also develop life skills that will help them deal with the unfairness of the world in which we live with a more positive approach. Yes, the world is not always a fair place; but it is a wonderful place.

Helicopter or Lawnmower Parents

These are the parents that are always around and will never allow their child to deal with failure or success on their own terms.

I am a big believer in WORDS and the impact that they can have – negative or positive. Throughout this book, I will use quotes that I have gathered during my years of coaching and teaching. **Epictetus,** a Greek Philosopher, taught that you lived out your philosophy during your life. A great quote of his is one of my favorites and cuts straight to the point.

***"It is not what happens to you but how you react to it that matters."* – Epictetus**

Most real lessons are learned through experiences and the outcome of how an individual copes or deals with these situations. If a child or player deals with the situation with a negative attitude, later he/she should evaluate that outcome. This evaluation begins to build a basis for reflection for future decisions. This PERSONAL POOL of REFLECTIONS is key in the development of life skills. If I am camping and I need to relieve myself, then the first time I decide to pee into the wind, I should learn that there is a better approach to urinating outdoors.

If one never has the need to deal with tough situations because their parents continually tell them what to say, then no learning takes place and there is no building of this PERSONAL POOL of REFLECTIONS. Do not let this line of thinking lead you to the wrong conclusion about parents attending games. Parents should be supportive and attend games whenever possible. One of the most emotional conversations that I have had the privilege to be a part of involved a 50-year-old telling me how his mother never missed a game during his entire career. He felt that support but was never robbed of the lessons that he gained from competition.

Parents should understand that there are situations that should be "team only time" and parents being in close proximity during these team moments can take away many opportunities for the development of coping skills and maturity. Think about this: Maybe you should let the child that you love so dearly experience an amazing activity that will help them in their daily lives even when you are not around.

Non-Involved Parents

These are the parents who are never around and do not ask the athlete about how things are going on the team.

Although this type of parent does allow the child to experience failures and success on their own, the problem arises when the athlete needs to feel supported, loved, and hear the voice of common sense. I have coached players who have quit the team simply because the parents did not see the value in playing and, therefore, would not transport their child to the necessary places. Non-involved parents also do not allow the player to have some proud moments that come from being a part of something special and sharing that feeling with their family.

A coaching colleague related a story to me of a sophomore player who had the potential to become a good player and possibly even get a college scholarship. This young man asked the coach if he could miss a very important game because it was Valentine's Day, and he wanted to take his girlfriend out to eat. The coach said,

"You have already quit one time and were allowed to return, so you need to make a commitment to this team. If you miss this game, just turn in your equipment." At this point, the voice of common sense should have come from the parents and said one day is not worth an entire career. You can take this girl out another day – instead the boy turned in his equipment and never played again. What a shame to give up a sport in which he could have experienced many opportunities for personal growth and learning for one day of fun, not to mention the possibility of college funding.

"Never give up what you want most for what you want today." **Neal A. Maxwell**

As a side bar to this story, the girl in question broke up with him a week later and ended up dropping out of school the next year.

Overprotective Parents

These are the parents who are always afraid that their child is going to get hurt either physically or emotionally.

Talk about robbing a child from a maturing experience when mom is always saying, "Are you okay, Johnny?" then complaining that he is being overworked. How is a youth ever to establish a solid work ethic? Besides, there will be times when he will not be OK in the moment – but that is OK because he will develop some desperately needed coping skills. I once had a player who spent more time in the training room and on the sideline than he did on the floor. I am by no means an unsympathetic coach, but some soreness will occur with almost any physical activity.

Often these overprotective parents will blame any level of failure on someone or something other than the child (i.e. referees, coaches, teammates, conditions). What parents must realize is what this behavior is really teaching your child is how to be a great excuse-maker. People who are great at making excuses are seldom great at anything else. Additionally, these parents who continuously complain about the officials or coaches are not laying the proper groundwork for respecting authority. Not showing proper respect can plant an unwanted seed toward voices of authority that will lead to many unpleasant situations in youth and adulthood.

These overprotective parents have a misguided love for their child. If you keep a bird in a cage, it will not learn to fly properly. Teaching my sons to swim was an interesting endeavor because it was a great experiment between protecting them from drowning and letting them learn how to tread water. Parenting is always a difficult balance between these concepts, but I am a firm believer in the idea that allowing them to fall from time to time is a better teacher than any words that a parent could ever speak. Yes, experience is the best teacher.

Meddling Parents

This group is always trying to control what happens on the team by any means at their disposal. These control freaks will ask for a conference with the coach in order to express their concerns (which are really demands).

I once coached a player who was a junior, and his parents scheduled a meeting with me. They brought their son – we will call him Johnny. They expressed to me that Johnny did not want to play unless he could start and be a star on the team. This young man was a reasonably good player and was playing valuable minutes coming off the bench. I discussed with the parents that every player has a role, and that Johnny should embrace his current role on our very good team. I reassured the player and his parents that he was improving and if that continued to do so, he would probably break the starting line-up at some time. I even told them that I thought Johnny would earn a starting position during the summer workouts and be a starter all year during his senior campaign. He stated that if he could not be a star right now, he did not want to play.

Johnny was athletic and, in my opinion, could have become good enough to get a scholarship to a small college, but because his parents could not control his role on the team, they encouraged him to quit. Not only did his parents not encourage him to work to earn the position that he wanted, they encouraged him to quit. So, he did just that and quit our team. Johnny was robbed of this experience which would have taught him the value of demanding work or an understanding of how important every role in a group really is to both the success of this group and the individual's personal growth. The actions of Johnny's parents also took away the possibility of him becoming good enough to earn a college scholarship. This to me is one of the major tragedies that I observed in my 30 years of coaching.

Meddling parents will often be very vocal during a game which is a huge distraction to the team and their child. I have heard parents yelling directions to their child during games – "Johnny, be selfish," "Sarah, don't pass it, shoot it," "Billy, just run over him" – sounds unbelievable but misguided love can cause parents to do farfetched things.

I once talked to a colleague of mine, Harold Stout, who is a hall of fame college baseball coach. Coach Stout told me the story of some of these meddling parents who met with him and stated that he was not getting the best out of their son, Billy. They told the coach that their Billy would produce better if he batted first in the lineup. Coach Stout told them that they were correct to say that he was not getting the best out of their son and because of that, they should take Billy to another school. He also stated that their son, Billy, would not have a scholarship at the end of the current semester. So, again we see parents who robbed their child of valuable life lessons in accepting a role and supporting the team. When I recall these kinds of situations, I often wonder if Johnny ever learned the value of a good work ethic or people embracing their role within a group.

Pragmatic Parents

Parents may feel that giving the child a dose of the real word is always a clever idea, but it is my belief that children of all ages need to dream and imagine. These thoughts may be unrealistic, and the parents should council the child at the appropriate time on what is the best route to success based on the skills and aptitudes that the child has displayed, but this counseling should be done at a suitable age.

My wife recently shared with me how a young lady that she worked with had begun using the Elf on the Shelf during the Christmas holidays. This Christmas tradition is of a magic elf that watches to see how the children behave and reports to Santa on their behavior. A small elf is placed in unique places around the house, and the child is told that he/she should not touch the Elf. This young mother became frustrated that her young child touched the elf and so she decided to take the Elf away and abruptly tell the child that she had caused this action. My problem with this mother's decision and substantive action is that it killed the child's imagination. It is well-documented that imagination is the building blocks of creative thinking, and that children who have large imaginations often become very successful adults. I see no problem in allowing children to believe in myths at an early age because it does foster imagination. Truthfully believing that one might be rewarded for being well-behaved and generous is not a bad concept – some would just call that karma.

As children begin to mature, then it will become time to council the young athlete toward areas in which they have shown potential, but this should be done with caution. I have had players who were a part of my team that did not play a lot of minutes, but they were a very important part of our program and cultivated life skills through this experience. I can recall some of these role players' specific instances who have gone on to become coaches themselves, when the parents supported this idea of being a part of something and contributing what they could. But I can also recall some instances where the parents did not allow their child to accept this role and forced their child to quit stating that their time could be better spent doing something else, thereby robbing their child of a chance to see what it feels like to accept a different role on a team. Although quitting might be a better option than becoming a continuous negative influence on the child's attitude, I strongly believe that supporting the child's choice to accept this role is much more valuable in the big picture of life.

During my 30 years in the classroom, I taught personal finance and Life Skills and within these classes, I always found a way to use Chad Foster's Curriculum on

Teenagers – Preparing for the Real World. Within one of the lessons, Chad shares a story about his boyhood friend who loved to juggle, and how his parents would often scold him for spending so much time juggling. His mother used to tell him that his juggling was never going to get him anywhere in the real world. Contrary to his mother's thinking, this young man became an entertainer on a cruise ship where he made a very nice living with his juggling. It is a good thing that he did not listen to his parents who tried to kill his dream when he was young. Being a realistic counselor is the role of a good parent; not a sarcastic critic who squelches dreams.

Parenting Lessons

Modeling

The most overwhelming experience that occurs in nearly every new parent is the realization that your child is watching and modeling your every move. One of the most memorable commercials that I recall was a public service announcement titled "like father like son." I watched this commercial numerous times; but when I first became a father, it hit home to me. I can still recall it vividly in my mind. The commercial depicts a father painting the house with his young son, then driving and washing his Ford Mustang which was my first vehicle. Later, they both sit under a tree to take a rest and the father takes out a cigarette, lights it and lays the pack on the ground where the young boy picks it up and looks up to his dad. This was a very powerful visual picture to me as I entered the world of parenting and faced the realization that I would be the biggest role model that my son had during his formative years.

This heightened consciousness can be overwhelming and lead to stress and indecision especially in young parents who want so much to embrace this extreme responsibility of parenting. It is important to realize that you as a parent are a role model, but that this is only a small piece of being a good parent which also involves wearing the hats of teacher, counselor, motivator, provider, protector, disciplinarian, and best supporter. All these roles are extremely important; but during the years that the child is involved in competitive athletics, the role of supporter and counselor become paramount to embracing the experience as a teaching ground for life skills.

There is a shelf in house that is used to display a picture of my father in his Navy attire, the flag that was presented to me upon his death, and this quote:

> *A father is neither an anchor to hold us back,*
> *Nor a sail to take us there, but always*
> *a guiding light whose love shows the way.*

It is very easy for a parent to get caught up in the role as a provider and continue to give things to the child.

I feel that one of the toughest things to grasp is when to expose your child to certain things and how to balance giving with teaching values. If we as parents give our children everything, it is easy to see how they will never stop taking; but in turn if we teach our children to work and be generous, it is very possible that they will never stop giving.

The absolutely amazing result of embracing this enormous role of being a great parent is that in the pursuit of this lofty goal, we become the best version of ourselves.

I am sure that most parents would agree that being a parent has made them a better person – so I challenge each of you to allow your child to experience athletics just as you have experienced parenting.

Evaluating

From an early age a child sees his/her parent as the chief evaluator of all people and situations in the world. You are basically building a filter that your child will use for much of their life which acts as a glass through which to view the world. This is a huge responsibility; and I believe that while we should teach our children good values, we must still teach them to think for themselves and evaluate the messages that they are hearing. I grew up in a Christian household in which we attended church regularly, and I still remember vividly my father telling me that I should listen to the preacher intently but then evaluate his message using my own research. We should teach our children to be free thinkers and to contribute positive things into this world in which we live.

Realizing that we as parents are the great evaluators, it is important that we do not over evaluate our own child especially at the wrong time. *Often the part of the athletic experience that the child hates the most is the ride home after the game.* In most of my positions as a public-school coach, I required that the athletes ride the bus to and from the game. This helped to achieve the mindset necessary before the game and provided a down time with the team for chemistry building and to desensitize their emotions before facing their parents. In one of my positions, the school could not provide transportation due to budget issues and I found it very difficult to build the positive relationships that are necessary for coaching due to the fact that these athletes were exposed immediately to the parent evaluator during the ride home from each game. It is a widely agreed upon fact that athletics can have a powerful role in building self-esteem, so parents should be careful not to destroy those building blocks that are being established through athletics.

This parental evaluation process is very important in the development of decision-making skills in the child. Being a coach, I believe wholeheartedly in practice, and at a young age I would allow my children to make decisions and then help them to evaluate their choices.

This "practice" of decision making is a great teaching ground for life, but as a parent we must evaluate when the child is ready to make certain decisions and when they need some help with the problem at hand. When TJ was around four years old, he decided to take the dog shampoo and turn the entire bathroom into a soapy playground. This activity was unbeknownst to me until I heard loud laughter coming from the small bathroom. As I entered the room, I saw a little boy having the time of his life and a room full of white bubbles and suds. I found this very amusing, but I realized that I had to come up with some punishment for this activity because it was going to be a major effort to get the bathroom back to a usable state. I thought of my educational training and the premise of allowing the child to set his own punishment, so I asked TJ what he felt like his punishment for creating this mess should be. He stared around at the room for a moment and then looked up at me and said, "I do not know, I am not a dad yet." As I worked hard to contain my laughter, I realized that he was not ready for this level of decision making – just yet. TJ is now the loving father of two beautiful daughters, so he is now making dad decisions of his own.

Create Teaching Moments

Being a parent is a very high honor and although there are many guides to parenthood, I feel that being a parent is very much like being a teacher or coach. There are techniques that can be a great help, but each parent must use their individual personality and then consider the uniqueness of each child to develop a successful parenting philosophy. Raising a child in the world today is a major challenge and those who just raise a child like they were raised should evaluate how these methods work with this generation in the world of today.

Being a parent of three very unique sons myself there have been numerous times that I had to evaluate my parenting methods toward each child in order to teach the life lessons that would lead to success. The parent's main objective is to teach their child to think for themselves and make good decisions using the information that they are provided.

While navigating through a difficult financial time in my life, I decided to use the Christmas season to teach my three sons a valuable lesson. I purchased for them some individual presents, but the largest box under the tree had all three of their names on the tag. They were very intrigued by this box and questioned me about its contents. My response was that this was a "share present," and that they would be expected to share all items that were in the box. When it came time to open the box, they were very excited as they saw that the box included not one large item but numerous small toys, sports jerseys, jack rocks, etc. Through this experience my sons learned to share and to appreciate both what they received, and the fact that they had brothers to share in the fun. Appreciation is truly a magical thing because it takes us to a place in which we are fully aware of the situation and can be content in that moment. When my sons speak of Christmas this is always one of their fondest memories and the discussion of the "share present" always brings about joyous laughter and detailed descriptions of the contents and the fun they had playing with the inexpensive contents.

Maintain Correct Perspective

There are many athletic youth organizations around the world that are in the business of supporting young athletes. At the heart of most of these organization are good principals and ideas about how youth sports should be conducted. Little League Baseball and Softball is one of these organizations and it is comprised of 180,000 teams, their motto is - courage, character, and loyalty. These are very admirable concepts that should build a foundation that would allow for the development of great learning experiences for young athletes. Problems often occur when the aforementioned robbing parents do not keep a solid perspective of what youth sports is all about. I do appreciate that many Little League and youth fields now are adorned with signs, similar to the one below, that are meant to help all parents keep perspective during the competitive contest.

> ## Attention Parent's
> ## Here are Some REMINDERS
> ## from YOUR Child
> - I am still a KID
> - It is just a GAME
> - My Coach is a VOLUNTEER
> - The Officials are not perfect - They are HUMANS
> - NO College Scholarships will be handed out today.
> - NO Professional Contracts will be signed today.
> - You are my biggest ROLE MODEL

Being not only a parent but a grandparent, it is easy for me to see how a parent who is observing their child, their most loved and prized possession, can see great difficulty in allowing said child to experience anything negative. But if parents keep the correct perspective, they will see the great value in teamplay, and this outlook will serve as a gatekeeper to out of control emotions. Parents must play the part of the ADULT and remember that perception is truth to a ten-year-old and they most often will model the behavior of their parents. The correct perspective might also be called WISDOM which is the ability to think and act using knowledge, experience, understanding, common sense and insight. Be a WISE parent.

Allow Failure

When teaching a child to walk, every parent will see times when the child falls and gets up and tries to walk again and again. This concept is also true as the child grows. As parents it can be difficult to watch our children fail at something but facing failure and then deciding to work hard or to try something else is a great teacher. The world is full of very successful people who developed perseverance from facing many failures. In baseball, hitters who succeed only 30% of the time are considered great. It is a well-documented fact that Michael Jordan was cut from his freshman basketball team. At that moment he could have decided to give up on the game and try something else but what he did was made a commitment to work hard and make the team on the following year. As you probably know, he did just that and went on to become one of the greatest players ever. Facing failure will happen in everyone's life at some time. Allowing your child to experience that when you as a parent are still able to help them to evaluate and move on is great preparation for what life has in store.

Allow Coaches to Coach

It is very important that parents teach children to respect authority and supporting the coach as an early authoritative figure is a great way to instill this concept into the athlete. I have seen and heard this statement from coaches at all levels.

> UNCOACHBLE KIDS become UNEMPLOYABLE ADULTS
>
> LET YOUR KIDS GET USED TO SOMEONE BEING TOUGH ON THEM —
>
> IT WILL PREPARE THEM FOR LIFE!

Regardless of how you personally view the coach's style of coaching, your child is going to need to learn to cope with it in order to be a part of the team. You will find in the world of coaching as many different styles as there are different people in the world. These styles can have a wide range of possibilities from too harsh to too kind. The tough thing about being the major line of support for the child is that if you do not support the coach, then your child has no chance to learn from the situation.

One specific experience that I had as a coach was when a player's mother did not like me correcting her son and she let that be known on several occasions to myself and my assistants. I always maintained the philosophy that I would never allow the behavior of the parents to change how I treated their child. Every athlete is of the same importance because the sport that you are coaching is only a vehicle to teach the player about life. Do not get me wrong. I coached to win which meant that I did assign roles and corrected bad decision making, but I tried to keep the main thing the main thing as we shared the journey of the season. On one occasion after a game when a mother had voiced her opinion loudly during the game, the young man asked me after the game if we could have a meeting. I of course obliged him and as we sat in my office and he fought to hold back tears, he asked me to please just ignore his mother – he stated that she just did not understand sports very well. It was easy to see that he was embarrassed by his mother's behavior and he took it upon himself to approach being on the team with the correct attitude. Case in point, if the parent allows the child to work through their own experience while providing strong support and unconditional love then it almost always becomes a positive learning experience for the player.

Parameters & Expectations

The truth is that parenting is not an exact science because every person is unique in their attitudes, philosophies, and talents, but there are some guidelines that parents should consider when counseling their child. When I was 11 years old, I was playing on a school team and I came home from practice one day and began to complain about practice and criticize the coach and quickly my father stopped me and stated that he was not going to listen to me complain. He said, "Son, you made the choice to be on this team and while you are on the team you will have a positive attitude, if next year you do not want to join the team that is your choice but while you are on the team I expect you to respect your coach and your teammates." If my father had listened to my grumbling and then agreed with me then I would not be writing this book today because my experience with athletics would have taken an entirely different route.

I shared this story with a friend and he shared a similar story about a time when he was criticizing his coach and his father stopped him and made this very profound statement: "Son, your coach may not always be right but he will always be COACH and you may have a boss someday that is not always right but he will be your boss and you must respect that authority." He stated that he never forgot that statement and that it has served him well through some difficult employment situations.

The lesson in these examples is that a young athlete is still a child that needs parameters and expectations. When these moments arise, they are great teaching moments and should be seized by the parent immediately for the purpose of teaching. You could talk to a someone for hours about respecting authority this real-life scenario through the magic platform of competitive athletics will be the kind of experience and lesson that sticks with someone for a lifetime.

Counseling/Teaching

Being an educator throughout my career, I have

always embraced the role of teaching and counseling as being one of immense importance and responsibility. A phrase that I used with the most talented players comes to mind – "To whom much is given much is expected" – this is a Biblical principal (Luke 12:48). As parents, we become the first teacher for our child, and we already have a vital part to learning in place. In 1995, James Comer stated one of the premises that I built my professional and private success around, he stated, "No significant learning occurs without a significant relationship." What better and stronger relationship than that of a parent and a child for learning.

It is a strong belief of mine that we are what we experience, and for that reason I am a big proponent of athletes playing multiple sports. Every team, every season, every practice, every social gathering, and every game provide opportunities for the development of life skills. I also know that a coach cannot recreate the pressure that real game competition can provide. I have seen first-hand how success in a pressure situation in one sport can help the athlete to preform successfully in another sport. I have had the privilege of coaching many college athletes and two professional athletes. Ninety-five percent of those who reached the college level chose to participate in multiple sports while in high school, so the idea that you need to specialize to reach the next level is totally wrong. I have also seen an increase in injuries of the athletes who choose to play only one sport – it makes sense that overuse will cause injury because they are using the same muscle groups all the time. Many people are touting the praise of cross training, but for some reason this does not translate into the encouragement of athletes to play multiple sports. In has been my experience that some high school coaches frown on the athlete playing multiple sports, but I contend that this mental and physical training is better for the athlete than specialization.

Empowering

Going hand in hand with counseling is the art of empowering children. This is the idea of giving your child a choice and many parents use this technique very successfully with toddlers, but I think it can be employed with older children as well. I would encourage parents to discuss which sports the child might be best suited for and then empower the child from day one by allowing them to choose between two or three sports. Once they have picked, then a parent can use their counseling skills to help the child to understand the enjoyment and commitment that come with participating. I always like sticking with the idea that once the commitment is made, then the child must finish one entire season before they are allowed to discontinue playing that sport.

Make Listening an Art

An extremely important part of supporting your child in athletics is listening. Often parents think that they are authorities on their children when they are looking at their child through colored glasses that distort the view. If your child is sharing things with you or you notice a specific behavior, then you should do your best to interpret these messages.

When TJ, my middle son, was playing for me, it became apparent that he could only play about three minutes at a time before needing a break. He played extremely hard and my initial reaction was that he was not in good shape, but I also began to notice that his sleeping patterns had changed drastically. As Christmas approached, TJ began eating cups of ice and I brushed it aside as just a teenage fad. Finally, after the first of the year, I decided to take him to the doctor. The doctor asked him a myriad of questions and when he revealed that he was eating ice the doctor immediately ordered some blood test. Sure enough, the test came back that TJ had very low levels of iron in his system which was causing the shortness of breath and the need for sleep. The doctor stated that craving ice is a symptom of low iron. I still wish that I had taken him to the doctor initially instead of dismissing his symptoms.

If your child is talking to you about his team or teammates or coaches, then parents should do their best to put a positive spin on the situation and encourage your child to grow with each challenge. If your child is revealing things to you through his actions as my son was, it would behoove you to take a closer look. It is normal for young athletes to have some ups and downs and emotional times. They will often overreact to a bad day but if a pattern emerges or something different is observed in your child, then I would advise you to ask numerous questions and listen closely to the answers as they are being shared.

Practicing Good Parent Posture

My advice to parents would be to embrace parenthood with your heart, your mind, and your hands. In other words, choose your attitude and behavior based on what is best for your child in the long run. This will take some practice and maybe some soul searching to truly embrace the correct posture with your mind and what is truly in the mind will manifest itself into actions.

Watch your thoughts for they become words,
watch your words for they become actions,
watch your actions for they become habits,
watch your habits for they become your character,
watch your character for it becomes your destiny.
– Ralph Waldo Emerson

Many parents follow their own parent's example of how to parent without evaluating these actions, so realize that you are raising your child in a different world than the one you grew up in which means that reflection is a necessary action if you are to practice good parenting posture. It is very evident that most parents do love their children, but that simple love can manifest itself into actions that are not in the best interest of the development of the child if reflection and evaluation are not included in the picture.

Embrace the role of a supportive parent and council your child and watch your child seize and enjoy each situation as they mature with each experience. Realize that even if a tough situation occurs, your child will just grow by learning to cope in the correct manner. If you cannot embrace the snapshot of a supportive parent, then your best option is to be supportive from a distance and just allow your child to deal with the experience; and through coping with this experience – grow and mature. A good parent would never steal from their children – so do not rob them of a valuable learning experience that is second to none.

It is imperative that parents understand that every child is unique in their talents and needs. I have enjoyed the immense pleasure of parenting three sons (Steve, TJ, and Ben), and all three played basketball for me during their high school days. These guys are extremely different in their demeanor, their priority interest, and their learning style. Each of these young men gained valuable lessons about life during their athletic careers, and they have a similar view on how to be successful and on how to set priorities within their chosen lifestyle. I am very proud of how they each handled the tough task of both being a part of the team and playing for their father – which adds difficulty to the situation.

Steve loved everything about basketball, he loved practice, working on the game, thinking about the game, shooting, and watching the game. What he needed from me as a parent was just solid support and encouragement. Steve is now the men's college basketball coach at Lees McRae College in North Carolina where his team recently set the single season school win record. TJ enjoyed the competition and loved to accept the challenges that each practice and game provided, but after formal practice other interest took the place of basketball. What TJ needed from me was solid support and encouragement toward accepting his role on the team and toward his approach to the experiences that being a teammate provided. TJ is currently living in Hendersonville, North Carolina and is an area manager for Empire Distributing. Ben enjoyed the joy of victory. He worked hard to be able to achieve victory at every turn and could raise his level of play when the situation called for it. He did not like to lose and got discouraged at times. What Ben needed from me was support and encouragement toward working hard and becoming the best player and teammate that he could. Ben played a year of college basketball until an injury lead to him pursuing a career in the hotel industry. He is now the general manager of three hotels in East Tennessee.

As you see, they are three unique people who approached athletics in different ways, but in the situation of athletics, they really needed the similar things from me as and my wife as parents. The conscious act of creating a solid home climate filled with – love, understanding, and encouragement, without judgment or negative criticism, builds a foundation for athletes to excel. When I say EXCEL, I am speaking of embracing the athletic competitive situation in such a way as to actively learn real life skills. This act of excelling will propel participants into a better and happier life. School administrators speak often that a school should be a climate for learning, and the same holds true for the home of an athlete. Simply put, a good positive supportive climate creates the best environment for dealing with success or failure in a way as to learn from each unique situation.

One key to actively helping your child which you should draw from your personal knowledge of your child is in the area of goal setting. Every athlete should try to develop both short and long-term goals, but the maturity level of the child will direct you as to where the main focus should lie. The norm for useful goal setting would be that the younger the player, the shorter and more focused goals should be. Parents should help their children set goals because obstacles are those terrible things that a young athlete sees when he takes his eyes of specific goals. Also, most failures occur because someone traded a long-term goal for short-term enjoyment.

I began my coaching career as a middle school coach at Hunter School in Carter County. While I was coaching there, one of our teams won the state tournament in Tennessee. For three years I had a vision of achieving this goal. Understanding that my team could not see that vision, I worked to keep their eyes on short-term goals and we celebrated our short-term successes. When we arrived in Murfreesboro, the big message that I gave to my team was – we get to stay another night if we win. The players on the team will tell you they never thought about winning the state championship until that last game – they just wanted to stay in a hotel together one more night. Short term goal setting achieved a bigger goal and it taught them to do the same thing in life. I often think that a life may look like chaos when you are in the middle of struggles, but if you stay focused on doing what is right in each small situation, things will turn out in a good way. Basically, that chaos looks like a beautiful picture when remembering it after enough time passes. What a great life lesson these young men learned firsthand about setting a daily goal and how it will lead to a greater success.

Let your child fall down but encourage him to get up. Let your child win and teach them not to brag. Let your child get frustrated and encourage them to work to improve. Let your child accept his/her role on the team and encourage them to embrace that role but be ready if that role changes. Let your child have the joy of being part of a team and teach them to support the endeavors of that team. Be a parent who displays wisdom.

TO MY ATHLETE

I always knew this day might come
When you'd want to play a sport.
If that is what you want to do,
You have all my support.

I'll try not to push you;
But advice I may give
To help you in the sport you play,
And every day you live.

I hope you always give your all
And work hard every day.
This can help you to grow
In so many different ways.

I hope that on those winning days
You always win with class.
As we all know, those winning streaks
May one day be in the past.

I know somedays that you'll fall down.
Mistakes you're going to make;
But they can cause you to be stronger
If you bend and do not break.

The Parents

They can help you evaluate
Where you know you must improve.
They can give you determination
That will help you make it through.

You may or may not be the star,
But you still can live your dream.
Just do your best in the role you have
Because it's all about the team.

You do your part, I'll cheer you on.
We'll do the best we can.
Win or lose I hope you know
That I'm your biggest fan.

– Lisa Lowe
www.lovinglinesandmore.com

Everyone Can Win

Chapter II. The Coach
The Most Important Model

Being a coach is an enormous responsibility that no one should take lightly. Players will listen to a coach as though every word that comes out of his or her mouth is absolute truth. Players will also watch the actions of a coach with the strong assumption that his/her actions are absolutely perfect given the set of circumstances. A coach should always consider what is best for their players as their first priority. The concept that John Wooden believed was that if things are done correctly with the right priorities, everything else will work out – and the wins on the court are a byproduct of doing things the right way. Great coaches understand that the wins are not measured at the end of the season, but 10 to 15 years down the road when one can see if the maturing process yielded a good harvest in the individual athlete. My greatest victories are the players who have gone on to become great people, and it is an honor when they always call me coach.

I had the privilege of coaching for 30 years, and I have many of those long-term success stories that I am honored to share. Many of whom are now coaching and parenting. One of those former players is Jason Witten who is the tight end for the Dallas Cowboys. Jason recently received the Walter Payton man of the year award, and it was satisfying to know that he was in our basketball program for four years during his high school career. His grandfather did an unbelievable job of being the key figure in establishing solid priorities in Jason's life. During Jason's high school career, I watched him begin to mature, and I am honored that our program reinforced the values established by the most important key – his parental figure – his grandfather Dave Rider.

Ego

I realize that society tends to place coaches on a pedestal, and at the college and professional level that they are compensated very well if they are winning games. But in my coaching career I never made a basket, got a hit, or served and ace. Coaching is really not about what you know but what you can impart to your players so if a coach is to be revered, it is because he/she is a good teacher/counselor. It is my opinion that society should laud good teachers, but they are not miracle workers but great communicators. There is no secret information that one coach has about his/her sport that makes them magician, so coaches should be keenly aware of keeping their personal ego in check. Ultimately, youth athletics should focus on the child.

As players move into high school competition, the expectations grow and often a coach may feel the need to push an athlete to help them reach their potential. This is the natural order of competition, but I caution coaches not to become a bully but to use motivational techniques to push high school athletes. A coach who is a bully will misguide his/her focus from the athletes toward creating a climate where the emphasis is on themselves. Modeling confidence IS extremely important but if you coach long enough there will be seasons when you win a lot of games and seasons when you lose a lot of contests. Ultimately, high school athletics is about the players, so I challenge coaches to give your players the chance to enjoy the journey which could become the experience of a lifetime.

Chemistry

Team chemistry is something that young coaches often overlook but it is a big key to laying the groundwork for the magic of personal growth to take place. Building team chemistry is a process and it can be greatly hampered by individuals who refuse to buy into the team concept. The special thing about good team chemistry is that it supercharges both game performance and personal growth. In my experience, the best way to build good team chemistry is to create moments away from the field of competition for the players to interact. Most of the seasoned coaches that I have been around realize the value of team chemistry and will make numerous decisions that are for the purpose of building this magical force.

The Connection

The beginning to any relationship is a connection. The relationship between a coach and a player is a special one, and the better the connection the more influence the experience will have on the athlete. This is also true of a teacher. A player who establishes a true solid connection with a coach/teacher will value the words, lessons, and routines of that leader above almost any other source. Today's world is full of technology, and we have spawned a very unique generation that has used technology in their formative years more than any other. This new X-Box generation, as I have nicknamed it, makes fewer personal connections than any previous group; therefore, a solid connection means more than it ever has in history. To be an effective coach, the connection is an absolute necessity (by effective I mean a true teacher of life skills).

At Lees-McRae, my son does a great job of embracing this X-Box generation and not losing sight of the personal time needed for a real connection. Steve will use every avenue available to help build this all-important connection with his players including embracing their current love for technology and social media along with the knowledge that there is no substitute for one-on-one time.

Coaches must value the maturing process and the teaching of life skills above the short run goals. Winning games is important to reinforce those essential life skills, but winning games must not be the ultimate goal. If coaches take the win at all-cost attitude, it will devalue the experiences that the athletes have as far as learning good life skills is concerned. Decisions made during the season should be made based on what will make the team better for competition. This is not a contradictory idea because athletes should learn that being productive is necessary if one is to be successful. What they should not be taught is to bend the rules of the game to get an advantage in order to win. They should be taught, as Vince Lombardi said, that there are no shortcuts to success, and that the only place that success comes before work is in the dictionary.

Feeding the hungry players is a fantastic way to make this necessary connection. From time to time I would take the teams out to a meal or have them over to our house for a meal. A good coach will understand that providing food is not the real goal in these situations but giving your most valued possession to your players is the real goal. Truthfully, a wonderful way to help build any relationship is to share your most valued possession – your time. Today's athletes are starving for a personal connection and they are not fed very often.

I can recall many of these team meals and the give and take and laughter that most always accompanied each meeting. One particular day was when our star post player chose to be the last through the original line to eat.

We had a rule that everyone received one portion first and then could return later for seconds from the remaining food. This player proceeded to hide one of the sandwiches on the top of the fridge which he, by the way, was the only one tall enough to see. Much later in the day when he emerged with the sandwich, his teammates proceeded to question where he found the extra sandwich. He had to tell the truth. What a great teambuilding moment. This became one of the closest groups that I ever coached. Spending personal time with your players will help make this vital connection strong. It does not always have to be for a planned event or an extended period of time.

Make <u>Listening</u> an Art

Coaches tend to be what I call 'speakers,' and not what I call 'sponges.' A speaker is just like the one in your stereo which blares out sound. A sponge is something that soaks up anything that it possibly can. Coaches need to learn to LISTEN to their players. A coach who is a sponge will make a strong connection with the athlete and will understand the motivation within the make-up of individual players. Just asking about things not related to the sport will very often cause the player to open up to the coach who is willing to take the time to listen. The sponge coach is not trying to become the player's best friend but seen as a caring adult who is interested in what makes that individual unique. Listening is a huge way to establish a connection, and it makes the player feel better about the coach.

When I first took a job in a new town, the Athletic Director wanted me to meet many of the leaders in the school system. As I met many of these stakeholders, we had an array of discussions; but there was one that particularly sticks out in my mind. I had a short meeting with one of these leaders on the street, and it seemed to go well at the time. Later, that same lady relayed to a good friend of mine what a great hire that I was, and that it was her perception that I was a great person. As I recalled the conversation, I realized that I did not say very much at all. What I did was listen intently to the lady as she told me about the area. A magical thing happened when I just listened – she perceived me to be a high-quality person. (Listening contains within itself magical powers). Coaches need any magic that they can possibly get their hands on, so I highly recommend becoming a huge sponge.

On one occasion when our team had just won the region tournament as we returned to the parking lot of our school, one of our players started saying something that I could not understand. ERRBODY HEERE was the sound that I heard. I asked him to repeat himself, and he said it again ERRBODY HEERE. Then one of his teammates said, "Coach, what he is saying is that everyone is here waiting on us to celebrate the victory." This began a great dialogue between me and this particular team. With each bus ride they proceeded to teach me slang words and new sayings, and I listened as they explained and laughed together. What great teambuilding moments we had as they talked and I became a sponge.

Speak in Different Tongues

A good coach must also be able to convey his beliefs and thoughts in many ways. I believe that a good coach is an outstanding teacher, and how much the coach really knows is not the most important thing because what is truly important is how much the coach can teach his players. So, really in the end it is not what the coach knows himself, but what the players absorb enough to put into practice that really matters. Good coaches will perfect numerous types of communication by learning to say the same thing in numerous ways in order to reach each particular athlete. If you realize that each person is an individual, you realize that to connect with each player, you will need to learn to speak 'their language.' You will also learn that having one way to communicate will not reach all the needed ears. Through speeches, individual talks, drills, situational play, practice, working the referees, and games, the coach should send the same messages in a million different languages.

A good example of this happened to me early in my coaching career. I was conducting an instructional camp in which we had boys from first grade through ninth grade in attendance. During the day I gave what I thought was a very motivational talk about setting your goals high

The Coach

and working to reach that goal. The next morning, I was greeted by a seven-year-old who told me he had made his dad put his goal up as high as it would go, so that he could work to make it. I obviously did not get the correct message across to this young man.

When coaching at the high school level, I had a few tricks up my sleeve to slow down the game and buy time for me to think the situation through clearly. I had a standing order that if you fouled out of the game, you should make yourself hard for the official to find because by rule, he was to tell you that you had reached five fouls and had to leave the game. My players got very creative at hiding on the other end of the floor or behind the largest player as time progressed. On one occasion, our team had suffered numerous injuries, and a freshman was forced to play in an unfamiliar role. When he received his fifth foul which disqualifies him from play, he came over to the bench. I whispered to him "go hide." The young man proceeded to sneak off the floor to our dressing room. The official was very confused when he found only four players on the floor. The young man was only doing what I had instructed him to do but I had not done a good job of checking for understanding of what the phrase go hide meant in this situation.

Again, the message that I had sent was not received in the manner in which I had hoped that it would.

While developing these different ways to communicate

to your players a coach must always be in the business of checking for understanding and this is where the connection plays a big part. Sometimes a very brief and low-key conversation can help a player to understand a concept or specific role.

Giving and Gaining Trust

Learning to trust your players is a big key to creating a good environment for communication and making the necessary connection. Of course, before totally trusting your players, you must be around them enough to get a true picture of their character. Trust builds solid relationships and helps both individuals share the responsibilities necessary for success.

On one of our team trips we traveled to a popular restaurant that is located near Knoxville and famous for their hamburgers. As we finished our meal and the players lined up at the register, I took my familiar position near the front to monitor the behavior of these athletes. As one of our team leaders, Shawn Witten, was returning his change, he told the waiter that he had been short changed on the money he received back. The waiter insisted that Shawn had given him a ten dollar bill, and Shawn insisted that he had given him a twenty. I asked my team leader if he was sure, and he told me that his mother had given him a 20 in order for him and his younger brother, Jason, who was also on the team, to both have enough to pay for their lunch. After hearing his committed tone, I then trusted my player. I asked to see the manager and told him that I believed this young man had indeed been shortchanged. The manager said that the only way they would return any money was to stop taking any money and count out the entire cash drawer. The line to pay was backed up through most of the restaurant, and many of my players were waiting to pay. I looked at Shawn, and he shook his head as to confirm that he was certain that he had given the waiter a 20 dollar bill. The manager insisted that he was not going to believe my player over his employee unless they counted out the drawer. I told him to count the drawer and we would wait. I instructed the remainder of our team to proceed in line to the second cash register.

After the waiter counted out the drawer, he realized that he was indeed ten dollars over. Therefore, he handed Shawn his extra change and Shawn took the money and gave it to his brother and stated to the manager that he should know that the customer is always right. I then told the manager that he should give these two fine young brothers a free meal or some compensation for being put through this embarrassing situation in front of their peers. The manager stated that they do not give free meals but after some continued conversations, he decided to give the two brothers numerous boxes of the best cookies in the world. As I carried these boxes onto the bus, the players erupted with celebration and screamed, COOKIES. Shawn and Jason shared these cookies with the team, and I learned a valuable lesson about trusting my players. If I had simply given the younger brother money to pay for his meal, I would have wasted a perfect opportunity for connecting with this team by trusting them. This became a great team-building experience because we stuck together through the pressure of this situation. The cookie story is one of my fondest memories of that particular team.

Celebration

Celebrating things together is a terrific way to help teams' bond together. Coaches should take every opportunity to celebrate with their team. I made the mistake once of talking to the press before entering the dressing room after our team won a championship and it taught me to keep the team as the priority and handle the press at a more appropriate time. After that experience, I made a point to celebrate everything that we accomplished.

One summer while attending summer camp at Tennessee Tech University, I entered my team in what was called the Overtime tournament. This event consisted of taking the teams that choose to play and placing them in a tournament bracket then progressing through this bracket to determine a winner. The winning team was then awarded enough pizza to fill up 12 teenage boys. Each contest began with a tie score and three minutes on the clock. I always placed my team in this event because it was a great platform to teach decision making under pressure. Consider this: how big of a life skill is decision-making under pressure? During this specific summer our team had progressed to the final game. We were down two points with six seconds on the clock and during the timeout I set up what we called our bomb play. This play was executed by the inbounder throwing a three-quarter court pass to our biggest guy and then he would look to the sideline for a shooter who would be running to the three-point line. Our inbounder made a good pass to Jason Witten and he went up and caught the ball. He turned and looked for our best shooter, Michael Morrell, who was defended so Jason made the decision to shoot from that distance. As the ball went through the hoop, the entire team screamed with Jason –PIZZA!! We celebrated like it was 1999.

This idea of celebrating success is a great team builder because every player can be involved at the same level in the celebration and every player on a team has the same importance. The morale of the team is the glue that will hold the team together through a grinding season. Basketball is a team game but not all players can be involved in the game at the same level, so it is important to have moments that allow everyone to be involved on an even playing field.

Empowering Players

Many authorities on leadership are huge proponents of empowering the stakeholders. This process of allowing stakeholders to be involved on the ground level in decision-making processes had proved to be successful. Many principals empower teachers by allowing them to develop improvement plans and in today's business landscape, CEO's often empower their staff. This principal can also be effective in the world of competitive athletics.

On one of my high school basketball teams I was very blessed to have some seniors who understood the meaning of leadership. This particular team had finished their junior campaign by winning the regional championship. I called a meeting of this group to discuss who would be our captain for the upcoming season. I was considering alternating captains because every one of this group could display leadership qualities on different occasions, but I wanted to get their thoughts about who displayed the qualities necessary to be called captain. During the meeting, Vince and BJ spoke up and stated that they thought that Jordan should be our captain. Vince was our 6'7" standout post player who later attended Liberty University and played professionally for the New England Patriots in the NFL. BJ was our leading scorer who attended Tennessee Wesleyan on a basketball scholarship. Jordan was our most versatile player, but at that time he was not our most outgoing or outspoken player. The other seniors all quickly agreed that Jordan should be the captain for their senior campaign. Walter, our point guard, stated that Jordan did everything on and off the floor that our coaching staff asked him to do. This meeting was a huge moment for our team and for Jordan. Our team had showed how they had matured in their view of what a leader should be, and by empowering Jordan, his confidence grew by leaps and bounds. He went on to have a great senior season and was the captain on a team that made the first state tournament appearance for our school in many years.

Peer Pressure

Coaches often talk about building a culture that helps the athlete to excel, another label that could be used is positive peer pressure. If the team culture is to work hard on your skill, then players who are not hard workers will normally subscribe to what the majority of the team is doing. Good coaches will use this idea of positive peer pressure as they build their team and this concept becomes a great way to hold players accountable. The correct use of peer pressure can be critical as players move up into more competitive situations, in my career I found that public criticism is something that coaches must be very careful about because this can move the peer pressure to a negative place. It is one thing to point out mistakes in a practice setting but pointing fingers during a competitive contest and embarrassing the athlete can be a slippery slope. Coaches and positive peer pressure should hold the athlete accountable for effort, but performance can vary from contest to contest. Every coach must develop their own unique personality and techniques to use peer pressure in a way that helps the athlete to develop.

Positive peer pressure can become the best friend of a coach because it can hold the athlete accountable without the coach saying a word. One of the key principals that I tried to teach each to my teams was to always be prompt. When I was the coordinator of cooperative education, I taught interview skills and the first steps to a successful interview is to be early and dressed correctly. This is also just a great life skill because no boss wants and employee who is continuous late. I felt that if we had a time to meet as a team for anything that the players should be early, it is actually rude to keep others waiting. I began using the saying, "if you are on time – you are late." This became a statement that my players would say to each other. I can clearly recall that on the occasion that a player would be late they would stay after practice voluntarily to make up for the missed time. There were occasions when I might have understood that some circumstances were out of the players control, but they took pride in putting in the same amount of time as their teammates.

Criticism

A major part of coach's duties is to put players into a situation where they can have an opportunity to be successful and to teach them how to make good decisions in that situation. In order to achieve that lofty goal, it is imperative that the coach know how to criticize the team and each individual in a way to help them grow as a player and a person.

It can often be helpful to allow players to see themselves through the eyes of an observer. On one of my more successful teams, we had a player who was a gifted offensive player. In his younger years he was almost always the leading scorer and considered the best player. Because of his history, he had developed a great deal of confidence which helped him to play to a high level. Also, as a biproduct of his history of success, he had not experienced frustration very often which meant that he would become exasperated when things did not go his way. Helping him to develop solid coping skills when presented with frustration was something that I knew as a coach was important to his life, his success, and the success of our team. As I tried different techniques to expand his coping skills, I considered who he was as a person and what motivated his success. This guy was a good kid and he thrived on his success and coming out of situations looking good, he was destined to be a college level player. So, I developed a plan to simply allow him to step back and see himself in a different light. On one evening I invited him to my house for a film study; I had prepared a series of video clips that did not show him in a good light. I simply played the clips and sat quietly with him as he intently watched himself trying to deal with frustration and often showing negative emotion. At the end of the viewing, he looked at me in a very humble way and stated, "Coach, I look like a jerk." He had looked at himself from the outside as an observer and it caused him to see his actions in <u>a different light.</u> This experience helped him to develop coping skills which he used on and off the floor in a way that led to a higher level of success.

I wanted our coaches to "Praise Loudly & Criticize Softly" and to help remind us daily of this philosophy, I made a sign with that phrase embossed clearly on it and placed it directly over the exit. Almost every high school coach uses the tool of video review whether with team meetings or individuals – I implore that coaches should consider what technique will work best in this session of reviewing the tape. The common idea of just attacking poor performance may not help to reach the goal of improvement. I do realize that many coaches quote the phrase, "the tape does not lie" and this is a true statement. But I feel strongly that discussing how to make better decisions in these situations will normally lead to a better outcome than the philosophy of simply pointing out mistakes. The goal is to teach players how to make good decisions. The great Larry Bird once made this statement in an interview: "Pressure? I don't know what that is." He made this statement because he prepared so well that he always felt like he knew what to do. PRESSURE is truly not knowing what to do, therefore good coaches teach decision- making skills so that their players will know what to do in any situation. It is important to build confidence in players so making it a point to not always talk about the negative but to accentuate the positive is very important.

The Coach

Coaches should always be in the process of evaluating – not just their team and their staff but ultimately themselves. When I first began my coaching career, I was set with the task of coaching young boys. Being very young and full of enthusiasm, I would often challenge the young men by raising my voice, as some of my coaches had done with me. This technique often worked in the short term, but I found that it did not reach my goal of teaching decision making and providing a groundwork for future improvement. At one point in my career, I was tasked with the job of coaching young girls in a program that had never been very successful. During the early stages of building this program just as we finished practice, I noticed one of my players, Amy, sitting by herself and crying. She was probably one of the toughest players that I ever coached (of any gender) so I was confused as to why she would be crying. I actually thought she had just completed a very good practice, so my curiosity drew me toward where she was sitting. When I approached her, she looked up at me and could not stop the tears from falling. I asked her, "Amy, why are you crying?" She stated to me, "You hurt my feelings." I explained to her that I viewed her as a fabulous person and a good player, and my words were meant to challenge her – not to hurt her feelings. I believe that this moment made me a better coach because I learned to make it a point to criticize the action, NOT the person when pointing out mistakes.

Overcoaching

I think many young coaches tend to overcoach their specific game. I was guilty of this, but as I became a more seasoned coach, I realized that allowing my players some creativity was a great thing. Giving them freedom within the team plan not only helped them to enjoy the game more, but it helped them to develop some unique skills. Watching players develop new skills was a joy for me and on occasion it actually changed my philosophy toward the game. Early on I thought that the closer you were to the basket, the better chance you had to make the shot. As my players developed better range, I realized that if you could make a shot seven out of ten times in game, then it was a good shot. I also believed that if you were on balance which I translated into jumping straight up, then you had a better chance of making the shot. My youngest son Ben developed a good floater which changed how I viewed being on balance. Regardless of the sport that you coach, I encourage you to give your players some freedoms within the system that you teach.

Be a Player Advocate

The relationship between a coach and a player is a special one that contains many facets and should be positively fostered as often as possible. I took it upon myself to stick up for my players as often as possible in public and address my concerns in a private setting. In the game of basketball, one of the most unselfish plays is the act of drawing a charge. In order to accomplish this, a player must establish correct guarding position and basically allow his/her opponent to run over them. It was a policy on my teams that if someone drew a charge the entire bench would stand up and cheer for their teammate's unselfish actions. I would take it upon myself to address the official when a player attempted to take a charge but did not get the call. My statement would be something like, "Mr. Ref, it is hard to get a kid to stand in front of a train." Even when I thought that the official had made the correct call, I would stick up for my player because of his/her effort.

Create Gateway Moments

We have all heard the phrase gateway drug which infers that use of a specific drug creates an easy gateway to much more potent and harmful drugs. My use of the term gateway moments is a play on that concept but in a positive way. The term is really an edification of what positive words or decisions from a coach to a player can mean to his/her self-esteem and ultimately future. When I was in the sixth grade, I was chosen to start at the point guard position on the eighth grade team. I truly was not a good shooter, but I had spent numerous hours working on my ball-handling skills in our basement on a 10x10 concrete slab. So, I was tasked with the ballhandling role by my coach. Up until this moment I played because it was just fun but at that moment, I began to believe that I could accomplish things that I had believed where clearly out of my league. This gateway moment built my self-esteem and laid the building blocks for my later decision to attend college rather than go to work (very few of my friends thought about attending college). This positive gateway moment was created by my coach's decision and encouragement.

Coaching is a huge responsibility, but it also offers a platform to raise up athletes. Coaches can work to create these gateway moments any time that they are around their team: in practice, in one on one discussions, in games, at social settings, etc. Encouragement goes a long way especially coming from the COACH. As you have read previously, coaches must evaluate and critique players, but the journey of a season will offer opportunities for gateway moments. It has been my experience that young players who have a positive experience early with a specific sport will have a strong drive to work on skills necessary to be successful. They tend to view the work as fun. So, as a coach you have the challenge of creating as many gateway moments as you can and remember that every member of your team could experience a positive gateway moment to their life while on your team.

Gateway moments can also occur with anyone who is supporting personnel – managers, stat keepers, ball boys/girls, etc. During my coaching career we involved many different students in roles that allowed them to contribute without being a player. In one of these situations we were blessed to involve a young man who had been diagnosed with cerebral palsy before he was one. Josh's condition meant that since the age of five, he has walked with the aid of forearm crutches. Although this disability prevented him from being a normal part of competitive teams, Josh's interest and the fact that his parents valued athletics allowed him to be involved on a different level.

Josh was a very special person and we enlisted him to be a part of our statistics crew. He became a normal part of our program traveling with us to games and events and playing a vital role by supplying our staff with critical statistics. I recently talked to Josh who is now a professor at James Madison University about that season with our program. He shared with me that the big lesson that he learned from that experience was how to be a part of something bigger that himself. Because of the challenges that his condition brought to him, most of the experiences that he was involved with were centered around him. Make no mistake about his level of involvement; our staff looked to him for correct statistical information at the half and after the game that helped us make decisions affecting our team. He took pride in getting things right and embraced the fact that we held him accountable. So, the gateway moment that our team provided for him helped him to experience what it was like to be a real part of something bigger than himself – what a great way to develop a life skill that he has never forgotten. The thing that sticks with me is that I feel so blessed to have gotten to know Josh. After all these years to hear him say that the experience in our program provided him an opportunity to develop life skills is more rewarding than winning 600 games. Dr. Josh Pate lives in Harrisonburg, VA with his lovely wife and two children. He works at James Madison University as an Associate Professor in The Hart School.

The thing to consider about these gateway moments is that a coach can create gateway moments for learning life skills, but it is still up to the young boy/girl to seize that moment with the correct approach. When the moment arrives, and the right approach is taken with the support of the parents, it can become that magical experience that will change one's perspective for life.

Motivation

Becoming a solid motivator is a big part of being a good coach and it is important to use your motivational skills year-round to get the athletes to train, work, and play at high levels. What good motivators are actually teaching is the life skill of using determination to overcome obstacles. The real effectiveness of a coach's motivation is in direct proportion to the strength of the player coach connection. Everyone who strives for success in anything will be forced to overcome some obstacles and this experience is great training for those times when life knocks you down. The best gameday motivator that I was ever associated with was Dave Rider, who was the football coach at Elizabethton High during my tenure there. Coach Rider was almost always able to create that magical focus that propelled his players to reach their potential on any given night.

The best motivation is self-motivation, but coaches can give good motivation that can truly help athletes to go beyond their normal boundaries. During one of the contests that I was coaching early in my career, one of our key players, John Malone, injured his arm while diving after a loose ball. At this time, we did not have a trainer who traveled with the team so when John came to me and said, "I think I can still play," I wrapped the arm and told him that he was a tough young man, and that I had confidence in him. Later I put him back into the game. He played well and actually got a steal that led our team to victory. After the game, I suggested that John get a professional to take a look at his arm. The next morning, he came to my classroom in a cast – the arm was broken. I felt so bad for allowing him to play but he was and still is proud that he was so determined that he was able to play well with a broken arm.

Good coaches often observe something that another coach is doing and then mold it to fit their philosophy. When Jason Witten was playing at the University of Tennessee, I was fortunate enough to attend their pregame routine and I was moved by the way the entire team quoted the team maximums together. These maximums were created by Robert Neyland during his time as the football coach. I took that idea and created our own version of these maximums and our teams would say those together before every contest. I challenged each player to commit to doing their best to carry out each of the maximums as they verbally stated them loudly. This proved to be a good reminder of our focus for the game and a good motivator just before we entered the arena.

Teamwork

Coaches at all levels of team sports talk about teamwork, but to instill this concept in an athlete coaches must approach it like teaching a skill. Skill work consists of repetition – hitting a ball, catching a ball, shooting a ball, kicking a ball, etc. Coaches should create teamwork activities in their practice, drills, warm up activities, skill work, on a consistent basis. The skill of teamwork is one that carries over directly into the world of work as anyone who is a good manager will tell you. By giving athletes multiple opportunities to build this teamwork skill, you are preparing them to embrace collaboration in their future career.

Support Staff

It is important to show your appreciation to all your support staff including your family because it will not only help YOU to have an attitude of gratitude, but it will help to model good behavior to your team and after all, your staff deserves the recognition. I was very fortunate in my coaching career to have some high-quality individuals as my support staff and I am indebted to them forever for all their help. I felt that it was important to hire good people first and then teach them the role that they should play in our program. I was also very lucky to have a spouse, the players called her Miss Linda, who took an active role in our team – she did everything from feeding our team, to running the hospitality room, to working in fundraisers, and attended the games. At the conclusion of any event that Linda was involved in, I would instruct my players to thank her personally – this gave her recognition and helped to teach gratitude to our team. I also employed this technique to help recognize other staff members, bus drivers, business owners, and others who supported our program. So, to all those who have helped me along the way, I again say thanks and I tip my hat to you for your kindness toward our players.

A Coach's Prayer

I am a follower of Jesus Christ and our programs did have prayer before the games. In today's political climate that might not be possible in many public schools. It is not my belief that God has a stake in the winner of a competitive contest, but I do believe in the power of prayer. Our teams would recite the Lord's prayer or one of the great team chaplains would pray. *"Brad Bryant and Dan Pratt were two of the amazing men who volunteered to work with our teams and they always prayed for the safety of all participants and that our players would play in a way that was pleasing in God's sight."* My private personal prayer would be very comparable to the team's prayer with a reflection of my favorite verses (Micah 6:8 & Colossians 3:17).

Programming Success

The real job of a coach is to teach players to become good decision makers. In athletics each player must quickly evaluate each situation and enact the behavior that creates the best chance for success.

Many coaches try to program the athlete like you would a computer giving them options for many situations. This concept may work in the short-run, but it does not help to prepare them for making future decisions. It is my contention that the more you put into the heads of young players, the slower their feet become.

Another method of programming athletes is to use fear as a motivator. Some coaches act as though they are dictators and that each player must follow their instructions and be successful in order to gain the favor of the ruler. Again, this method may work in the short-term but will not last and does not teach the player to make life decisions.

It is my belief that a coach should set parameters that have positive and negative outcomes. One of the best tools that I embraced as a basketball coach was what came to be known as a brick/save chart. It was the job of the team manager to keep this chart during practice. The coaches could assign a brick for an unwise decision and a save for extra effort or great decision making. At the end of each practice, the manager would total the chart by subtracting the saves from the bricks. Each player would then run a sprint for his total. If a player had more saves than bricks, he could give his teammates that save to prevent them from running (this promoted team unity). This simple tool helped our coaching staff to avoid having to spend an inordinate amount of time verbally criticizing performance but to spend more time teaching the correct decision making.

To be truly successful, each coach must always keep the main thing the main thing – and that is to develop players into great people. Consider short-term and long-term statements that coaches hear from parents.

Short Term:
You are a good coach because we won a lot of games.
You destroyed my son's confidence.

Long Term
You were the most positive influence on my son in his formative years.
You destroyed my son's life by treating him like a pawn.

It is often difficult to make coaching decisions and it has been said that coaches can make 40,000 decisions in a days' time. That makes it critical to keep the main thing the main thing when programming success into your players and your program.

Choose Your Legacy

With all the media outlets now it seems that every day someone is trying to start a conversation with – "What will a specific coach's legacy be?" As a coach you really have the advantage of choosing your own legacy which goes against what society wants to discuss. Allow me to explain what I mean by engaging in this exercise that I have seen in numerous places with ideas for coaches including the coachingtoolbox.net.

Name the top two winningest coaches in NCAA football, baseball, and basketball.
Name the three winningest coaches in high school sports in your state.
Name the two winningest coaches in jr. high sports in your area.
Name the last two championship coaches in your local youth club organization.

OK – Now see how you do with these questions.

Name a teacher and a coach who helped you to believe in yourself.
Name two friends who you would help on a minute's notice.
Name two people who have inspired you.

Name two people who made you feel appreciated.

I would bet that the second list was easier – so the real heroes in life are the people who actually care. I have always defined my success based on if I make a positive difference in a young person's life. Our society would truly be better served to change how we define success. Those folks who go out of their way to care enough to spend their life in teaching, serving, coaching, and doing it the right way with a caring heart are the real success stories of our lifetime.

When asked at the local barber shop if it was going to be a good season my patented answer would be "ask me in five or ten years when these players grow up." It may take that long for these experiences to resonate into positive growth.

There is a truism or quote that has been attributed to many people over the years including President Theodore Roosevelt, John Maxwell, Earl Nightingale, and others. I would challenge every coach at any level to keep this concept in mind as you lead young athletes.

> *"People*
> *don't care how much you know,*
> *until*
> *they know how much you care …*
> *about them."*

The Best Teacher

The great Roman Leader Julius Caesar is attributed with first stating the proverb, "Experience is the teacher of all things." This idea has been stated in many forms and fashion, but the concept remains the same. The absolute best way that I have gained knowledge and wisdom in my life is from personal experience. But, early in my teaching and coaching career, I began each lesson or practice with a quote for the day. I have walked into McDonald's and had a former student ask me for the thought for the day – so at least I relayed the idea that beginning something with a positive or wise thought can help to get things going in the right direction.

This exercise of using quotes forced me to do some research on these figures whom I was quoting. Basically, I hoped to gain wisdom from the experiences of others and not just waiting for life's lessons to teach me individually. When you look at the wisdom in a great quote, it is easy to see that the person who coined that phrase was going through a time that created some amazing insight. This simple way to start an exercise has definitely served me well through the years. To that regard and to get your mental wheels turning I have shared twenty of my favorite quotes below.

I will begin with my absolute favorite.

"Success is a journey, not a destination. The doing is often more important than the outcome." – **Arthur Ashe**

"A coach will impact more people in one year than the average person will in an entire lifetime." - **Billy Graham**

"Make each day your masterpiece." – **John Wooden**

"Success comes from knowing that you did your best to become the best that you are capable of becoming." - **John Wooden**

"The most important thing in good leadership is truly caring." – **Dean Smith**

"I would never recruit a player who yells at his teammates, disrespected his high school coach, or scores 33 points a game and his team goes 10-10." – **Dean Smith**

"We must combine the toughness of the serpent and the softness of the dove, a tough mind and a tender heart." – **Martin Luther King, Jr.**

"It's not whether you get knocked down, it's whether you get up." – **Vince Lombardi**

"The quality of a person's life is in direct proportion to their commitment to excellence, regardless of their chosen field of endeavor." – **Vince Lombardi**

"You cannot help men permanently by doing for them what they could and should so for themselves." – **Abraham Lincoln**

"We can do no great things – only small things with great love." – **Mother Teresa**

"Courage is the resistance to fear, mastery of fear, not absence of fear." – **Mark Twain**

"It is not the size of the dog in the fight, it is the size of the fight in the dog." – **Mark Twain**

"Those who dare to fail miserably can achieve greatly." - **John F. Kennedy**

"Even if you are on the right track you will get run over if you just sit there." – **Will Rogers**

"Tomorrow hopes that we have learned something from yesterday." – **John Wayne**

"The price of greatness is responsibility." – **Winston Churchill**

"The reward of a thing well done is to have done it." – **Ralph Waldo Emerson**

"Happiness lies in the joy of achievement and the thrill of creative effort." – **Franklin Roosevelt**

"Genius is one percent inspiration and ninety-nine percent perspiration." – **Thomas Edison**

Practicing Good Coaching Posture

Modeling is a great way of teaching and once an athlete is committed to a team the coach often becomes the most important role model in his/her life. The coach should always consider personal positive coaching posture – during games, during practice, during team social events. This posture will change according to the event, but good coaches are mindful that they are modeling behavior that they expect to see in their players. On one specific team, I had emphasized sportsmanship and explained that we would always shake the opponents' hand at the end of the game I was pushed into the modeling position. We had just won a hotly contested game and as I walked over to shake the coach's hand, he turned and walked into his dressing room avoiding my handshake. When I turned to my team, I saw that they were all watching me intently, so to make sure that I followed through, I then followed the coach into his dressing room and stated, "Great game coach" and then proceeded to shake his hand. It is very counterproductive when a coach tries to hold his players up to a higher standard than he holds for himself. This holds true for many things including - promptness, appreciation, language, servanthood, and proper etiquette.

I do feel that it is the job of a coach to point out mistakes and offer alternative decisions, but I do not feel that it is necessary to subject an athlete to public humiliation. Strong coaches use well-defined expectations to lead the athlete down a path that will correct behavior. When people apologize, learn, or grow, then one should expect to see a change in behavior. Coaches must correct decisions and performance, but they should never lose site of the big picture – which is the who each athlete becomes because of their experience competition is more important than what happens in the next practice or game.

Coaching is a very honorable vocation that demands a great deal of dedication, humbleness, and selflessness. Consider that true caring parents are hoping and often praying for a coach that will lead and develop their child during his/her adolescence. What a huge honor and responsibility coaches have to their players, the parents, and even to our society.

A Coach

A coach is like a teacher,
Teaching many skills;
Not only about the game he plays,
But about the way life is.

A coach is like a friend.
He's there right by your side
In good times and bad times,
In times you laugh or cry.

A coach is like a counselor.
He listens every day.
He helps you solve your problems.
He knows the words to say.

A coach is like a doctor.
He has to find what's wrong.
He has to make it better,
So, the team can move along.

A coach will help you deal with loss
And teach you how to win.
He'll take the team that once was boys
And turn them into men.

Lisa Lowe
© Loving Lines and More
www.lovinglinesandmore.com

Everyone Can Win

Chapter III. The Player

The Approach is Key

Each player should make a commitment to him/herself to give their best effort daily, physically and mentally working toward personal and team goals. A key to having the correct approach is the development of a true appreciation for your gifts and for those who guide you. *Sincere gratitude has a truly magic effect on how you view the world.* When you choose this approach, it will clear a path for an amazing transformation to take place during your personal journey. The WHO you become while pursuing these goals will develop a guide that you will refer to for the remainder of your life.

Trophies

As a player you must realize that kids who participate in athletics get way too many trophies. In a world where kids need self-esteem to succeed, I do understand the idea of giving kids trophies, but if they get a trophy for everything that they do, then what is the reward if they are successful? Each of my sons played numerous sports growing up and therefore our house was full of trophies and when each of them moved out, they did not take these trophies. They did not place enough value on them to even keep them. The truth is when we eventually moved to a new town, we sold many of them in our moving yard sale for pennies. I have heard many parents say that their son/daughter had a room full of trophies that proved that their child was a great athlete. Getting a trophy does not make you a good player so value the experience and the lesson you learn from each experience, not a piece of metal that they presented you at the end of the season.

Triple Check

I was involved in competitive athletics at a young age and one of the most lasting experiences that taught me about responsibility happened when I was in the eighth grade. Our team was playing in a division tournament game. The school that I attended did not have a lot of funding for athletics, but we enjoyed wearing different uniforms (as athletes do today). Coach Norman White tried to compensate for our desire to wear new uniforms by often alternating shorts and jersey colors to help us to feel like we had four different uniforms. On the night in question, I was so excited to play in this game because I was a 7th grader and starting on the 8th grade team that I inadvertently packed the wrong color of shorts for this contest. When our team was dressing, Coach White realized that I had on the wrong color shorts, so he instructed one of the players to give me his red shorts and he was to wear my white ones. When I became a coach, I realized that the official could start the game with a technical foul because of the uniform problem so I assumed that Coach White did this because I was a starter and that boy who traded shorts with me was not a starter. I felt so bad at the time because I knew that it was my mistake and that my teammate should not have to wear a different color. After this contest a picture was taken and you can tell that my teammate is wearing non-matching shorts. To this day I still feel bad about this mistake but the life lesson that I learned still holds true to me today – anytime I travel I always double and TRIPLE check my suitcase to make sure that I have the essential clothing for the trip. WHAT a great personal lesson about responsibility that I learned during my seventh-grade basketball season at Unaka Elementary School.

Earn It

Having taught public school for over thirty years I have observed a great change in the perception of public school. At a young age I was taught to respect my parents, teachers, and coaches, but at the age of ten this training began to take a true hold as I developed independence. I never wanted my parents to see a need to talk to the teacher or coach because I had such respect for these role models and I definitely did not want to disappoint my parents. Therefore, I felt that I must earn my grades, my spot on a team, and any privileges that I would receive.

As I began my teaching career, I quickly saw that the landscape for how many parents and children viewed education was changing. The 'No Child Left Behind' mentality began to develop and along with that came the word that is now used often by educators – entitlement. Players, let me say it bluntly, if you have the belief that you are inherently deserving of privileges or special treatment without earning it then you need to do some soul searching. Don't expect anything without work – except the love of your family. I truly love Christmas, but families tend to go overboard with the presents – many children do not really value what is given to them but – let them earn it and they will treasure it.

So, PLAYERS, YOU are not ENTITLED to be on a team, or start every game but you can earn it with a four-letter word called WORK.

If you want to make the team and wear the uniform – work to develop the mindset and skills that are necessary.

If you want to be a good player – work on your skills and embrace competition that will make you better.

If you want to be a great player – work on your skills when others are not, seize competition whenever available, study the nuances of the game, learn to be a leader, embrace making others around you better.

If you truly earn things a magical thing will happen on the way to achievement – you will learn unmeasurable life skills and the WHO you will become will smile at you in the mirror.

Embrace Competition

This is a concept that can be misinterpreted into a 'Win at all Cost' mentality, but we must consider that winning a game is not the big picture objective. The contentment and the opportunity to learn truly lie in the competition itself and are not held only for those who win on a specific day. Embracing competition means giving your best effort AND respecting the opponent, it is playing to win AND showing great sportsmanship. This approach has mystical powers that can ffect your individual life journey by actively engaging you in the life skills learning experiences. One of my former players, Dustin Brown, became my assistant for a year after he graduated from college. When Dustin and I talked about his time in our program he stated that he had never played the game to win until I explained to him the correct approach. Playing to win with the correct approach served him well in his four-year career at Maryville College and in helping him to become the outstanding man that he is now.

In my coaching career I have seen many different types of personalities and qualities in players but those who truly embrace competition always improve their level of play. When I say embrace, I am not just referring to competing in games, but in drills, in practice, and wherever the opportunity presents itself. Ben, my youngest son, loved competition wherever it occurred – drills, practice, summer camp, or games. This love of competition allowed him to perform at a high level under the highest level of pressure. In his sophomore season we played the defending state champions lead by Dane Bradshaw and they were at an entirely different level than our team was at that time, they finished the season with a record of 36-2. Although our team did not fare well in that game, Ben competed and connected on five three-point shots. He was the kind of player that always wanted to take the shot that could win the game (make or miss he wanted to take the shot). By embracing competition again and again his level of play grew high enough to become a college level player. What a great lesson as too always giving your best effort in whatever you attempt.

Building Confidence

If you want to become a good player in your sport you will need to develop an inner belief that you can be successful. Developing confidence goes hand in hand with the previous two sections. Working to perfect your skills then using them to be successful will build confidence. Vince Lombardi is created with the expression "the only place that work comes before success is in the dictionary." In the world of basketball, where I spent most of my coaching career, skill work is translated into repetitions. If you want to be able to make a free throw when the game is on the line, then you should shoot as many as it takes to get you confident in that skill.

The normal goal for our players would be to make seven out of ten on a daily basis but to get to that level of accuracy one might have to shoot hundreds a day building up to that consistent goal.

I have seen numerous examples that repetitive work pays off in many players and even in my own sons. My oldest son, Steve, never missed a chance to work on shooting the basketball and I still remember many nights in the gym with just the two of us. I would rebound while he took shot after shot to perfect this craft. Steve went on to win the three-point contest at the Arby's tournament which is still today one of the most highly regarded high school tournaments in the country.

BJ Miller, who is now in the hall of fame largely because of his shooting prowess, had a game early in his high school career when he was not shooting the ball very well. When I replaced him with another player, he came to the bench and approached me and almost had tears in his eyes from frustration. He looked at me and said, "Coach, what am I doing wrong?" I sat down beside him and looked him in the eyes and said, "It looks to me like you need to spend some time in the gym." The next day BJ called me and requested to get into the gym and work on his shooting – that was a big turning point for him because it drove him to always look to take extra shots whenever time allowed.

Seize the Day

Each unique situation that a player experiences provides a unique opportunity to learn. This opportunity will not only help you in the sport that you are involved in but in developing life skills. If you find yourself on a team and playing a role that you do not like, then you have the opportunity to work on your skills and to prove that you can handle a different role, but you should immediately embrace that role and be the best that you can in your current role. Abe Lincoln is attributed with the quote, "Whatever you are be a good one." If you do embrace a role, it only helps to prepare you for future roles.

One of my coaching colleagues relayed to me a story of a basketball coach whose team had progressed to the state tournament. During this season, many parents had approached the coach with demands that their son should be a starter on the team. The coach had tried to explain to each of these parents that being successful requires that everyone play a different role and sometimes that role can change from game to game. This group of parents continued to pressure the coach even leading into this state tournament game. So, to begin the game, the coach sent all ten players out onto the floor to start the game – of course the official would not start the game and stated to the coach that he must send only five players onto the floor. The coach then walked calmly over to the stands and stated loudly, "I have tried to explain to you that they all cannot start." This is a practical example of a fact. Instead of spending time wishing for a bigger role – spend time embracing each situation fully – this approach will absolutely lead to improvement and growth.

Desire Coaching

It is a universal concept that if you want to learn something, ask someone who has done it or someone who has studied in the field. It has always been amazing to me that many fans who watch a game believe that they could be a successful coach. With that logic, everyone who goes to school could be a great teacher, everyone who watches a movie could be a great actor, everyone who watches the Kentucky Derby could be a great jockey or everyone who watches golf could be the next Tiger Woods. I implore all players to look to your coach for real guidance on your game, he/she has that position for a reason. Good players want to be coached and to become great, you must hear the truths that your coach is relating to you and work continuously to improve.

Intense Listening

Intense competition creates a need for quick decision making and a player should work to develop good decision-making skills of their own and utilize them during the game. On the occasion that the coach is making a decision as to how to proceed, players should listen intensely and give their best effort to complete the immediate task that the coach has given to them. My coaching philosophy included the concept that during the game while a player is on the court or field, they should listen to a coach's instructions and complete the task to the best of their ability – if the athlete has questions or discussions about something, then that conversation should occur at a later time.

Buck VanHuss was a legendary basketball coach in East Tennessee and along with his legendary winning ways go many stories that have been passed down about his career. On one occasion, Buck was so excited during a game that he found himself in the middle of the playing floor. The official in charge was very familiar with Coach VanHuss and he stopped play and instructed Coach that he was going to assess him a technical foul for every step that it took him to get back to his proper position on the bench. Buck, in a moment of quick decision making, instructed his players to pick him up and carry him to the bench. His players where not sure what the official had said to Coach VanHuss but they did as he instructed. Of course, a technical foul was assessed but this story shows how during a game the legendary coach's players listened to his instructions without question.

Defining Moments

A defining moment is one that changes WHO we are inside. This moment can be a specific moment in time or an experience that causes the individual to reflect while we undergo a specific period in our life. These are essential moments to true growth in the depth that we possess as a person. The true thing about these defining moments is that they occur more often than not when we are highly challenged, something negative happens, or we fail altogether. Therefore, it is imperative that a player always maintain a big picture view of what the current experience offers in terms of possible growth.

So, HOW you approach this challenging situation is crucial not only to how you deal with the day to day, but what you learn from the experience. The very famous Michael Jordan quote (listed below) highlights the fact that failure can lead to success when each failure is approached with the attitude of put in the work and learn from each failure.

> I've missed more than 9,000 shots in my career. I've lost almost 300 games. Twenty six times I've been trusted to take the game winning shot and missed. I have failed over and over again in my Life.
>
> That is why I succeed.
> Michael Jordan

Over the years I have used many quotes and slogans to define an instructional camp, team goals or motivate our players in a specific direction. Once when I took a new position, I used the slogan "attitude is everything" because my initial goal was to change the culture of the program. A former coach, who later became a good friend, expressed to me that his wife expressed the view that this slogan seemed to say that it was okay to lose. So, we approach the idea of what is winning and losing and the realization that the very often short-term goal of winning games and the long-term goal that will allow everyone to win can be at odds with each other. It is my strong belief that embracing the philosophy of ATTITUDE IS EVERYTHING can lead to success in the short term and will definitely lead to success in the long run. Embracing a positive attitude daily and backing that attitude up with persistent work and continuous action will always lead to a player's personal success. Therefore, when it comes to progressing as a player, your attitude is everything and you must constantly be evaluating and adjusting your approach. Do not be afraid to take an honest look in the mirror because this will lead to improvement both in the short run and in the big picture of life. Your defining moment might come from self-reflection if you are brave enough to do a sincere evaluation and then alter your approach based on that assessment.

Time Management

Being a competitive athlete of any age is an exercise in time management. Once you decide that you are willing to put in some work to become the best that you can, then you must prioritize your time and consider your life as it is now and your goals for the future. Most players will say that they want to be good and that they are willing to work to be good, but not all truly mean what they say. If you have a goal of developing the skills that will make you a solid player or a star in your sport, then you must realize that this means that you will need to spend time working on those skills. I have often seen players who talk a good game about work ethic but when it comes to deciding how to spend their time, they choose many other things over focused practice. In the field of economics there is something called Opportunity Cost – which in simple terms is when I am presented with two opportunities, I cannot do both so the price of doing one is not being able to do the other. I like to say, "Do not trade WHAT you want most for what you want in this moment." The benefits that one gains from setting a goal and making time management decisions based on those goals are life-changing. What a great opportunity it is to develop solid life skills through the experiences that competitive athletics offer.

Honesty

We have all heard the famous Ben Franklin quote

The Player

"honesty is the best policy" but as a player, you must embrace this idea on more than one level. First, of course, you should be honest about physical things, but you must also do an honest evaluation of yourself, your skills, your efforts to improve, your attitude, your approach, and your level of gratitude.

As I previously mentioned, I began my coaching career in middle school. While traveling with this program we often stopped at McDonald's after the game and I always made sure that each of my players had money to eat. On this particular night, I noticed that the twin guards who played on this team were not in line to get food, so I walked up to John and Jeff Cyphers and I asked them if they needed money. If my recollection serves me correctly, it was Jeff who stated that they had forgotten to ask their parents for money, so I began to give them some cash so that they could eat with the team. John stated that they would pay me back tomorrow and Jeff concurred strongly. I never begrudged a single penny that I gave to any of my players. I counted it a privilege to be in the situation, but most of the time it just became a gift and I saw it as such. The next morning while standing outside my classroom I saw the Cyphers walking toward my door and they handed me the money that they had borrowed, just as they had promised as they each said, "thanks Coach." I could see true gratitude in their eyes. I knew at that moment these two young men were different from many young men. I also felt that they would embrace their time on this team and get everything that they could out of this experience. These young men were a joy to coach and I count it a huge honor to have had a ring-side seat to watching them grow up into outstanding men.

Being honest with self can be a much more challenging task than being honest about physical things. If as a player you practice evaluating your efforts daily, then you will begin to get a much truer picture of the player and person that you are now. The awesome thing about this self-evaluation is that it will push you into a path of growth. Develop a pattern of assessment and ask yourself specific questions: for example, was my mind focused today in practice, did I mentally prepare before the game began, did I do anything to develop my skills today? As a young player, if you can just begin to take an honest look at yourself, you will start to see growth as a player, but more importantly, as a person. Remember the entire process is just helping you develop into the best version of yourself for life.

Practicing Good Player Posture

The American Chiropractic Association defines posture as the position in which we hold our bodies while standing, sitting, or lying down. The association goes on to say that without posture and the muscles that control it, we would simply fall to the ground. I would say that the same is true for a player. Without good player posture, one will most certainly fail. Coaches often talk about body language because it speaks the truth about a player's attitude at that moment in time. So, to have good player posture you must first begin by considering the physical cues that you give off during competition. If you are dropping your head or showing negative emotion, it is easy to see that you are not dealing with disappointment or frustration in a constructive manner.

To truly practice good player posture, one should embrace the attitude that the platform of sport offers – it is a sport and not life and death. It is true that one must have a serious approach to competition and embrace the values of it, but this should happen without placing your self-esteem on one play, one game, or even one season.

Being a good teammate is essential and that includes how you support others when you are not in the game. Choosing to cheer for your teammates, listen to your coach, and actively stay engaged in the game are essential to growth. Players who choose to pout or laugh while teammates are playing are not only disrespecting the team but creating habits that will prevent the development of sportsmanship in themselves.

When an individual realizes that someone is looking up to them as a role model, it almost always leads to some inner self examination. I challenge each player to realize that you are a role model to someone and do not just show up but look to walk the walk and talk the talk of being a positive role model.

Everyone Can Win

Chapter IV: Teachers/Administrators/Extended Family

The Safety Net

Most athletes have what I like to call an extended family and this support group can have a huge effect on the development of a competitive athlete. Having taught public school for a long time, I have had the privilege of seeing how many teachers and administrators choose to take an active role in the support of specific players. I have also seen positive influence come from another adult who genuinely cares about the development of an athlete. The great thing about this situation is that they can often be a voice of reason when the athlete is going through a difficult patch.

I would caution this group to maintain a big picture view of how to advise the specific athlete. I have experienced situations when athletes would consider making a decision that might seem to help in the short term, but in the long run it would destroy the opportunity to embrace a learning moment. It may be difficult for athletes to see that the WHO they become by experiencing a growth process is way more important than any specific performance on Friday night. This is why this group that make up a safety net should support and care for the athlete in the short run and encourage them in making decisions that are going to help them in their development into a successful adult.

Common Sense Approach

This chapter is concise in its content but highly important in the concept of the entire book. When working with student athletes the thread that ties all the theory and educational philosophy together must be a common-sense approach. Educational studies are constantly developing new theories on how to motivate a child or teach them in a unique way – these are often very innovative and useful to educators. The problem with pushing something on a student athlete is that anyone working with a student athlete must keep in mind that no two students are exactly alike. I have seen some theories that approach coaching or teaching like it was a factory and the children are raw materials that should be molded into whatever society decides is a good thing – this philosophy is totally flawed. I have listened to some very wise elders who often state that if you had 50 children, none of them would be the same. Therefore, this all-important group who comprise a safety net for student athletes must take a common-sense approach to being supportive and embrace the uniqueness of each of athlete. Taking some time to get to know the player can yield a valuable vision into how to best be a positive supporter with a common-sense view.

Encourage Leadership

Players are often encouraged to have a good consistent work ethic on their sport specific skills, and they should also be encouraged to become potential leaders. Competitive athletics can be a great breeding ground for leaders. Many times, members of the support group make the mistake of thinking that the best player will be the best leader. It would be great if the best player was the hardest worker and the best leader, but that is often not the case. It has been my experience that good leaders can come from a variety of places including bench players, statisticians, role players, and even managerial staff. This group of supporters should encourage athletes to be leaders in areas that are not sports related to help them expand their life skills training and grow in confidence and abilities.

The Critic

Those who make up this safety net must first consider that their job is in part to be a critic – but not to be critical of performance. I have experienced numerous occasions when members of this safety net with good intentions tried to become a coach and in doing so, they actually do more harm than good when it comes to the development of the athlete and the person. The job of this support team is to do just that, support the athlete through his/her personal journey through their competitive experience. Encourage the athlete to dare to be great and to bring their best effort mentally and physically everyday toward this goal – the result will always be a positive experience – personal growth.

Teachers/Administrators/ Extended Family Members

"It is not the critic who counts; not the man who points out how the strong man stumbles, or where the doer of deeds could have done them better. The credit belongs to the man who is actually in the arena, whose face is marred by dust and sweat and blood; who strives valiantly; who errs, who comes short again and again, because there is no effort without error and shortcoming; but who does actually strive to do the deeds; who knows great enthusiasms, the great devotions; who spends himself in a worthy cause; who at the best knows in the end the triumph of high achievement, and who at the worst, if he fails, at least fails while daring greatly, so that his place shall never be with those cold and timid souls who neither know victory nor defeat."

– **Theodore Roosevelt**

Practicing Good Support Posture

This group of individuals are in a great position to only be an encourager to the athlete. Proverbs 25:11 states that *"A word spoken at the right time is like gold apples in silver settings" (Christian Standard Bible Translation).* This is so true when spoken to an athlete – a kind supportive word is like a huge rock tossed into a quiet pond – the positive ripples can go on almost forever. Being in this position is great because it takes away any negative and can truly help the athlete to have a better inner voice concerning their own worth. Confidence is a key element in becoming a good player and if your inner voice is telling you that you can accomplish something, you have much better chance of being successful. It is my strong belief that positive thinking will help an athlete to be successful in the short run and a stronger person in the face of life's adversities. If you think that you can accomplish something, you have given yourself a real chance to be successful, but if you think that you cannot do something, you will almost always fail in the attempt.

Chapter V: Why Competitive Athletics
The Great Life-Skills Platform

At this point some of you might be thinking, "Why should I encourage my child to be involved in competitive athletics?" The answer to that is at the root of this book – competitive athletics is a great teacher of life skills. I maintain that in our society today, it is the absolute best vehicle available because a child will become actively involved in the learning process and any educator will tell you that active learners are at the pinnacle of the learning process.

The experiences that I had in competitive athletics changed my life. I grew up in a humble home with a great father who valued hard work and was a great provider and a loving mother whose life was rooted in the teachings of the Bible. Neither of my parents graduated from high school on a normal path – Dad joined the Navy as a junior in high school and they awarded him his diploma and Mom went back to school when I was young and earned her GED. They did value education, but there was never an expectation for me to go to college. I did not even know if I would be able to pass any classes. My early success in sports gave me the confidence that I needed to enter school at ETSU and later Lincoln Memorial University. It is 100% true that involvement in competitive sports not only prepared me for adulthood but played a big part in the direction of my life.

There is a plethora of educational and sports research on the value of children playing sports. Below is a list of my top 25 reasons to encourage your child to play sports.

Increases Confidence	Improves Self-Esteem	Builds Character
Teaches Respect	Reduces Depression	Teaches Teamwork
Develops Coping Skills	Develops Resilience	Promotes Social Skills
Builds Friendships	Develops Decision Making	Teaches Values
Develops Communication Skills	Improves Academic Performance	Develops Critical Thinking Skills
Develops Leadership Skills	Reduces Stress	Develops Healthy Lifestyle
Gives a Sense of Belonging	Improves Physical Fitness	Teaches Sportsmanship
Develops Healthy Acceptance of Criticism	Teaches How to Develop and Pursue a Goal	Teaches Time Management Skills

AND THE ULTIMATE REASON:
It will change their life because it
*TEACHES **CRITICAL** LIFE SKILLS!!*

Forbes Magazine Top Twenty Skills You Need to Succeed at Work

The Ability to Relate to others	Strong Communication Skills	Good Judgment	Negotiation Skills
Patience with Others	Active Listening Skills	The Ability to Persuade Others.	Awareness of Body Language.
The Ability to Trust Others	Genuine Interest in Others	Honesty	Proactive Problem Solving
Knowing How and When to Show Empathy	Flexibility	The Ability to Persuade Others	Leadership Skills
Good Manners	The Ability to be Supportive and Motivate Others	Knowing Your Audience	A Great Sense of Humor

Forbes - November 2013

I do not claim to be a psychologist or a sociologist, nor am I a self-proclaimed genius but in my humble opinion, it is impossible not to see the parallels between these two lists. If a parent wants to help their child to develop into a person armed with the skills that will lead to success, it is very evident that competitive athletics is a solid choice as a platform for development. It is my contention that our society should embrace this platform to that end and if our society embraces competitive athletics as a way to prepare children for the real world, then the approach to sports will change. As more and more parents and business owners assert the value of this training ground, then more and more parents and players will have a positive approach to the entire process. I dream of an entire society that praises young athletes for embracing the process and not only lauding the stars or those who win games.

As we all go through our individual life's journey, we are going to learn from our experiences, good and bad, and we are going to build a filter that we will use to view future experiences. If we build a filter with a common-sense approach and positive outcomes, then we are much more likely to make informed intelligent decisions as we progress to our own personal level of success. If our entire support system is based on encouraging our individual journey, then the positives are magnified.

One of the young men that I had the privilege of

coaching was Bradley Brown. During his high school years, it was easy to see that Bradley was a very intelligent young man which would lay the building blocks for great success. Bradley's parents not only encouraged him along his academic journey but encouraged him to participate in athletics. Bradley was truly a joy to coach but in my communications with him, I needed to be very specific about the expectations that I had for him in each of the offensive and defensive sets that our team used. In our family we actually coined the phrase that we still use today "Bradley Brown Smart" which infers – in the highest category for intelligence. I can still recall the day that Bradley took the ACT – when he returned to practice, I asked him how he thought he did on the test and he stated, "Coach I know that I missed ONE." Whenever I took any standardized test my mind was mush for at least a day. The reason that I wanted to mention Bradley was that he and his parents alike saw the value in competitive athletics. They embraced the life-skills training and wanted Bradley to become a well-rounded adult – which has worked out quite well. Bradley attended Massachusetts Institute of Technology (MIT) and has an MBA from Harvard Business School. He was previously an Investment Banking Analyst for Goldman Sachs and is now a Principal at KKR.

Job Readiness

If I was the CEO of a multilevel corporation or the owner of a small business, I would put a section in the job application that allowed for the discussion of high school activities because I would hire individuals who had learned to be team players and problem solvers. When interviewing prospective employees, I would refer to this section and listen closely to how they described their experiences. This process would reveal more about the prospective employee's readiness for success than a traditional interview or a call to a reference that has been provided by the prospect.

Interpersonal Skills

We are living in a time with the highest use of technology and this climate does not induce our youth into face-to-face communication. The majority of this new X-Box generation, as I call them, would almost always choose to become entranced with using a device over having a conversation, especially with an adult. It is not the fault of our youth, it is the times in which we live. Every generation has faced challenges to personal development from a child into a success- ready adult, but this high technology climate proposes huge challenges to the development of interpersonal skills. This is precisely why I believe that it is critical that the X-Box generation seize the platform of competitive athletics.

Along with being a parent, coach, and a husband, I am an amateur musician – meaning I enjoy playing the guitar and sometimes it can be okay to listen. During a recent conversation with one of my music colleagues who has played for many years, he brought to my attention that former athletes make much better band members than someone who has not developed their social skills through competition. It comes down to accepting different roles at different times. In a band there are moments when a different instrument might need to lead and times when that same instrument might need to take a secondary role. My friend's experience had taught him that a musician with a background that included being on a team would be much easier to work with than one who had not experienced real life teambuilding. This might best be illustrated in the type of music call bluegrass. If you watch bluegrass performed live, it is easy to tell when each of the musicians take the lead because they will step forward and when they are very content taking a supporting role. they will step back from the front of the stage. This is a great example of how being on a youth team can help develop social skills that will later help one to cope with many experiences that the future may hold.

Help for Today

As I reflect on the numerous teams that I have had the privilege of coaching, there are always some unique personalities and situations that come to mind. I often had players who accepted their role on the team but could have played a bigger role if they had been on the squad during a different year. It was often the case that these great team players went on to be great team players in life and many of them are coaching on different levels.

This is a direct result of embracing competition in practice and continuous teamwork with the right approach to the current situation.

Considering the immediate positive effect that competitive athletics can bring, I reflect to numerous players who stayed out of trouble or even graduated from high school only because they were involved in athletics. These players were often on the cusp of traveling down a bad road but stayed close enough to the mainstream because of the positive influence that their team had on their immediate life. I recall one specific young man who came from a single-parent home which presented him with a lot of challenges. He had a difficult time controlling his anger and one occasion had to suspend him from our team for an incident in practice. I escorted him into the dressing room and instructed my assistants to continue with practice. When I asked him about his outburst, he immediately took responsibility for his wrong actions and stated to me, "Coach, I realize that I must accept the punishment for my actions but please do not throw me off the team because basketball is all I have, and I believe it can save my life." The young man realized that the discipline and parameters of being on the team brought to his life were of irreplaceable value. As I interviewed numerous people about their personal reflections, I came across many former athletes who stated that they would have never stayed in school had it not been for being a part of a specific team.

First Hand

The root of the fire that pushed me to write this book is the first-hand experiences that have shaped my life. Having watched players experience athletics in a positive way and seeing how it has had such a positive effect on their personal growth, I had to find a vehicle to share what this amazing journey can produce. Imagine having a first-hand view of a mystical event, I have been blessed to be a part of so many of these journeys to maturity it is only fitting that I share what competitive athletics, done with the right approach, can do to help the world.

Perspectives

I previously mentioned that as a high school teacher, I often used the resource written by Chad Foster entitled <u>Teenagers Preparing for the Real World.</u> In this book, Chad describes how he researched many successful people to find out what they had in common. I have had the idea for this book in my head for numerous years and I adapted his philosophy a long time ago to question those ultra-successful people that I would meet about their growth to success. In all these years, I have yet to meet ONE person who did not have some competitive or challenging experience that helped to propel them to the top. If this is true of ONLY 60% of the success stories that we see, then why would we as a society not embrace what competitive sports have to offer? Why would we as parents not encourage our children to be involved in competitive sports and embrace the lessons that they can learn? Why would we as coaches not make sure that we keep our focus on the big picture when running our program? Why would we as players not embrace the competitive nature of athletics and be enthusiastic about the ups and downs of the experience?

Below is a small sampling of paraphrased excerpts taken from the numerous live interviews with people from all walks of life that I have conducted while preparing to pen this book. These discussions were often filled with passionate statements and vivid descriptions of personal experiences. My personal goal in these conversations was to simply be an active listener while recording advice that they would give to those involved in sports or as they described the main takeaway that they had from their experience while involved in competitive sports.

Hall of Fame Baseball Coach

*** No good can come from a culture that says if you win the game great, however, if you lose, let's blame another player or the coach. My son was an average player, but boy did he enjoy playing and learning so many lessons for life from sports.

Stay at Home Mom

***   Some simple advice

   -to the player – work hard, play hard, and you will learn much.

   -to the parent – a kind word of support goes a long way.

Accountant
***   I have encouraged my son to be involved in athletics because my parents pushed me to stay involved in athletics and it was a vital part of my personal development during my teenage years.

Contractor
***   It is my belief that athletic teams are a great teaching field for the youth of today. Learning some of life's lessons during high school athletics can prevent having to learn these lessons later from experiencing the hard knocks that life can bring.

Bar Manager
***   Being a teenager can be tough! It is easy for me to see how many of my former friends got into trouble and really did not set out to cause trouble. Teenagers need goals and a positive group in which to belong. Without this group, many teenagers will find other not so positive groups to which they can easily belong.

Electrician
***   From being a part of a team, I learned CHARACTER – and character to me is simple "if IT is to be… IT is up to Me" – I learned to take responsibility for myself.

Restaurant Chain Owner
***   In my current business we look to hire former athletes because we have had trouble in the past with employees who did not function well in an environment based on teamwork.

CEO
***   The values that I learned from being involved in sports have been the building blocks for my entire professional career. Simply put, if I had not grown up playing sports, I would not be successful today.

Salesman
***   To me, the greatest thing about being on a team in high school was the camaraderie, the forging of relationships together while going through adversity was second to none in instilling the skill of relationship building that I use as an adult.

Gym Owner
***   I was an introvert in school and sports really brought me out of my shell which helped me socially by leaps and bounds.

Musician
*** Being a high school athlete was a real-world experience in time management, balancing school work, practice, games, and social life was a challenge.

Nurse Practitioner
*** It may sound cliché but to me teamwork was the huge lesson, and I have never had a job in which you did not need good teamwork skills to be successful.

Business Owner
*** To me, the major thing that I learned from sports was discipline – how to control my actions and the great value it brought.

Engineer
*** It is easy for me to pinpoint one thing that sports taught me – leadership. I learned how to assume an active leadership role.

Regional Insurance Manager
*** I loved competing and how to work on a team would my first takeaway but the one that really sticks with me is – how to accept constructive criticism and use it to improve.

Coupling my first-hand experiences and these testimonials along with numerous others, it is very evident to me that nothing that we can get our kids involved in compares to the platform of competitive athletics. Where else can today's youth get the skills that prepare them to be successful in the future. A lifetime farmer may have said it most profoundly when he stated, "We have just got to get our kids off video games and involved in sports."

Chapter VI: The Conclusion
Everyone Can Win

The true mission of this manuscript is to show the value of competitive athletics when those involved truly embrace the process as a training ground for adult life. Kids begin playing sports because they enjoy it and there is no better way to learn than to be engaged in an experience that you enjoy. In today's educational landscape, many educators subscribe to a philosophy that can be summed up by a Ben Franklin quote: **"Tell me and I forget, teach me and I may remember, involve me and I learn."**

Hey folks – did you hear that loud and clear?

INVOLVE ME!

This concept is why choosing to be involved in competitive athletics is such a great chance to develop life skills that will help carry an individual through their entire life.

Would any good parent take away something from their own child that was teaching them valuable skills and the child enjoyed?

We have this great vehicle before us to teach our children how to be successful so we must use it correctly.

It is my strong belief that if all stakeholders – parents, coaches, players, teachers, administrators, officials, and fans have the correct approach to competitive athletics that everyone will benefit from the experience. Everyone who has ever competed knows that there is a winner and a loser a specific contest and comparably in real life you will not always get that job that you wanted, but with the correct approach you will develop determination to go for the next job available. What this type of WINNING looks like is that the competitor will become a solid citizen, equipped for success.

The competitor is WINNING!

In the world that we live in today, society certainly needs individuals who are willing to have a great work ethic, accept roles, and become leaders.

Society is WINNING!

Competitive athletics not only teaches life skills, but it has become a great platform in the prevention of prejudice, and it is my contention that this occurs because when an athlete totally embraces a team, then every member of that team becomes family. If you are all in, then you are taken to a new and unique place and one cannot help but be changed by intense experiences. It is very much like travel – it often puts you in a different mindset and your previous view is altered. Mark Twain is one of my favorite authors and his eloquence goes far beyond anything that I could ever hope to achieve.

"Travel is fatal to prejudice, bigotry, and narrow-mindedness, and many of our people need it sorely on these accounts. Broad, wholesome, charitable views of men and things cannot be acquired by vegetating in one little corner of the earth all one's lifetime."

Mark Twain

Conclusion

The awesome thing that happens to all the stakeholders in an athlete's circle is that they all can experience the same benefits as the athlete. If these true supporters maintain a close relationship to the competitor during their experiences and constantly with an open-heart share, then they too can learn the lessons right along with the athlete. It has been my true experience that I have learned much more from my sons and other athletes that I have had the privilege of coaching than I ever taught anyone myself.

All the stakeholders are WINNING!

I am a lifetime educator and I spent 31 years in the classroom which I embraced as I tried to impart knowledge to all my students, but a funny thing that I learned on my way through that journey was that I learned more from teaching than I had ever learned sitting in a classroom. The great Roman leader Julius Caesar is credited with recording the first know version of this concept when he stated, "Experience is the teacher of all things." Do not get me wrong, there is great value from embracing the classroom but the lifelong skills and the world views and the lessons that we never forget are best taught by personal experience. You may recall the Epictetus quote from earlier, **"It's not what happens to you, but how you react** to it that matters." This is profound and it is the backbone of growth that competitive athletics have to offer. By entering the arena, you have the chance for life-guiding growth – but only if you take the correct approach.

It is imperative for the personal growth of each young athlete that everyone involved keep a BIG PICTURE VIEW and play their role correctly. Many coaches talk about body language and how it does not lie about the attitude that an athlete has at that moment. I have included a section about correct posture in the beginning chapters of this manuscript to help guide each of the stakeholders toward making the most of their role in this life- changing experience of competitive sports. The posture of each individual within this community of supporters for a specific athlete will either help or hamper the learning experience that this awesome platform of competitive athletics has to offer.

The idea that everyone can win is not one that society would initially embrace because we are all about celebrating those who win games. But it is my strong belief and mission of this book that competitive athletics can CHANGE THE WORLD. When discussing this work with one of my close friends he suggested an alternative title because he felt that "Everyone Can Win" might not be taken seriously enough. His suggestion was "Redefining Winning" and I do feel that this would also be very appropriate because my hope is that everyone will begin to take a different view of competitive athletics which will create a better climate for the young athletes. As I attempt to put into words how this book is truly redefining winning within youth sports, we must create a new definition. This new definition of winning would be – the positive growth that occurs while embracing the journey of competitive sports **correctly** and moving toward becoming the best person that you can be – that is truly WINNING.

So, parents, coaches, players, teachers, administrators, and extended family – I challenge each of you to strongly consider the opinions that these reflections have presented to you and look at athletics in a different light.

Making a mindful choice to have a positive approach can be a life-changing event that can lead to contentment in this crazy world. When anyone greets me with the question like "how are you doing today?" my response is almost always, "Loving life." To me it is both an expression of gratitude and a choice that I make daily to embrace the experiences that each day allows. To be truly honest, there have been days that saying that out loud is a motivational speech to myself, but I do believe that our approach to sports and life is a choice. This book offers true stories that can lead each stakeholder toward self-examination which can in turn lead to altering one's approach.

It is my great dream that competitive athletics will become a revered place for the training of our youth. This correctly approached platform can teach our youth to become personally successful and vital positive citizens of society.

If each and every stakeholder makes a continuous conscious choice to take the correct approach, then we can **TOGETHER** change the landscape of youth sports and ultimately alter lives in a positive direction.

I challenge everyone to embrace this platform of competitive athletics enthusiastically so that we can all enjoy the benefits of WINNING!

About the Author

Tony holds a Bachelor of Science Degree in Business Education from East Tennessee State University, a Cooperative Education Certification from the University of Tennessee, and a Master of Education Degree from Lincoln Memorial University.

The author is a lifetime educator whose coaching career spanned more than three decades. In that time, he has coached numerous sports with basketball being the mainstay of his experiences. His hoop teams amassed over 550 victories and he has garnered numerous Coaching Honors along with Teacher of the Year and Hall of Fame status. His experiences as a parent and a coach give the reader a firsthand look at competitive athletics. Having been a cooperative education coordinator he brings a unique perspective and gives great insight into how the correct approach to athletics can yield life changing positive results.

Tony is married to the former Linda Campbell and has three adult sons: Steve who is married to the former Tanaka Andrews, TJ whose wife is the former Stephanie Edens, and Ben whose girlfriend is Nicole Lawrence. He has been blessed with five grandchildren; Lyla, Veda, Campbell, Hazel, and Claire. He loves spending time with the family which includes his sister Lisa, who penned some of the poems in this manuscript, his Godly mother Virginia, and his niece Kristen Shepard and her family, along with numerous cousins and extended family members.

Tony is also an amateur musician who has published an original CD of acoustic music. He is a follower of Jesus Christ and his approach to life is to love life and seize each moment as a gift.

Conclusion

Made in the USA
Columbia, SC
10 June 2019

A Guide for Business Writing

Write to Learn—Edit to Clarify

COMPOSE FEARLESSLY • Write Like a Pro • EDIT RUTHLESSLY

About the Author

Dona Young is a teacher, facilitator, and writing coach who believes that writing is a powerful learning tool as well as a key to career success. Young has her M.A. from The University of Chicago and is the author of the following professional writing books:

Angry E-Mail: How to Put a Lid on It

Eleven Steps to Instantly Improve Your Writing

The Writer's Handbook: Grammar for Writing

The Mechanics of Writing

Business English: Writing for the Global Workplace

Foundations of Business Communication: An Integrative Approach

Business Communication and Writing: Enhancing Career Flexibility (2012)

And on the lighter side:

The Princess and Her Gift: A Tale on the Practical Magic of Learning

The Little Prince Who Taught a Village to Sing (with *Andrew's Story*)

To Charley, Rose, and Robert Lee

Brief Contents

Introduction ix
Pre-Assessment xi
Acknowledgements xvii

Chapter

1	Process and Purpose	1
2	The Sentence Core	21
3	Conjunctions	41
4	Comma Rules	51
5	Semicolons and Other Marks	75
6	Verbs	91
7	Active Voice	109
8	Parallel Structure	123
9	Pronouns	133
10	Point of View	147
11	Conciseness	157
12	Tone	175
13	Paragraphing and Formatting Basics	193
14	Formatting Letters, Memos, and E-Mail	205
15	Persuasive Communication	219
16	Writing Persuasively	237
17	Best Practices for E-Mail	263
18	Job Search Tools	277

More Mechanics 303
   Part 1:   Capitalization and Number Usage 305
   Part 2:   Quotation Marks, Apostrophes, and Hyphens 323
   Part 3:   Similar Words and Spelling Tips 335

Quick Reference to Similar Words 341
Keys to Exercises 357
Index 375

Introduction

This book is for those who need to write effectively to survive on the job or pursue higher education.

Though writing is an art, editing is a science. Effective editing takes the mystery out of how to produce clear, correct, credible writing. Each time that you apply a proven editing principle, you will see results. As you develop expert editing skills, you also gain more insight into how to use writing to build strong client relationships.

A Guide for Business Writing starts with the simple elements of writing. By revisiting core principles, you are able to fill *learning gaps* that now hinder your progress. Trust the process: to transform your writing, focus on the simple, not the complex. This book walks you step by step through a process, giving you all the tools you need to succeed.

If you now make writing decisions on the basis of *guesses* rather than *educated choices*, you are cheating yourself. For example, one of the biggest myths of writing is that commas are placed on the basis of pauses. When you find a pause, how do you know whether to place a comma, a semicolon, or a period at the break? In fact, how do you know that you are even pausing at a *grammatical* break?

- In about an hour or two, you can learn how to punctuate correctly, saving yourself time and frustration from that point on.
- As you learn how to punctuate correctly, you gain a sense of structure, with natural breaks in grammar becoming apparent.
- As you develop a sense of structure, principles of editing, such as active voice and conciseness, become easy to apply.

No magic bullet exists; but if you do the work, you will see results. Spend an hour or less on each chapter, and the world of editing will open for you: you will gain a new lease on writing and the potential it offers your life and career.

Follow the plan below:

1. *Before you start the first chapter, complete the pre-assessment.*

   The pre-assessment is on pages xi through xvi. Feel free to copy the assessment. Your score will indicate your current skill level, revealing your learning gaps. When you complete the book, take the post-assessment and compare your results. (Go to www.commasrule.com for the post-assessment and additional practice worksheets.)

2. *Complete the brief exercises interspersed throughout each chapter.*

   The *Practice* exercises give you an opportunity to apply new principles. The keys are located at the back of the book.

3. *Do the* **Writing Workshop** *and* **Editing Workshop** *exercises.*

   At the end of each chapter, the *Writing Workshop* gives you a reflective topic for journaling. The *Editing Workshop* gives you drafts and revisions: work on drafts *before* reviewing the revisions.

4. *Apply the principles in your own writing.*

   Learning involves change: give yourself time to improve. In general, it takes about a week to become comfortable applying a new principle. When you do not apply what you are learning, the knowledge quickly becomes lost: *if you don't use it, you lose it.*

If writing has always been a challenge, give this method a chance—the way the topics are sequenced support you in your success. Thousands of business professionals have improved their writing skills using this approach. In some ways, the plan is foolproof, so do not second-guess yourself or cut corners.

For a quick review, see the abridged version of this book, *Eleven Steps to Instantly Improve Your Writing*.

Good luck on your journey: practice makes progress—repetition is key to improving any skill. You may find that building editing skills turns you into the writer that you have always wanted to be. In the process, you may also become an incurable editor.

Do the work, and you will see the results—go for it!

Pre-Assessment

Complete the following pretests to identify your strengths and diagnose your learning gaps.

As you make more effective writing decisions in each skill set, the overall quality of your writing will improve. By the time you have worked through this text, you will make effective writing decisions confidently.

Designing Your Learning Strategy

Each pretest measures a different skill set relating to proofreading and editing. Design your learning strategy on the basis of your pretest results.

Skill Profile Part 1: Proofreading Skills

    Pretest No. 1: Grammar Skills

    Pretest No. 2: Punctuation Skills (commas and semicolons)

    Pretest No. 3: Word Usage Skills

Skill Profile Part 2: Editing Skills

    Pretest No. 4: Editing Skills

    The Editing Inventory

To improve your skills:*

- For Pretest 1, Grammar Skills, work on chapters 2 and 6 through 10.
- For Pretest 2, Punctuation Skills, work on chapters 2 through 5.
- For Pretest 3, Word Usage, work on Part 3.
- For Pretest 4, Editing Skills, work on chapters 7 through 11.

*For best results, work on the chapters in sequence: each chapter builds on the next, untangling grammar for writing. The key to improving editing skills is to stop editing as you compose; the key to improving grammar is punctuation because punctuation reinforces the sentence core.

Pretest 1: Grammar Skills

Instructions: Underline each error in the following sentences; write the correction in the space provided. If there is no error, just write OK.

1. The issue should remain between Jim and yourself. 1. _____
2. If you want the promotion, take their recommendations more serious. 2. _____
3. Your department did very good on last week's report. 3. _____
4. The funds in our department will be froze until next quarter. 4. _____
5. Thank you for inviting Charles and I to the discussion. 5. _____
6. The customer should of enclosed the check with the application. 6. _____
7. Her and her manager will achieve their goals by working together. 7. _____
8. They gave us the project at the most busiest time of the month. 8. _____
9. Mr. Brown asked you and I to design the workshop. 9. _____
10. My supervisor has spoke about that policy many times. 10. _____
11. Everyone in the marketing department felt badly about the problem. 11. _____
12. The new accounts should be divided between Bill and I. 12. _____
13. Seth is the person that made the referral. 13. _____
14. If you have more experience than myself, you be the project director. 14. _____
15. If Tim was available, he would accept the challenge. 15. _____
16. The manager has not yet given the information to no one. 16. _____
17. When you need assistance, call Joe or myself. 17. _____
18. We would have been pleased if the pilot project had went better. 18. _____
19. Don't Ms. Becker need to approve the proposal before we accept it? 19. _____
20. Ed, along with his team, are going to the conference. 20. _____

Pretest 2: Punctuation Skills

Instructions: Insert commas and semicolons where needed in the following sentences.

1. If you are unable to attend the meeting find a replacement immediately.
2. Should Bob Jesse and Marlene discuss these issues with you?
3. As soon as we receive your application we will process your account.

4. Your new checks were shipped last month therefore you should have received them by now.
5. Will you be attending the seminar in Dallas Texas later this year?
6. Fortunately my manager values my efforts and believes in my ability to do quality work.
7. Mr. Anderson when you have time please review this contract for me.
8. We received his portfolio on May 15 and we promptly developed a new strategy.
9. Ali brought her report to the meeting however it was not complete.
10. Ms. Suarez sent a letter to my supervisor the letter was very complimentary.
11. The merger however required that each corporation learn to trust the other.
12. Thank you Mrs. Dodd for supporting our quality assurance efforts.
13. I am not sure about the costs but I recommend we consider this proposal.
14. You must file your application by July 15 2012 to meet all requirements.

Pretest 3: Word Usage Skills

Instructions: Correct the following sentences for word usage.

1. The policy changes will effect every department in the company.
2. The total amount reflects your principle and interest.
3. He ensured his manager that the project would be completed by June.
4. The title of the report did not accurately reflect it's content.
5. Our assets may not be sufficient for the bank to loan us the capital we need.
6. The finance department has to many new policies to consider before the merger.
7. There interests are not being taken into consideration.
8. What references do you plan to site?
9. You can reach me this Wednesday some time in the afternoon.
10. We ensure the quality of all items we carry.

Pretest 4: Editing Skills

Instructions: Revise the following sentences for structure and style. (Sentences may be grammatically correct but still benefit from editing.)

1. Bob was the right person for the job because he is the most qualified.

2. The supervisor asks that every manager report their findings by the 15th of the month.

3. Improving writing skills promotes critical thinking, will enhance career opportunities, and develop confidence.

4. Working right up to the deadline, Marie's presentation was finally completed.

5. The contract was negotiated by the attorney and corporate representatives for hours.

6. Concerned managers asked for changes in company policies, are appealing recent decisions, and will plan to schedule a meeting to discuss their recommendations.

7. Management will begin the implementation of the new policies in June.

8. Account managers purchased new software from a reliable source that cost only $2,000.

9. It is Gerald's recommendation that the executive committee take into consideration the proposal.

10. Per our discussion, the corrected form is being sent to you by our customer service department.

Editing Inventory: A Self-Assessment

Based on the challenges you had on *Pretest 4, Editing Skills,* rank your knowledge of the following editing topics.

On a scale of 1 to 5, 1 means little or no competence and 5 means complete competence. Your self-assessment of these topics will help you develop a learning strategy. If you don't know what a category means, rank it as a "1."

1. Controlling Sentence Structure   1   2   3   4   5
2. Using the Active Voice   1   2   3   4   5
3. Using Real Subjects and Strong Verbs   1   2   3   4   5
4. Being Concise   1   2   3   4   5
5. Being Consistent with Point of View (pronouns)   1   2   3   4   5
6. Using Parallel Structure   1   2   3   4   5
7. Avoiding Misplaced Modifiers   1   2   3   4   5

Total Skill Profile

How did you score?

The keys to the pre-assessment are located on pages 371-373. For each incorrect answer, deduct 2 points and then subtract your total points from 100. (Total points x 2 subtracted from 100.)

Part 1   **Score**

Pretest 1: Grammar Skills   _____ incorrect (20 possible)   _____

Pretest 2: Punctuation Skills   _____ incorrect (20 possible)   _____

Pretest 3: Word Usage Skills   _____ incorrect (10 possible)   _____

                                              Total Points _____

Part 2

Pretest 4: Editing Skills   _____ corrected sentences (10 possible)

Editing Inventory   _____ self-assessment average (1 to 5)

Acknowledgements

At one time, writing was an excruciatingly painful experience for me. That's because I would try to edit my words while they were still in my head. I also thought that when I sat down to write, I should have the answers. I did not understand that writing itself was a problem-solving activity, a discovery process.

When my teacher Dr. Ralph W. Tyler told me that he spent part of every day writing himself clear-headed, I listened. He also said, "The house you live in is your mind, your own integrity—don't worry about the rest."

The more I wrote, the more I was able to write. Writing helped me learn what I needed to know. You see, the way to learn about a topic, even if it is your own life, is to write about it. As John Dewey once said, "You become what you learn."

Writing was not enough, though. Once my words were on the page, I had no clue how to edit or revise them. I felt like a "broken record" and based my decisions on guesses; this approach was frustrating and made me want to give up. So I took classes and read books and learned to edit; I also taught others what I was learning, and they in turn taught me: my best teachers have always been my students.

In time, I realized that learning how to edit was the key that unlocked my ability to write. Editing allowed me to push the pause button between my thinking and my writing. Editing kept me engaged with my topic in a different way from the way writing did. With each edit, I reached a deeper understanding and expressed myself with more clarity.

Writing, or composing, is a reflective process but one that is highly focused: when you stop to think about what you are writing, you lose your thoughts. In contrast, editing gives you tools to work with your words in slow motion, allowing you to revisit your ideas to refine and clarify them.

To those of you who think that you are not writers, know that writing is a gift available to all who beckon its call; and learning to edit effectively will give you access to writing in a fresh and exciting way. To those of you who think that building your editing skills will not improve your critical thinking skills, keep an open mind.

You do not need to be a creative writer to reap the benefits of writing, which are intellectual, emotional, and spiritual. As you write, if you listen closely enough, you will hear a still, small voice that will lead you to the answers that you seek. Writing makes it easier to hear that still, small voice because writing, similar to reading, is a meditation.

When you can take the words that are in your head and put them on the page, you will have begun to liberate yourself from whatever is holding you back. Writing will help you find the truth, writing will help you find hope, and writing will even help you find yourself.

My teachers, my students, my friends, and my family have all helped me on this journey. Thank you.

Write to learn—edit to clarify.

Dona Young

Contents

Introduction ix

Pre-Assessment xi

Acknowledgements xvii

Chapter 1 **Process and Purpose** 1

Composing vs. Editing 2

Planning Tools 3

Purpose and Process 6

Micro-Messages 9

Reader Expectations 10

Style, Voice, and Audience 11

Critical Voices 14

Quantum Learning 15

Recap 16

Writing Workshop 16

A Sample Journal Entry 18

Editing Workshop 19

Chapter 2 **The Sentence Core** 21

What Is a Sentence? 21

What Is the Sentence Core? 22

What Is a Subject? 24

What Is a Grammatical Subject? 25

What Is a Real Subject? 26

What Is a Verb? 27

What Is a Compound Subject? 30

What Is a Compound Verb? 31

What Is a Compound Sentence? 32

What Is a Phrase? 33

Why Is the Sentence Core Important? 35

Recap 37

Writing Workshop 38

Editing Workshop 39

Chapter 3 **Conjunctions** 41

Why Are Conjunctions Important? 41

What Are Coordinating Conjunctions? 42

What Are Subordinating Conjunctions? 42

What Are Adverbial Conjunctions? 44

What Is a Fragment? 46

How Do You Correct a Fragment? 46

Recap 48

Writing Workshop 49

Editing Workshop 49

Chapter 4 **Comma Rules** 51

Rule 1: The Sentence Core Rules 52

Rule 2: Conjunction (CONJ) 53

Rule 3: Series (SER) 55

Rule 4: Introductory (INTRO) 57

Rule 5: Nonrestrictive (NR) 58

Rule 6: Parenthetical (PAR) 60

Rule 7: Direct Address (DA) 63

Rule 8: Appositive (AP) 64

Rule 9: Addresses and Dates (AD) 66

Rule 10: Word Omitted (WO) 67

Rule 11: Direct Quotation (DQ) 68

Rule 12: Contrasting Expression or Afterthought (CEA) 70

Recap 70

Comma Rules (chart)   71
Writing Workshop   72
Editing Workshop   73

Chapter 5   **Semicolons, Dashes, and Ellipses**   75
The Semicolon   76
Rule 1: Semicolon No Conjunction (NC)   76
Rule 2: Semicolon Transition (TRANS)   78
Rule 3: Semicolon Because of Comma (BC)   79
The Colon   81
The Dash   83
The Ellipses   84
Writing Style: Punctuation and Flow   85
Recap   87
Semicolon Rules (chart)   87
Writing Workshop   88
Editing Workshop   89

Chapter 6   **Verbs**   91
Action Verbs (list of)   92
Verbs in Past Time   93
Regular Verbs in Past Time   93
Irregular Verbs in Past Time   95
The −S Form: Third Person Singular   97
Linking Verbs   98
Subjunctive Mood   99
Past Subjunctive   100
Present Subjunctive   101
Recap   102
Writing Workshop   102
Editing Workshop   103
Irregular Verb Inventory   104 / 105

xxi

Irregular Verb Chart   106
Standard Verb Tenses   107

Chapter 7   **Active Voice   109**
Grammatical Subjects Versus Real Subjects   110
Active Voice   111
Passive Voice, the Tactful Voice   113
Nominals   114
Style, Tone, and Meaning   118
Style and Process   119
Recap   119
Writing Workshop   120
Editing Workshop   121

Chapter 8   **Parallel Structure   123**
Noun for Noun   124
Adjective for Adjective   126
Phrase for Phrase   126
Clause for Clause   127
Tense for Tense   128
Correlative Conjunctions   129
Recap   130
Writing Workshop   131
Editing Workshop   131

Chapter 9   **Pronouns   133**
Personal Pronouns: Four Cases (chart)   134
Subjects Versus Objects   135
Pronouns Following *Between*   138
Pronouns Following *Than*   139
Who, Whom, and That   141
Indefinite Pronouns   143

Recap 144
Writing Workshop 145
Editing Workshop 145

Chapter 10 **Point of View 147**
Pronoun and Antecedent Agreement 148
Point of View and Consistency 150
Point of View and Voice 152
Recap 154
Writing Workshop 155
Editing Workshop 155

Chapter 11 **Conciseness 157**
Compose to Learn—Edit to Clarify 158
Put Purpose First 158
Eliminate Redundant Pairings 159
Cut Redundant Modifiers 160
Cut Vague Nouns 162
Eliminate the Obvious 163
Update Outdated Phrases 163
Avoid Legalese 165
Use Simple Language 166
Modify Sparingly 167
Modify Correctly 169
Edit Out Background Thinking 170
Leave Out Opinions and Beliefs 170
Recap 171
Writing Workshop 172
Editing Workshop 173

Chapter 12 **Tone 175**
Client Relationships and Trust 176

xxiii

Micro-Messages 177

Diversity: A Catalyst for Misunderstanding 177

Generational Diversity 178

Cultural Diversity 180

Personal Diversity: *Thinkers* and *Feelers* 181

Analytical Versus Global Learners 182

The *You* Viewpoint 183

A Positive Focus 184

Clear, Accurate Language 185

Apologies Necessary 186

Bad News Messages 188

Recap 190

Writing Workshop 190

Editing Workshop 191

Chapter 13 **Paragraphing and Formatting Basics 193**

Paragraphs 194

Information Flow 197

E-Mail Messages 199

Side Headings 199

Formatting Features and Marks 200

Bullet Points and Numbering 201

Recap 201

Writing Workshop 202

Editing Workshop 203

Chapter 14 **Visual Persuasion:**
Formatting Letters, Memos, and E-Mail 205

White Space and Balance 206

Computer Settings 207

Business Letters 208

Standard Business Letter (example) 209

E-Mail Messages 210
E-Mail Formatting 211
Fax Cover Sheet Format 212
Business Letters: Connect – Tell – Act 213
The Direct Message 214
The Indirect Message 214
Recap 215
Writing Workshop 216
Editing Workshop 217

Chapter 15 **Persuasive Communication 219**
The Process of Persuasion 220
The Role of Trust in Informal Persuasion 220
Guidelines for Informal Persuasion 221
Client Relationships 224
Formal Persuasion 224
Purpose 225
Audience 225
Motivation 226
Resistance 227
Evidence 228
Benefits 228
Credibility 229
Action Plan 229
Customer Loyalty 230
    Customer Feedback 230
    Disenfranchised Customers 231
Visual Persuasion 232
    Paragraphing 232
    Headings and Subheadings 232
    Subject Lines 233
Recap 233

Writing Workshop 234

Editing Workshop 235

Chapter 16 **Writing Persuasively 237**

Routine Requests and Favors 237

Feasibility Memos 240

Complaints or Claims 241

Sales and Marketing Letters 248

Writing a Proposal 249

Client Relationships 250

Cover Letter 251

Formal Proposals 251

Letter Proposals 254

Team Writing 258

Recap 259

Writing Workshop 260

Editing Workshop 261

Chapter 17 **Best Practices for E-Mail 263**

E-Mail Facts 264

E-Mail Format 265

    Salutations 265

    Closings 266

White Space 267

E-Mail Guidelines 268

E-Mail Versus Text Messaging 270

Thinking Points 270

Recap 274

Writing Workshop 274

Editing Workshop 275

Chapter 18 **Job Search Tools** 277
  Career Portfolio 277
  Skills, Not Titles or Degrees 279
  Transferable Skills 279
    Working with People 279
    Identifying Knowledge You Can Apply 281
    Working on Tasks 282
    Identifying Personal Qualities 284
    Asking for Feedback 286
  Work Experience 286
  Business Cards 288
  Networking 289
  Job-Search Letters 290
  Cover Letters 290
  Follow-Up Letters and Thank-You Notes 292
  The Résumé 294
  Chronological Formatting 294
  Electronic Formatting (E-Résumés) 296
  Quick Skills Pitch 298
  Recap 299

More Mechanics 303
  Part 1 **Capitalization and Number Usage** 305
    Capitalization 305
    Proper Nouns and Common Nouns 306
    Articles, Conjunctions, and Prepositions 307
    First Words 308
    Hyphenated Terms 308
    Organizational Titles and Terms 309
    Two Common Capitalization Errors 310
    Global Communication and the Rules 311
    Number Usage 312

Ten Basic Number Rules 312
Dates and Time 315
Address and Phone Numbers 315
Two-Letter State Abbreviations 317
Recap 319
Writing Workshop 320
Editing Workshop 321

Part 2   **Quotation Marks, Apostrophes, and Hyphens 323**
Quotation Marks 323
Quotation Marks with Periods and Commas 324
Quotation Marks with Semicolons and Colons 324
Quotation Marks with Questions and Exclamations 325
Short Quotes and Long Quotes 325
Quotation within a Quotation 325
Apostrophes 326
Possessives 326
Inanimate Possessives 328
Contractions 328
Hyphens 329
Word Division 329
Compound Modifiers 330
Numbers 330
Prefixes 331
Recap 332
Writing Workshop 333
Editing Workshop 333

Part 3   **Similar Words and Spelling Tips 335**
Pretest 336
Spelling Tips 337

A Sampling of Roots, Prefixes, and Suffixes 338

Recap 340

Quick Reference to Similar Words 341

Keys to Practice Exercises 357

Index 375

1

Process and Purpose

Are you more focused on the *product* than you are on your *process*?

1. Do you try to figure things out before you put your words on the page? Do your ideas dissolve before you get them down?
2. Do you stop to correct grammar and punctuation *as you compose*?
3. Do you send out your writing without proofreading or editing it?

If you answered *yes* to any of the above, you may think that you have *writer's block*. However, writer's block is the inability to produce new work, and none of the above relate to writer's block: they all relate to *editor's block*, which is far more common. Editor's block results in part from being overly concerned with product at the expense of process.

- *Editor's Block Type A*: You edit as you compose, and your ideas get jammed in your head or dissolve before they reach the page.
- *Editor's Block Type B:* You do not proofread or edit your work because you feel anxious about mistakes or are unsure of what to correct, so you hold your breath and click *send*.

You can overcome **Editor's Block Type A** by separating composing from editing, which is discussed next. You will overcome **Editor's Block Type B** by improving your editing skills, which each chapter of this book addresses.

Let's get started by gaining insight into the writing process and then work on *purpose*, the most important element of all writing.

Composing Versus Editing

Writing is not a neat and tidy activity: writing at its best is messy. To make progress, learn to let your ideas to flow; allow your draft to be detailed, wordy, and incorrect.

If you now edit in your head, you need to retrain yourself:

> Compose freely—edit ruthlessly.

When you edit, you can cut, correct, and shape your writing for your readers. Move back and forth between composing and editing. The key is staying focused on only one type of activity at a time.

By composing freely, you will overcome *Editor's Block Type A* and see an immediate difference in your writing. You will produce more in less time; you will also feel less frustrated and, ultimately, more confident. The planning and composing tools in this chapter will help you with this type of editing block.

To overcome *Editor's Block Type B*, you need to take the time to proofread and edit each piece of writing that you produce. By developing your skills, you will understand the principles that lead to correct, clear, and concise writing. Building your skills is not as challenging as you fear—this book teaches you editing principles step by step, one principle at a time.

Eventually, editing will be easier than composing. Editing gives you clear-cut answers that take the mystery out of how to produce effective writing. You may also find that building editing skills gives you a fresh way to think about writing. As you edit, you reach clarity; but more important, you shape your writing for your readers so that it gets right to the point in a clear and concise style.

When you stop editing as you compose, and composing still feels excruciatingly difficult, focus on the *thinking behind the writing* and do some *prewriting* activities.

- *Pre-writing:* reading, researching, discussing, thinking reflectively, planning, taking notes, and mapping.

Manage the writing process effectively as you master editing skills, and you will see results. Each of the following chapters develops a different aspect of grammar or style; but first, learn to compose freely using the tools discussed below.

Planning Tools

Planning tools focus your attention to the problem at hand and add creative energy to open up your critical and creative thinking. Use them throughout the writing process as you go back and forth between composing and editing.

Mind mapping   To get your ideas on the page in a quick, spontaneous way, write your topic in the middle of the page, circling it. Finally, free associate ideas and cluster them around your topic.

Figure 1.1 | Mind Map: What is difficult about writing?

Once you select your topic, spend about 3 minutes getting your ideas on the page: no pauses, no corrections, and no criticism.

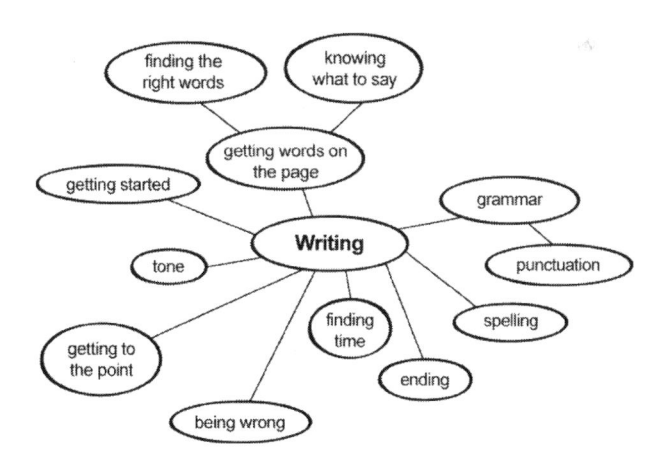

If you have great ideas but cannot seem to get them on the page before they dissolve, mind mapping is one part of your solution.

Also use mind mapping as a time management tool; use it to plan your day or an important phone call. Select a topic and spend 3 minutes doing a mind map.

Creating a Scratch Outline   Rather than doing a formal outline, simply list your ideas. Keep a notepad close at hand so that you collect your insights as they come to you.

Freewriting   Allow your words to flow freely: take whatever thoughts that are in your head and put them on the page. Pick up a pen and start writing or *free type* on your computer. As you freewrite, you learn to compose freely while blocking out the compulsion to correct your writing.

If you have never tried freewriting, set the clock for 10 minutes and start writing. Freewriting clears the head so that you gain focus and renew your energy.

Focused writing   Choose a topic and write about only that topic for about 10 to 15 minutes or 3 pages. Focused writing helps you make good use of small amounts of time that would otherwise be lost. Focused writing can also help you jump-start a project that you have been avoiding.

At the end of each chapter, you will find a focused-writing activity.

Page mapping   Use key points from your scratch outline or mind map to create **side headings**. Put each key point along the side of a blank page, and then fill in the details that you know. This technique helps eliminate one of the biggest fears of any writing task: starting with a blank page.

Fishbone Diagramming   A fishbone diagram is also known as a *root-cause diagram* because it forces you to probe deeply into a problem you are actively working to solve.

First, identify the problem. Next, if there are major components of your problem, identify them. For each component, ask *why* five times.

4 *A Guide for Business Writing*

You can apply this tool in a simple format to solve daily problems. For example, let's say you have difficulty completing a writing task. Start by turning it into a problem statement and then work through it by asking the question *why* five times.

Problem statement: I am having difficulty with this writing task.

Why?	I am having trouble getting started.
Why?	I am feeling as if it is out of my control.
Why?	I don't understand the topic well enough.
Why?	I haven't done my research.
Why?	I haven't taken the time to find resources.

Finish your fishbone diagram by defining your next step:

Next Step: Do research today from 3 to 4 p.m.

Answering Journalist's Questions   Journalists focus on the *who, what, when, where, why,* and *how* of an event. When you find yourself stuck, frame out the relevant questions.

See beyond the various angles, and put yourself in your reader's position. As you argue a point or try to persuade your audience, include the opposing argument and then show how your points are superior.

Use these planning tools to get started quickly, stay focused, and develop a creative response. *Creativity is listening to the obvious and responding with a unique and effective solution.* Focus on solving the problem, and your writing will flow. However, there are times when getting started is especially difficulty. At those times, you may feel anxious.

Think of this anxiety as a *signal anxiety*, a unique kind of anxiety that tugs at your sleeve, reminding you to start working. If you use signal anxiety as a call to action, you will feel relief and see results.

Some writers, however, need the extra boost of adrenaline that an impending deadline creates. If that is the case with you, set your own *internal deadlines.* Start writing, but do not try to start from the beginning: write about what you know first.

Writing is a discovery process, and one idea will lead to the next. Writing is a also a problem-solving activity. Once you start writing, you gain deeper insight, even when you are not thinking about your topic. Writing forces you to make progress by pulling you to deeper levels of understanding. That is why writing sometimes feels painful: putting critical thoughts on paper takes courage because you are forced to take positions, make decisions, and think clearly.

If you have the time now, select one of the tools that you have just learned and try it. Incorporate these tools into your daily routine, and you will see a difference in how you get your words on the page and how you solve problems.

Next, let's look at purpose, a critical element of writing . . . and life.

Purpose and Process

Business writing depends on context, and *purpose creates context*. The most important editing step you can take is to identify your key points and make them easily accessible, if not instantly visible, for your reader.

Once readers understand purpose, details make sense. However, when details appear *before* the point that they are illustrating, readers find difficulty understanding their relevance.

Readers want to know the outcome, not "how come." They want to know the end point, not all the points leading up to it. Most important, they want to know what you need from them so that they can respond.

In contrast, as a writer, you are unlikely to be clear about your exact purpose when you start writing. Your thinking is likely to be full of details—some relevant and some *not*.

Once you articulate your key point clearly, begin to edit your document: your key point delineates information that is important from information that is not important. Unimportant information is irrelevant and even irritating to a reader.

Until you identify your key point, identifying relevant information is a difficult task—all information can seem important as you compose.

When you start editing, ask these questions:

- What is the most important issue?
- What are my outcomes and conclusions?
- What action do I want the reader to take?

As you read the following message, look for the key point and identify information that you can cut.

> Dear Ms. Holloway:
> My name is Donald Draper, and I recently met an associate of yours at the Chicago Trade Fair. His name is Roger Sterling, and he was representing your company at the Trade Fair. Mr. Sterling suggested that I write you about your intern program. To give you a little background about myself, I am currently a graduate student at Best University and will receive my master's degree in marketing next spring. My purpose in writing you is to find out if you have any openings in your intern program this coming winter. I would be pleased to send you my resume. I look forward to hearing from you.
> Sincerely,
> Donald Draper

Before looking at the revision on the next page, do the following:

1. Identify the key point.
2. Bring the key point to the beginning of the message.
3. Cut unnecessary information.

Here is the revision with the key point up front:

> Dear Ms. Holloway:
>
> Your associate Roger Sterling suggested that I write you about your intern program.
>
> If you have an opening, please consider me an applicant. I will receive my master's degree in marketing next spring. My management and computer skills are excellent as are my people skills.
>
> Attached is my resume. If I do not hear from you within a week or two, I will follow up with you.
>
> Best regards,
>
> Don Draper

Does starting with key information make it easier to identify irrelevant, empty information?

When starting a message, do not state the obvious, such as "my name is" or "my purpose for writing is." Your name will appear in the sign-off; and by stating your purpose directly, the reader will pick up on it.

Also notice how the second message breaks the message into parts by making use of **white space**.

White Space   *White space* is the blank space on the page that gives readers a chance to rest their eyes. Create white space in an e-mail by leaving one blank line between parts.

White space aids readers in understanding your message by breaking it into digestible parts. In fact, white space even contributes to the credibility of writing, making it look professional.

When writing is bunched together, the reader sees at a glance that the compacted message is more difficult to understand. For example, refer back to the original message on page 7 and then its revision on

8   *A Guide for Business Writing*

page 8. Notice how the draft is one long paragraph; in contrast, the revised message is broken into short paragraphs that give the impression of a *beginning*, a *middle*, and an *ending*.

Become aware of how you use white space, and experiment adding white space where needed. For more information, turn to Chapter 13, "Paragraphing and Formatting," which gives precise instructions on how much white space to use for e-mail messages, letters, and other business documents.

Next, let's examine purpose on a broader level than key points and formatting. For example, purpose is the umbrella under which everything you are communicating resides.

At times, the unspoken message speaks louder than words. Those unspoken messages are called **micro-messages**.

Micro-Messages

Micro-messages are the intangible messages that occur "between the lines," for example:

- You forget to respond to a colleague's urgent message.
- You respond to a message without answering questions posed.
- You tell a client about a mistake and copy the client's supervisor.

Or maybe you are on the other side, being the recipient of any of the above. Without doubt, e-mail has the potential to destroy a person's day and even disrupt business relationships.

An underlying purpose of all business communications is to build relationships based on trust. That is because business transactions are only partly based on information flow, with another important part depending on the relationship among the players.

And let's face it, anyone can easily forget to respond to a message or overlook answering questions. How you respond to others in these situations and how they respond to you makes a difference in the relationship.

When relationships are in good standing, a sense of trust and respect exists; and, when needed, each person is likely to give the other *the benefit of the doubt.* However, when relationships are not in good standing, the benefit of the doubt ceases to exist. In fact, suspicion can seem to linger in every communication. When things go wrong, the blame game begins. When this dynamic takes over, business suffers.

Screen your e-mail for micro-messages:

1. Ensure that your communications do not include blame.
2. Do not write with emotion—do not try to "prove a point."
3. Focus on the solution, not the problem or the person who may have caused it.
4. Elevate the mission, not the issues; find common ground.
5. Give the answer, but don't tell the story; giving too many details can sound defensive and even make things worse.
6. Separate personal feelings from business relationships; the job needs to get done regardless of whether clients are personable.
7. Understand and respect diversity, such as generational and cultural differences.
8. Phone your client, rather than send an e-mail, when tensions run high.
9. Apologize when the situation calls for it.
10. If you would not say it face to face, do not write it.

Though uncomfortable to think of them this way, relationships are in constant flux; in general, the latest communication has the biggest influence on current feelings.

By pulling communication toward a positive, problem-solving focus, everyone benefits. Human elements such as pride and fear are present even when they are not visible. At times, a human voice can melt barriers that written words cannot.

Reader Expectations

To adapt to your audience, learn more about what they expect. In part, you can tune in to what your readers expect by identifying what *you* expect and value.

For longer documents, ask yourself if your readers are experts or novices. Experts expect technical details. However, a general audience does not relate well to a lot of specific detail.

If you are writing an e-mail, you are not likely to lose a reader for too little detail (unless you are rude or abrupt). When readers do not get enough detail, they ask for what they need. However, you can lose a reader in a nanosecond by filling an e-mail with unnecessary details. Too much information (TMI) leads some readers to save the long-winded message until later, but later may never arrive.

Readers also prefer writing that is correct, clear, and concise. Therefore, once you have drafted your idea, edit your writing until your words on the page are not only correct but also sound as fluent as they would if you were speaking.

Diversity is another element to consider: we differ in small and large ways through generational, cultural, and personal diversity as well as diverse learning styles. For example, global learners need to see the big picture and analytical learners prefer detail.

Many use the Golden Rule to meet another's needs: "Do unto others as *you would have them do unto you.*" However, the Platinum Rule works more effectively in diverse environments: "Do unto others as *they would have you do unto them.*" By understanding the lens through which your clients view the world, you are more likely to give them what they need and expect.

By appreciating what is important to someone else, you are more able to adapt your writing to their expectations and mirror some of their preferences. To learn more diversity, see Chapter 12, "Tone." Next, let's look at creating a reader-friendly writing style.

Style, Voice, and Audience

Voice is an elusive element of writing that speaks to a reader, engaging the person as well as the intellect. Voice is the connective tissue of all types of writing, including professional writing.

When you write about unfamiliar topics, your writing is more likely to sound complicated. That is partly because you do not yet understand your topic well enough to present complex information in a simple way. Writing about a topic is the best way to learn about it;

when you get stuck, read about your topic or discuss it with a colleague. If your writing tends to be more complicated than your speech, keep the following in mind:

> If you would not say it that way, do not write it that way.

Right now, you may be going out of your way to make your writing sound formal, using words such as *utilization* instead of *use*. Or maybe when you write an e-mail you are using canned phrases such as *attached please find* and *per your request*. Would you ever sit across from someone at lunch and say, "Per your request . . ."?

Readers do not connect with writing unless it is alive and in the moment. To improve your writing style, let go of artificial, canned language and instead say what you mean in a clear, direct voice. As you write more, this kind of simple writing will come natural to you. By the way, to avoid using *per*, simply say, *as you requested*; to get rid of *attached please find*, simply say, *attached is*.

When you write to your manager, your writing may also become complicated because you feel anxious. Regardless of whether you are writing to a peer or a superior, clear and simple writing is best.

Getting past the stage of complicated writing may seem challenging at first. The only solution is writing freely and frequently, which will eventually bring your writing to a higher level of skill and comfort. However, perhaps complicated writing is not your issue. Instead, does your writing sound too *informal*? For example, do you use slang or incorrect grammar? If that is the case,

> Just because you would say it that way
> does not mean that you should write it that way.

At face value, this advice seems to contradict the previous. However, different writers have different issues. Even though a different issue holds you back, your solution is the same: *write freely and frequently*.

Finding your voice is not a one-time event: *voice* is a process in which you reconnect with yourself, your topic, and your readers every time that you sit down to write.

To find your voice, stay committed to the process:

- The first step is to write frequently so that you become as comfortable writing as you do speaking.
- The next step is learn a topic well enough to write freely about it.
- The final step entails editing and revising your writing until it meets the needs of your audience.

When you compose, do not worry about your voice. Once you are able to write freely, your voice will appear. First get your ideas, your insights, your reflections on the page.

Others may still not hear your voice until after you edit your work. As you edit, cut and reshape your words so that they connect with your readers. One editing tip that you can apply immediately is to keep your sentences at a reasonable length, therefore:

> Limit your sentence length to 25 words or fewer.

For example:

> Sentences that are much longer than 25 words have a tendency to confuse readers because by the time that they get to the end of a long sentence, many readers have already forgotten what the beginning of the sentence was about and need to go back to the beginning and reread it again, which can be very tedious. (57 words) *What do you think?*

Less is more. When you write long or complicated sentences, count the number of words. If the sentence is longer than 25 words, cut words or break the information into shorter sentences. At times, you will need to do both.

Eventually, you will know whether you are speaking from your voice as you compose. Even then, you will need to edit out the clutter so that your voice becomes strong and clear. You see, you find your voice through composing, but you clarify your voice through editing.

Critical Voices

As you write, are you critical of yourself? Are there times when you feel like giving up?

Writing is difficult, and all writers face what they feel to be insurmountable roadblocks—that is, until they write their way out of them. And then what seemed to be impossible has developed into a deeper understanding and a more effective solution.

The creative part of the self is *hyper-sensitive*. When you criticize yourself, you effectively drain your energy and motivation, not only sabotaging your passion but also possibly your life's mission.

Shutting down your inner critic is more difficult than dealing with criticism from others. In fact, the worst part of being criticized is that it triggers self-criticism. When you feel especially critical of yourself, write about it. Writing about your fears and your feelings helps you to process them so that you do not get stuck, feeling like a victim.

According to Byron Katie in her book *Loving What Is*, negative thoughts should be challenged.[1] The next time that you have a negative thought, ask yourself, "Is that true?" Then ask again, "Is that *really* true?" If you cannot prove that a negative thought is true, let it go. And even if you can prove that it is true, dwelling on it only does you harm.

Your first step is becoming aware, your second step is claiming ownership, and your third step is empowering yourself to change: *name it, claim it, change it*.

Also, do not set yourself up to be disappointed. Learn to accept feedback without expectations. Show your writing to others only when you feel confident because confidence enables you to accept feedback gracefully.

In fact, an unconscious *fear of criticism* is worse than criticism itself: once you hear the actual words, you can regroup and emerge stronger. In contrast, fear is paralyzing, and the only way to combat fear is to take action. Start writing, even if you are writing only about your own fears. As you write, your topic takes on a life of its own, becoming ever larger as you follow your insights; even subtle insights can lead to profound understanding.

Fear of criticism goes hand in hand with an expectation of perfection. When you are disappointed with yourself for not being perfect, you are setting yourself up:

> Perfect writing does not exist.

Perfection exists only in the mind, so do not beat yourself up for being human. Instead, expect challenges and even embrace them because they will haunt you until you address them anyway.

Ernest Hemingway faced his fear by saying, "Do not worry. You have always written before and you will write now. All you have to do is write one true sentence. Write the truest sentence that you know."[2]

Each time that you embrace a difficulty, you have the opportunity to do more than overcome a weakness; you have an opportunity to build your own character. As Colin Powell once said, "There are no secrets to success. It is the result of preparation, hard work, and learning from failure."

Embracing mistakes as learning opportunities is a critical life lesson. Let's look at what learning involves.

Quantum Learning

Quantum is an impressive word that has diverse meanings. One of its meanings relates to big things, and the other to small, minute things. For learning, does it refer to the big things or the little things?

First, *learning involves change*; when there is no change in skill, behavior, or thinking, learning did not occur. Little changes, however, even when they are immeasurable or barely visible, create the foundation for big improvements.

Writing involves a multitude of decisions: each effective decision contributes to improving your writing as a whole. What appears to be a quantum leap in skill development actually consists of many little changes that finally come together to make a big (visible) impact.

In fact, when writing feels frustrating—or when you continue making the same mistakes—it may be that you have a *learning gap* that hinders you from making progress. If you find that you need to work on basic principles of grammar and punctuation, work in a systematic way until you fill your learning gaps. *Persistence* is the most important quality in achieving success in the long run.

Success is a matter of time and commitment; failure results from giving up before you reach your goal. Apply every principle that you learn: knowing something means little until you apply it. The saying, "If you don't use it, you lose it," is true. The sooner and more often you apply it, the more your skill grows.

Just as writing is difficult, so is learning. In fact, some types of learning involve building new channels in the brain, which is why *repetition* is such an effective tool. Think of it this way: with each repetition, you are creating a deeper pathway that eventually results in deeper understanding, new insight, and improved skill.

Learning also involves patience to see progress, courage to try new ways of doing things, and motivation to keep trying even when a goal feels out of reach. Writing is a powerful learning tool because writing leads to insight. *Insight* is a unique and genuine form of learning because the learner generates knowledge from within.

If you do not appreciate every new change that you make in your writing (however small), you are not likely to become an incurable editor; and becoming an incurable editor is what will turn you into the expert writer that you deserve to be.

Writing taps into critical thinking skills in a unique way. Have you ever noticed that you can think about the same problem all day only to end up feeling drained and helpless? Once you start writing, your mind will either pull you toward solving a problem or to releasing it so that your mind can return to the present.

Every time that you write, you draw upon your critical and creative thinking skills, making them stronger and gaining insight in the process.

Recap

The more you write, the more your skills will improve.

- Do *not* edit as you compose: *compose freely—edit ruthlessly.*
- Compose for yourself, but edit for your reader.
- Do pre-writing activities and use planning tools such as mind mapping and page maps.
- Put purpose up front, making it easily accessible to your reader.
- Keep your sentences to 25 words or fewer.

Chapter 2 reviews sentence structure, enabling you to analyze sentences so that you gain control of your editing skills. Follow the plan outlined in this book—no excuses and no shortcuts. *Do the work, and you will see the results.*

Writing Workshop

At the end of each chapter, you will find a *Writing Workshop* that presents a focused-writing topic. These activities give you practice building your ability to compose freely while blocking the compulsion to correct or edit your writing.

Topic: Journaling for Insight

Journaling is a potent form of self-reflection. As an ancient saying tells us, "If you hold it in, it destroys you; if you let it out, it frees you."

To maximize the benefits of journaling, here are two suggestions:

1. Write at least 4 times a week for 10 minutes or 3 pages each time.
2. Get a notebook so that you stay organized.

If you have never written in a *free flow of consciousness* style, now is the time to try it. By releasing stress and the emotions that go along with it, you will clear your head.

Or you may choose to take a more structured approach:

- *Write your memoir one page at a time.* Focus on one experience at a time; writing will help you discover your own story.

- *Keep a work journal.* Gain insight into how to improve work processes, solve work-related problems in a consistent way, and keep track of ideas so that you take action.

Writing about your experiences opens the process so that you can let go of unproductive ways of thinking that hold you back. Write until you see the connection between doing the work and seeing the results.

Journaling helps you find your voice and gives you experience composing freely as you use writing as a problem-solving tool.

A Sample Journal Entry

> Today I woke up very early. I was surprised when I opened my eyes, and it was still dark. I tried to go back to sleep, but I wasn't tired anymore. For half an hour, I tried to go back to my dreams, and suddenly I found myself thinking about my life, my past, my present, and my future. My mind—like the sand, the wind, and the sea—was trying to mix everything together into an eternal philosophy of loose thoughts.
>
> It was a long time since I opened my eyes and looked into my soul. In that personal world, I started to live reality in another dimension—a dimension so unique, so beautiful, so deep that it couldn't even take the best hours, the best writings to describe it. It is the dimension of personal analysis where you can judge your actions and your world with only your consequence. It is a dimension that tells you who you really are, what you really do, and where you are going with your life. It is a dimension full of truth, sadness, and happiness.
>
> In this dimension, I passed two hours of my early day, and I was very happy with myself. I felt as though a stone had been removed from my back. I had so much energy and courage that I felt as if I could take on the whole world. I had so much energy because I was happy. I understood that every day could be a beautiful day as long as I am in touch with my spirit when I wake up.[3]
>
> --D. M.

Editing Workshop

At the end of each chapter, you will find an Editing Workshop. Each Editing Workshop contains a draft and a revision.

Work on the draft before looking at the revision that appears on the page following the draft.

Draft

Instructions: Edit the following message. Put purpose up front and then cut unnecessary information. (See the next page for the revision.)

In fact, as you read the message below, imagine that you are the recipient—when do you finally understand what Mallory needs from you?

> Max,
>
> I am not sure if you are aware of the meetings scheduled to begin next week between my department and the sales representatives. Let me give you some of the background. We have organized a meeting with the sales reps to discuss each product that we are selling so that we can discuss strategies, goals, and how these products are doing currently in the marketplace. I am currently gathering information to finalize my report and would like to have you look it over to make sure that the financials are up to date—you're the expert in that area! As you review my report and update the numbers also let me know if you have any ideas on how to make it more effective and to add any information you think necessary.
>
> Attached please find my report; let me know any changes you might be so kind to suggest by Friday. I know this is short notice, so thank you in advance for your help.
>
> Mallory

Revision

Your revision may be different from the key below; in general, there is never only one right answer, but instead many good options.

> Max,
>
> Can you give me your feedback on the attached by Friday?
>
> Look at the financials, and let me know if they are correct. Any other suggestions you can give me would also be helpful.
>
> I'm using the report in a meeting with sales representatives next week. If you can't give me your input by Friday, please let me know so that I can make other arrangements.
>
> Thanks for your help—please call me if you have questions.
>
> Mallory
>
> PS Since this is such short notice, I also left you a voice mail!

End Notes

1. Byron Katie, *Loving What Is: Four Questions That Can Change Your Life*, Three Rivers Press, 2003.
2. Larry W. Phillips, Editor, *Ernest Hemingway on Writing*, Scribner, New York, 1984, page 28.
3. D. M.'s voice comes through with clarity and authenticity—don't expect this kind of writing from yourself, especially at first.

2

The Sentence Core

If you think that you need to become a better writer to produce writing that gets results, your focus is wrong. Writing is an elusive process that even the best writers never master. However, editing is a tangible skill that brings immediate results.

Effective editing reshapes writing until it achieves the desired effect. When you have stopped editing *as you compose,* you are ready to develop your editing skills in a serious way. However, if you think you can become an expert editor without being able to analyze the most simple elements of a sentence, you are also incorrect.

The base of editing is the sentence, and the most powerful unit of editing is the *sentence core.* However, off the top of your head, can you even say with confidence what a sentence is? In fact, what is the *sentence core*?

Even though you might be a bit stumped for the answers, you still might be feeling annoyed and saying, "I don't want to waste my time reviewing information this basic."

If you are like most writers, you have *learning gaps*; and those learning gaps will hinder you until you correct them. Keep an open mind, start from the beginning, and expect some surprises.

What Is a Sentence?

OK, leave your ego at the door—can you define what a sentence is? What about qualities of well-written sentences—can you name a few?

Before you turn the page, jot down the words or ideas about sentences that pop into your mind.

If you feel at a loss for words, you can begin to understand why this chapter may contain some useful information. Here is the definition of a sentence:

> A *sentence* consists of a subject and a verb and expresses a complete thought.

Even if your definition does not match this definition exactly, it can still be correct. For example, some people use the word *noun* instead of *subject*. Some use the word *predicate* instead of *verb*. Some use the phrase "can stand on its own," rather than "complete thought."

Another term for sentence is *independent clause*. The word *clause* refers to *a group of words that has a subject and verb*. When a clause cannot stand on its own, it is a *dependent clause*. Here is a recap:

- *Independent Clause*: a group of words that has a *subject* and *verb* and expresses a complete thought; an independent clause is a complete sentence.
- *Dependent Clause*: a group of words that has a *subject* and *verb* but does not express a complete thought; a dependent clause cannot stand on its own.

When a sentence consists of an independent clause and a dependent clause, the independent clause is the *main clause*.

What Is the Sentence Core?

Together the *subject* and *verb* form the **sentence core**. The sentence core is the critical point at which grammar and writing style cross paths.

At this point, bad memories of diagramming sentences may be haunting you. However, understanding the sentence core is a much simpler and effective solution than diagramming. Here's the good news:

> By gaining control of the sentence core, you gain control of grammar and your writing style.

Here are few points about subjects and verbs:

- In sentences, the subject almost always precedes the verb.
- The verb determines the subject of the sentence.
- The verb also determines the object, if there is one.

The first step in analyzing sentences is identifying the core: statements are generally structured as subject – verb – object (S - V - O).

In the following examples, the <u>verbs</u> are underlined twice; the <u>subjects</u>, once; and the **objects** are in bold typeface; for example:

>Marcus attended the **conference**.
>S   V   O

While all sentences have a subject and verb, not all sentences have an object (in fact, the object is not a critical element of the sentence core):

>The <u>train</u> <u>arrived</u>.
>   S   V

To form a question, use a helper verb and invert the subject and (part of) the verb:

>Did the train arrive?
>V   S   V
>
>Has Marcus attended the **conference**?
>V   S   V   O

To identify the subject and verb of a question, invert the question back to a statement; for example:

>The train did arrive.
>
>Marcus has attended the conference.

In practice exercises, identify the verb first and then its subject:

1. The verb is usually easier to identify than the subject.
2. The verb of a sentence determines its subject.

After you identify the verb, work backward in the sentence to find its subject.

Now let's look at subjects in more detail. To start, are you aware that the *grammatical subject* of a sentence may not be its *real subject*?

What Is a Subject?

Ideally, the subject of a sentence drives the action of the verb and answers the question "*Who* or *what* performs the action of the verb?"

As Karen Gordon explains in *The Deluxe Transitive Vampire*, "The subject is that part of a sentence about which something is divulged; it is what the sentence's other words are gossiping about."[1]

The subject of a sentence usually comes in the form of a *noun* or *pronoun* or *phrase:*

- A noun is a person, place, or thing, but it can also be an intangible item that cannot be seen or felt, such as *joy* or *wind* or *integrity*.
- A pronoun is a word that can be used in place of a noun, such as *I, you, he, she, it, we, they, who,* and *someone,* among others.
- A phrase is a group of related words, but a phrase does not have a subject and verb and cannot stand alone.

Knowing whether a subject is a noun or pronoun or phrase can be helpful at times; however, knowing the role the subject plays in relation to the verb is ultimately more valuable. Here are the two types subjects that are vital to understand when it comes to editing:

- Grammatical Subject
- Real Subject

Knowing whether a subject is *grammatical* or *real* or *both* is essential for analyzing sentences. Once you understand the difference, you will have learned a key principle for editing effectively.

What Is a Grammatical Subject?

Every sentence has a **grammatical subject**, defined as *the simple subject that precedes the verb in a statement*. The grammatical subject is simply referred to as "the subject." In fact, the grammatical subject is not always stated in the sentence and is sometimes *implied* (such as "you understood" and "I understood").

A **complete subject** *consists of the simple subject and all the words that modify it*. For writing purposes, the simple subject is important for a few reasons, but primarily because the simple subject must agree with its verb.

In the following sentences, the simple subject is underlined once:

>The new <u>manager</u> will chair the committee.
>
>All <u>members</u> of the task force are in the conference room.
>
><u>They</u> are working diligently.
>
>Her <u>honesty</u> is admirable.
>
>(<u>You</u>) please give the information to Marie.
>
>(<u>I</u>) Thank you for your help.

Here is a recap:

- A grammatical subject precedes its verb in a statement.
- When the grammatical subject is not present in the sentence, it becomes an *implied subject*.
- Implied subjects come in the form of *you understood* or *I understood*.
- *You understood* is displayed as follows: (You)
- *I understood* is displayed as follows: (I)

The subjects discussed so far (grammatical subjects: complete, simple, and implied) all relate to structure. The type of subject that more directly relates to writing style is the *real subject*.

What Is a Real Subject?

You may not have been aware that the *grammatical subject* of a sentence was not necessarily its *real subject*. In fact, "real subject" may be an unfamiliar term.

The real subject becomes critical to understand when it comes to editing or improving your writing style.

- The real subject drives the action of the verb.
- The real subject is the "who" or "what" that performs the action of the verb.

In the following example, the real subject and grammatical subject are one and the same; the subject is underlined once, the verb twice:

> <u>Billy</u> <u>threw</u> the ball.

In the following sentence, the real subject "Billy" is still performing the action; however, "Billy" is now in the object position.

> The <u>ball</u> <u>was thrown</u> by Billy.

When the person or thing performing the action is not the grammatical subject, a sentence is considered **passive**. When the person or thing performing the action is the grammatical subject, the sentence is considered **active**.

Here is a recap:

- The grammatical subject precedes the verb.
- The real subject drives the action of the verb.

When the real subject and the grammatical subject are the same, sentences are written in the **active voice**. Sentences written in the active voice are more clear and concise than those in passive voice.

You gain more practice with real subjects and the active voice in Chapter 7, "Active Voice." Now let's learn a few details about verbs, but just enough to help you recognize them.

What Is a Verb?

The verb drives the action of the sentence, determining the subject and the object, if there is one. The *verb* is the **simple predicate**; the **complete predicate** *consists of the verb and other elements of the sentence such as objects or modifiers or complements of verbs.*[2]

In English, verbs indicate time: the form of the verb tells you whether an event *happened* yesterday, *is happening* now, or *will happen* tomorrow. In fact, the verb is the only part of speech that changes time—that is why verbs have *tenses*.

You learn more about verbs in Chapter 6, "Verbs"; until then, here are some details to help you recognize verbs easily:

- All verbs have a *base form*; *to* plus the base form of a verb is its *infinitive: to go, to see.*
- All verbs have a *gerund form*: a *gerund* consists of *ing* plus the base form of the verb: *going, walking, being.*
- Verbs often string together, most often showing up in pairs (as in *will go* or *does know*).
- Common helping verbs are *to be* (is, are, was, were), *to have* (has, have, had), and *to do* (do, did, done).

Here are some tips to help you recognize the verb of a sentence:

1. Look for a word that expresses action, such as *speak, implement,* or *recognize.*
2. Look for a word that tells time and in doing so changes form, such as *speak, spoke, spoken,* and so on.
3. Look for the words *not* and *will*:
   a. You will generally find a verb after the word *will*, such as *will implement, will speak, will recognize, will find,* and so on.

b. You will generally find a verb before and/or after the word *not*,* such as *did* not *go*, *has* not *recognized*, *has* not *implemented*, *has* not *spoken*, am *not*, and so on.

Here are a few more examples:

Expressing Action:

Michael *finishes* his projects on time.

The committee *meets* every Friday.

I *complete* the inventory monthly.

Changing Time:

Michael *finished* his projects on time.

The committee *met* every Friday.

I *will complete* the inventory.

Preceding/Following *Not* or *Will*:

Michael *will finish* his projects on time.

The committee *did* not *meet* every Friday.

I *will* not *complete* the inventory.

In the following sentences, the verb is underlined twice, the subject once:

Alexander watched the PowerPoint presentation.

My manager will apply the policy to everyone in our department.

The meeting is not scheduled for May 29.

He discovers errors in our reports every week.

At times, a verb will need a *helper*, which is also known as an *auxiliary*. When you see a *helper verb*, look for another verb to follow it.

*Note: The word *not* does not function as a verb; instead, *not* modifies a verb and negates it.

Here are common helping verbs and their various forms:

Infinitive	Verb Forms
to be	am, is, are, was, were
to have	have, has, had
to do	do, did, done

Because the verb *to be* does not transfer action, it is a *linking verb*. Since *to be* is also an irregular verb, you will have an easier time if you memorize its various forms: *am, is, are, was, were*. (When you work on Chapter 6: "Verbs," you learn more about linking verbs, which are also called *state of being* verbs.)

In the following examples, verbs are underlined twice and subjects once:

Marc had offered to prepare the agenda.

The meeting was cancelled.

The change did not affect our schedules.

Take a few minutes to complete the practice below.

PRACTICE 2.1

Instructions: Identify the sentence core in the following sentences. First identify the verb by underlining it twice; next identify the subject by underlining it once, as shown above.

For example: Please send me my invoice by Friday.

(You) Please send me my invoice by Friday.

1. The order contained too many unnecessary products.
2. I thanked the new engineer for fixing the electrical problem.
3. Thank you for asking that question.
4. Our new program will begin in one month.
5. Examine the order carefully before sending it out.

Note: See page 357 for the key to the above exercise.

What Is a Compound Subject?

A compound subject consists or two or more words or phrases, for example:

> <u>Alice</u> and <u>Joyce</u> <u>planned</u> the reunion.
>
> Your <u>brother</u> and <u>sister</u> <u>can assist</u> you with the family reunion.
>
> My <u>manager</u> and the <u>vice president</u> <u>will attend</u> the meeting.

Writers sometimes use compound subjects that are redundant, such as:

> My <u>thoughts</u> and <u>ideas</u> <u>are</u> clearer today than they were yesterday.
>
> The <u>issues</u> and <u>concerns</u> <u>were discussed</u> at the last meeting.

Why not simply say,

> My <u>thoughts</u> <u>are</u> clearer today than they were yesterday.
>
> The <u>issues</u> <u>were discussed</u> at the last meeting.

Edit your writing closely so that you cut redundant subjects.

PRACTICE 2.2

Instructions: Identify the sentence core by underlining the verb twice and the subject once; then cut redundant subjects.

Weak: My <u>plan</u> and <u>strategy</u> for running the campaign <u>caught</u> their interest.

Revised: My <u>strategy</u> for running the campaign <u>caught</u> their interest.

1. My friends and associates tell me now is a good time to buy gold.
2. The details and specifics about the project were fascinating.
3. Visitors and guests should sign in at the front desk.
4. My goals and objectives reveal my dreams.
5. The results and outcomes reflect our success.

Note: See page 357 for the key to the above exercise.

What Is a Compound Verb?

A compound verb consists of two or more main verbs along with their helpers, as in the following:

> My associate had called and asked me for a favor.
>
> Hard work causes me to apply myself and focuses my attention.
>
> Jogging improves my health, motivates me, and encourages me to eat less.

As subjects can be redundant at times, so can verbs:

> I read and analyzed the report.
>
> The assistant listened to their responses and recorded them.

Why not simply say,

> I analyzed the report.
>
> The assistant recorded their responses.

Be sure that when you use compound verbs, each verb has a reason to be in the sentence. Of course, a sentence can have a compound subject and a compound verb, for example:

> Margie and Seth opened the invitation and expressed their surprise.

After you complete the Practice below, you will review compound sentences.

PRACTICE 2.3

Instructions: First identify the sentence core by underlining the verb twice and the subject once; then identify and cut any redundant verbs.

Weak: Mary identified and requested the rooms for the conference.

Revised: Mary requested the rooms for the conference.

1. Milton's decision uncovers and reveals his true motives.
2. Mark's actions surprised me and caught me off guard.
3. We started the project and worked on it for two hours.
4. I understand and appreciate your commitment to our mission.
5. Melanie greeted us and welcomed us to the banquet.

Note: See page 357 for the key to the above exercise.

What Is a Compound Sentence?

A compound sentence contains two main clauses, as in the following:

> <u>Joe</u> <u>called</u> about the opening in marketing, and <u>he</u> <u>expressed</u> an interest in applying for it.

> The new <u>ad</u> <u>will</u> <u>run</u> for two weeks, but then <u>we</u> <u>will</u> <u>need</u> a new one.

> My <u>manager</u> <u>asked</u> me to include the details, so <u>I</u> <u>presented</u> the entire report.

When writing a compound sentence, make sure that you are writing about only *one topic* and not randomly connecting ideas, for example:

> Joe called about the opening in marketing, and we need to run a new ad.

What is the above sentence leading to? Why are these two ideas linked? Disjointed ideas are fine if you are speaking with someone face to face; however, when you write, stay focused until your ideas are fully developed.

In the next chapter, you learn about conjunctions and how they effectively link ideas and show relationships, improving the flow of sentences.

What Is a Phrase?

A phrase is a group of related words that does *not* have a subject and a predicate and thus cannot stand alone. Here are two important types of phrases and their definitions:

- *Infinitive phrase:* an infinitive along with its object or complement and modifiers. An infinitive is the word *to* plus the base form of a verb, as in *to go, to walk,* and *to speak.*

- *Gerund phrase:* a gerund along with its object or complement and modifiers. A gerund is formed by adding *ing* to the base form of a verb, as in *going, walking,* and *speaking.*

Infinitive Phrases	**Gerund Phrases**
to go to the store	*going* to the store
to buy what you need	*buying* what you need
to attend class daily	*attending* class daily
to inform the staff	*informing* the staff

In addition to gerund and infinitive phrases, you are probably somewhat familiar with **prepositional phrases**. Here is a brief reminder of how to identify a prepositional phrase:

- *Prepositional phrase:* a preposition along with a noun and its modifiers. Some common prepositions are *between, from, to, on, under, with, by,* and *along.*

Prepositional Phrases

on the table	*behind* the desk
to the store	*by* the bookcase
after the meeting	*between* the two of us

In general, gerund and infinitive phrases need special attention. For example, use gerund and infinitive phrases consistently within a sentence or in a list.

In the examples below, notice how the inconsistent list becomes reader friendly when the phrases are presented as gerund *or* infinitive phrases:

Inconsistent List:
1. Maintenance of client list.
2. Expense accounts calculated.
3. Travel arrangements.

Gerund Phrases:
1. Maintaining client lists.
2. Calculating expense accounts.
3. Making travel arrangements.

Infinitive Phrases:
1. (To) Maintain client lists.
2. (To) Calculate expense accounts.
3. (To) Make travel arrangements.

When you list items, use gerund phrases *or* infinitive phrases, remaining consistent with one or the other. Consistency ensures that you achieve **parallel structure**, which means that you represent your words and phrases in the same grammatical form. (For more information and exercises, see Chapter 8, "Parallel Structure.")

PRACTICE 2.4

As shown in the examples above, use either gerund or infinitive phrases to make the following lists consistent and thus parallel. (Hint: Identify the action being performed first; for example, "office supplies need to be ordered": "ordered" is the action, which can be represented as "to order" or "ordering.")

List 1:
1. Office supplies need to be ordered
2. Appointment scheduling
3. Certificate renewal

List 2:
1. Coordination of schedules
2. Supplies distributed
3. Phone follow-up with clients

List 3:
1. Staff training
2. The development of policy
3. Profit and loss reconciliation

Note: See pages 357-358 for the key to the above exercise.

Why Is the Sentence Core Important?

The sentence core consists of the subject and verb: together the subject and verb convey meaning. One without the other, and meaning is incomplete. In fact, readers become confused if the sentence core is presented ineffectively. Let's start with an example:

> My associate Jane Culver, who has worked with me on several projects in the last few months and who has a great deal of expertise in the field of writing as well as consulting, will be our keynote speaker.

Does the above sound wordy and confusing? Was the sentence clear from the beginning? Now read the revision:

> My associate Jane Culver will be our keynote speaker. By the way, she has worked with me on several projects in the last few months and has a great deal of expertise in the field of writing as well as consulting.

Is the revision easier to understand? The major difference relates to the sentence core:

> <u>Jane Culver</u> <u>will be</u> our keynote speaker.

In general, the closer the subject and verb are to each other, the easier it is for a reader to understand meaning.

Here are some editing tips on presenting the sentence core effectively:

1. Keep the subject and verb close to each other.
2. Keep the sentence core close to the beginning of the sentence.

To further enhance the sentence core, focus on using **real subjects** and **strong verbs**. While most verbs are action verbs, the following verbs are considered weak verbs: *make*, *give*, and *take* as well as the verb *to be*: *is*, *are*, *was*, and *were*. Here are a few examples of sentences that have a weak sentence core:

Weak: We *will give* you the information you need.
Revised: We *will inform* you.

Weak: *Take* that into consideration when you apply.
Revised: *Consider* that when you apply.

Subjects can also be weak. When possible, avoid using *it* or *there* as a subject. Here are a few examples:

Weak: It is time for change.
Revised: The time for change is now.

Weak: There are many decisions pending.
Revised: Many decisions are pending.

Consider the above points as an introduction; the next few chapters cover more detail about developing a strong sentence core.

Complete the exercise that follows to gain practice with real subjects and strong verbs.

PRACTICE 2.5

Instructions: Edit the following sentences by changing the sentence core so that it consists of a real subject and strong verb.

Weak: It was a decision that Mr. James regrets.
Revised: Mr. <u>James</u> <u>regrets</u> the decision.

1. There are five orders that need to be filled by customer service.
2. It is an electrical problem on the fifth floor that caused the outage.
3. Randy will make a revision of the document today.
4. There is a new report that arrived earlier today.
5. You can make a decision tomorrow.

Note: See page 358 for the key to the above exercise.

Recap

This chapter has focused on sentence structure and the sentence core, which consists of the verb and its subject.

- To identify the sentence core, identify the verb first and then work backward to find its subject.
- To identify a verb, look for a word that expresses action and that changes form when it changes time (past, present, or future).
- Write sentences in which the grammatical subject and real subject are one and the same.
- Avoid writing sentences that begin with "it is" or "there are"; instead write sentences that have a *real subject* and *strong verb*.
- When you write a sentence that has a compound subject or verb, check for redundancy.
- When making a list, use gerunds *or* infinitives so that your writing remains parallel.

Writing Workshop

Topic: What do you value?

Frederic M. Hudson and Pamela D. McLean discovered, after studying hundreds of biographies of successful adults, that people evaluated their lives based on some combination of six core values.[3]

- *Personal Mastery: to know thyself* (self-esteem, confidence, identity, inner motivation, a positive sense of self, and courage)
- *Achievement: to reach your goals* (working, winning, playing in sports, getting results and recognition, being purposeful)
- *Intimacy: to love and be loved* (bonding, caring, feeling close, making relationships work, being a friend, being connected)
- *Play and Creativity: to follow your intuition* (being imaginative, spontaneous, original, expressive, artistic, funny, curious, child-like, not being purposeful)
- *Search for Meaning: to find wholeness* (spiritual integrity, unity, integrity, peace, an inner connection to all things, spirituality, trust in the flow of life, inner wisdom, connecting with nature, connecting with a higher power, focus on being)
- *Compassion and Contribution: to leave a legacy* (improving, helping, feeding, reforming, leaving the world a better place, serving, social and environmental caring, institution-building, volunteering, engaging in activism)

Which core value is most important to you? That's your key source of energy and passion. By focusing on activities that are congruent with your most important values, you find more energy and satisfaction. In turn, when you focus on activities that are incongruent with your values, your energy and passion are sapped.

Rank order the core values listed above to identify which are most important to you at this point in your life. (1 = most important; 6 = least important). Also write a few comments to describe how you express each value.

Prioritizing core values involves difficult choices but helps you make important life adjustments. As John Dewey once said, "You become what you learn." *Who do you want to become?* Is there something that you need to learn to bring your life to a higher level of congruence leading to more joy and satisfaction?

Editing Workshop

Draft

Instructions: Based on what you have learned so far, edit the following message, keeping these principles in mind:

- Put purpose up front.
- Keep phrases parallel.
- Use a strong sentence core.

After you work on the draft below, review the review the revision on the next page.

> Bart,
> It was brought to my attention that you have the following items available in your office.
>
> 1. Policy manuals that have been revised.
> 2. Flyers to promote our new product line.
> 3. To keep things in order, new ½ inch binders.
>
> I need 100 sets of materials. If you do in fact have these items available, it would be greatly appreciated if you could send them to me so that I receive these items by Friday. We are having a staff meeting on Monday, October 14, and your sending me these products will help me in my preparations.
>
> At our staff meeting, we will discuss our new products as well as the revised policies.
> J.T.

Revision

How does your revised message compare with the following? Though your message may not be the same, what changes did you make?

Bart,

Can you send me 100 sets of the following by Friday afternoon:

1. Revised policy manuals.
2. New product promotion flyers.
3. One-half inch binders.

I'm having a staff meeting on Monday, October 14, to discuss new products and revised policies.

If you cannot help me with this, please let me know as soon as possible.

Thanks and hope your day is going well.

J.T.

End Notes

1. Karen Elizabeth Gordon, *The Deluxe Transitive Vampire*, Pantheon Books, New York, 1993, page 3.
2. Sidney Greenbaum, *A College Grammar of English*, Longman, New York, 1989, page 27.
3. Frederick M. Hudson and Pamela D. McLean, *Life Launch: A Passionate Guide to the Rest of Your Life*, The Hudson Institute Press, Santa Barbara, CA, 1995.

3

Conjunctions

Think back—do you remember the Sesame Street song, *Conjunction Junction*: "Conjunction Junction, what's your function?" If you remember the song, you may begin to smile as the tune sets in.[1]

On face value, conjunctions do not seem to be a vital part of speech, when in fact conjunctions play a critical role in writing. Besides being bridges and connectors, the following three types of conjunctions also play a critical role in punctuation:

- Coordinating
- Subordinating
- Adverbial

Thus, conjunctions have the power to reduce your frustration with commas and improve your writing style, all at the same time. In this chapter, in addition to conjunctions, you also learn how to transform fragments into complete sentences. So let's get started.

Why Are Conjunctions Important?

Conjunctions play a critical role in punctuation and writing style:

- Conjunctions show relationships and bridge ideas, adding smooth transitions to choppy writing.
- Conjunctions pull the reader's thinking along with the writer's intention.
- Conjunctions signal when to use commas and semicolons.

Conjunctions place focus on key points so that writing becomes clearer and easier to understand. By pulling the reader's thinking along with yours, you help the reader draw conclusions.

As you use conjunctions more effectively, your writing style improves. The first step is becoming familiar with the terms and learning a few examples in each category. In the next two chapters, you use conjunctions as signals for placing commas and semicolons. In other words, the work you do in this chapter makes your work in the next two chapters that much easier.

And though you still might prefer to skip ahead, realize that with a bit of practice, you will use the terms *coordinating*, *subordinating*, and *adverbial* with ease. Now let's get to work on conjunctions.

What Are Coordinating Conjunctions?

Coordinating conjunctions connect equal grammatical parts. There are only seven coordinating conjunctions, and they are as follows:

        and   but   or   for   nor   so   yet

The acronym FANBOYS makes it easier to remember all seven of them: For, And, Nor, But, Or, Yet, So; however, the most commonly used coordinating conjunctions are *and, but,* and *or.*

The equal grammatical parts that coordinating conjunctions connect are *sentences*, *words*, and *phrases*. Thus, coordinating conjunctions play an important role in maintaining parallel structure as well as punctuation, which is covered in detail in Chapter 4, "Comma Rules."

What Are Subordinating Conjunctions?

Subordinating conjunctions show relationships between ideas and, in the process, make one idea dependent on the other.

By drawing connections for the reader, subordinating conjunctions help improve the flow of your writing.

Here are some common subordinating conjunctions:

after	because	since	even though
although	before	so that	when
as	until	though	while
as soon as	unless	whereas	if

The above list is not complete; for now, select a few, and memorize them. You can test whether a word or phrase is a subordinating conjunction by placing it at the beginning of a complete sentence. If the sentence no longer sounds complete, the word is likely a subordinating conjunction (SC), for example:

Complete sentence: Bob walked to the store.
SC added: *If* Bob walked to the store . . . *what then?*

Complete sentence: My manager arrived late.
SC added: *Since* my manager arrived late . . . *what then?*

Complete sentence: The sale begins today.
SC added: *Even though* the sale begins today . . . *what then?*

Subordinating conjunctions do what their name implies: "to subordinate" means "to make less than." In the examples above, you have seen that when you place a subordinating conjunction at the beginning of a complete sentence, the sentence is no longer complete. The "incomplete sentence" becomes a **dependent clause**. Here are more examples:

Complete sentence: The attendant asked for my receipt.
Dependent clause: *When* the attendant asked for my receipt . . . *what then?*

Complete sentence: Our car is parked in the lot.
Dependent clause: *Since* our car is parked in the lot . . . *what then?*

Complete sentence: Our team meets on Friday.

Dependent clause: *After* our team meets on Friday . . . *what then?*

Punctuating a dependent clause as if it is a complete sentence results in a *fragment;* a fragment is a common grammatical error, but a serious one.

Write a sentence or two, and then go back and place a subordinating conjunction at the beginning of each, as shown in the previous set of examples. Do you see how a subordinating conjunction affects both the grammar and meaning of a sentence?

Now let's take a look at adverbial conjunctions.

What Are Adverbial Conjunctions?

Adverbial conjunctions bridge ideas, and they are known as *transition words*. Here are some examples of common adverbial conjunctions:

however	therefore	thus	for example
consequently	in summary	hence	in conclusion
as a result	in general	finally	in other words

Adverbial conjunctions help pull the reader's thinking along with the writer's intention. Use them at the beginning of a sentence to *introduce* it, in the middle of a sentence to *interrupt* the flow of thought, or between two sentences to *bridge* the sentences and link them together:

Introducing: *Therefore,* I will not be able to attend the conference.

Interrupting: The Jones Corporation, *however,* is not our vendor of choice.

Bridging: George will attend the conference in my place; *as a result,* I can assist you on the new project.

44 *A Guide for Business Writing*

Here are more kinds of transitions that adverbial conjunctions make:

Compare or contrast:	however, in contrast, on the other hand, on the contrary, conversely, otherwise, nevertheless
Summarize:	in summary, in conclusion, as a result, thus, therefore, hence
Illustrate:	for example, for instance, hence, in general, thus, mostly
Add information:	in addition, additionally, furthermore, moreover, also, too
Show results:	fortunately, unfortunately, consequently, as usual, of course
Sequence or show time:	first, second, third, finally, meanwhile, in the meantime, to begin with
Conclude:	finally, in summary, in conclusion

Adverbial conjunctions appear as single words or short phrases. As a reader, use these transition words to identify key points. As a writer, use these transition words in a conscious way to pull your reader's thinking along with yours.

Next, let's take a look at fragments, one of the most common types of writing errors; but first, complete the exercise below.

PRACTICE 3.1

Instructions: Revise the following paragraph by adding conjunctions, thereby improving its flow.

> The construction for the 9th floor conference room was extended two more weeks. We were not informed until Friday. Our meetings for the following week needed to be reassigned to different rooms. None were available. Jane Simmons agreed to let us use her office. Several serious conflicts were avoided.

Note: See page 358 for a key to the above exercise.

What Is a Fragment?

A **fragment** is an incomplete statement that is punctuated as if it were a complete sentence. Most often, fragments come in the form of gerund phrases, infinitive phrases, or dependent clauses. Below are examples of fragments broken down by type (*gerunds*, *infinitives*, and *subordinating conjunctions* are shown in italics):

Gerund Phrases:	*Walking* slowly to the beach on a sunny day
	Following a list of directions precisely
Infinitive Phrases:	*To walk* slowly to the beach on a sunny day
	To follow a list of directions precisely
Dependent clauses:	*When* I walked slowly to the beach on a sunny day
	After Bob followed the list of instructions
	that you gave him

Notice that gerund and infinitive phrases do not contain a subject and a verb. However, when a gerund or infinitive phrase is long, writers can incorrectly punctuate it as a complete sentence.

How you correct a fragment depends on the type of fragment that you are dealing with. Let's take a look at how to use a simple solution to correct a serious grammatical error.

How Do You Correct a Fragment?

You have already seen that three common types of fragments are gerund phrases, infinitive phrases, and dependent clauses.

To correct a fragment consisting of a gerund or an infinitive phrase, use the phrase as the <u>subject</u>, add a <u>verb</u>, and then finish your thought, as follows:

<u>Walking slowly to the beach on a sunny day</u> <u>feels</u> good.

<u>To walk slowly to the beach on a sunny day</u> <u>is</u> recommended.

Another way to correct a gerund and an infinitive fragment would be to use the fragment as the object of a sentence (objects are shown in bold below) by adding a <u>subject</u> and a <u>verb</u>, as follows:

> George's favorite <u>activity</u> <u>is</u> **walking slowly to the beach on a sunny day.**
>
> <u>I</u> <u>prefer</u> **to walk slowly to the beach on a sunny day.**

Here is how to correct a fragment resulting from a dependent clause:

1. Use the dependent clause before a main clause to introduce the main clause,
2. Use the dependent clause after a main clause as a finishing thought, or
3. Remove the subordinating conjunction at the beginning of the clause.

In the sentences below, each dependent clause is italicized:

> *When I walk slowly to the beach on a sunny day*, my mind always wanders.
>
> I left work early *because I finished the list of instructions precisely as given.*

When the subordinating conjunction is removed, a dependent clause can become a complete sentence; for example:

> ~~When~~ I walk slowly to the beach on a sunny day.
>
> ~~Because~~ I finished the list of instructions precisely as given.

Get some practice turning fragments into sentences by doing the exercise that follows.

PRACTICE 3.2

Instructions: Use your creativity to turn the following fragments into complete sentences.

Incorrect:	Finding enough time to complete the report.
Revised:	<u>Finding enough time to complete the report was</u> a challenge.
Revised:	My <u>challenge was</u> to find enough time to complete the report.

1. Making the right decision at the right time and feeling good about it.
2. Because he finished the project much earlier than anyone expected.
3. After I made the decision to reclaim my initial investment in the stock.
4. To show interest in a project that no longer had merit.
5. Going slower than planned but staying under budget.

Note: See page 358 for a key to the above exercise.

You have now done the pre-work necessary to start your work with commas. In fact, this work will assist you with using all types of punctuation marks correctly.

Recap

In this chapter, you have refreshed your understanding of the various types of conjunctions; you have also worked on correcting sentence fragments.

- ➢ Conjunctions build bridges between ideas and signal key points for readers.
- ➢ A *dependent clause*, also known as a *subordinate clause*, begins with a subordinating conjunction.
- ➢ Phrases and dependent clauses that are punctuated as complete sentences are *fragments*.

Writing Workshop

Topic: Writing Your Story

Write a six- to ten-page paper on the story of your life. In particular, explore the following areas:

- Recall the earliest instance when you declared what you wanted to do in life. Write how your vocational declarations deepened or changed over time.
- Describe the influential people in your life and the impact they have had on your life.
- Explain the major events that had a life-changing effect on you.
- Describe the natural talents that other people notice in you (go as far back as you can remember). We all have natural talents. Since these gifts are natural, they are often overlooked by us.

To get your words flowing, complete the following:

When I was a child . . .

The best advice anyone ever gave me . . .

My passion in life . . .

I wish that I were able to . . .

If I could have any job in the world . . .

Editing Workshop

Draft

Instructions: Edit the following message by getting to the point and adding white space; can you use conjunctions to improve the flow?

> J.T., in your last message, you requested 100 sets of materials. I do have some materials to send you. I will also have a meeting with my staff next week. I cannot send you all of the materials that I have available. I would not have enough for my meeting. I do not have enough binders. I can send you only 70 complete sets. You can have as many revised policy manuals and new product flyers as you need. You will only need to purchase 30 binders from your office supplier. Bart

Revision

How does your revised message compare with the following? Though your revision may not be the same, what improvements did you make?

Conjunctions are shown in italics; notice how they add flow to the choppy writing in the draft.

> J.T.,
>
> *Since* I do not have enough binders, I can send you only 70 complete sets.
>
> *However*, you can have as many revised policy manuals and new product flyers as you need. *If* you purchase 30 binders, you'll have everything that you need.
>
> I hope this helps—good luck with your meeting!
>
> Bart

End Note

1. Just for fun, check out *Conjunction Junction* on this You Tube video: http://www.youtube.com/watch?v=7TQByv_xkuc.

4

Comma Rules

Oscar Wilde illustrated the confusion about commas and pauses perfectly when he said, "I have spent most of the day putting in a comma and the rest of the day taking it out."

That commas are not placed on the basis of pauses is a revelation to most writers, even seasoned ones. If you have been placing commas on the basis of pauses, the time to break your habit is now. Part of the problem lies in the fact that there is some truth to the "pause rule." You see, grammar creates natural breaks in structure, and those breaks generally occur between clauses.

Now that you have worked on independent and dependent clauses, identifying those natural breaks should seem easy for you, but do not rely on them. Instead, let go of just about everything that you thought that you knew about commas. Start fresh, keeping the following in mind:

When in doubt, leave the comma out.

When you do not know the rule that justifies the use of the comma, either revisit the rules or do *not* use the comma. The method applied here is foolproof. Here is what you need to do:

1. Go through this entire chapter quickly—within one or two sittings—and do the exercises.
2. Then, for the next few days, avoid using a comma unless you know the reason why you should use it.
3. When you use a comma, force yourself to specify the rule that justifies the comma use.

You still may be asking yourself, "Why are commas so important?"

Here's why: As you work on commas, *you learn the sentence core at a deeper level.* As a result, working on commas also prepares you to write powerful sentences that are also simple, clear, and concise. As you gain control of structure, you also gain control of your writing style.

To enhance what you learn in this chapter, identify the sentence core of each of the practice sentences. In the answer keys, the verb of each sentence is underlined twice, and the subject once.

In addition, this book attaches a name to each comma rule based on its function along with an abbreviation; for example, *comma conjunction (CONJ), comma series (SER), comma introductory (INTRO),* and so on. As you complete the practice exercises, identify the reason (or name) for each comma that you use.

In total, you have 12 comma rules to learn. However, the first rule tells when *not* to place a comma, with the remaining 11 rules indicating when to use commas.

Rule 1: The Sentence Core Rules

Do not separate a subject and verb with only one comma.

Though this is a rogue rule in that it does not indicate where you need to place a comma, this rule keeps you from making serious errors.

As you already know, the sentence core is the critical point at which grammar and writing cross paths; the sentence core is also the most powerful element of any sentence.

As you work through these comma rules, you will find that setting off information with a pair of commas is acceptable. However, if you find yourself placing *one comma* between a subject and verb—take out the comma *or* see if a second comma is needed.

Incorrect: George, signed the contract.
Corrected: George signed the contract.

Now let's review the remainder of the 12 comma rules, all of which give you guidance on when to use commas.

52 *A Guide for Business Writing*

Rule 2: Conjunction (CONJ)

Use a comma to separate two independent clauses when they are joined by a coordinating conjunction (and, but, or, nor, for, so, yet).

As you read the examples below, notice that the subject is underlined once and the verb underlined twice, making the sentence core apparent at a glance.

>Bill stayed late, *and* he worked on the proposal.
>
>The book was left at the front desk, *but* George did not pick it up.

Be careful not to add a comma before a coordinating conjunction when only the second part of a *compound verb* follows it, for example:

Incorrect: Bob worked on the proposal, *and* sent it to my attorney.

Corrected: Bob worked on the proposal *and* sent it to my attorney.

However, put a comma before a coordinating conjunction when an independent clause precedes it and follows it, for example:

Incorrect: The idea to implement the project was good *so* we plan to start next week.

Corrected: The idea to implement the project was good, *so* we plan to start next week.

The sentence above marked "incorrect" is an example of a **run-on sentence**: *two or more sentences coming together without sufficient punctuation.*

After working on the exercise that follows, you learn another comma rule that is also based on the use of coordinating conjunctions, Rule 3: Comma Series.

PRACTICE 4.1

Rule 2: Conjunction (CONJ)

Instructions: Identify the sentence core and then place commas where needed in the following sentences.

Incorrect: Jodie assisted with the last project so Christopher will help us with this one.

Corrected: Jodie <u>assisted</u> with the last project, so <u>Christopher</u> <u>will help</u> us with this one. (CONJ)

1. Mary O'Rourke is the new district manager and she starts on Monday.
2. Mary will be an inspiration to our staff and an excellent spokesperson for our product.
3. You can leave her a message but she will not be able to reply until next week.
4. The office in St. Louis also has a new manager and his name is Alessio Rivera.
5. You can mail your information now and receive a reply next week.

Note: See page 359 for the key to the above sentences.

REVIEW POINT

To get the maximum from the practice exercises, take the time to identify the verb and subject of each sentence.

- Identify the verb first and then the subject, which precedes the verb in statements.
- Remember that at times the subject of a sentence will be *implied* or *understood*.

Therefore, when you have difficulty identifying a subject that precedes the verb, ask yourself if the subject could be an implied subject such as *you understood* (You) or *I understood* (I).

Rule 3: Series (SER)

Use a comma to separate three or more items in a series.

A series consists of at least three items, and you may have learned that the comma before the conjunction is not required. That is true. Although the comma before the conjunction *and* is not required; for clarity, the comma is preferred, for example:

>I <u>brought</u> potatoes, peas, *and* carrots to the pot luck.
>The <u>estate</u> <u>was</u> <u>left</u> to Robert, Rose, Charles, *and* Sophie.
>My favorite activities are walking, doing yoga, and swimming.

In the first example, would you prepare the "potatoes, peas, and carrots" separately or mixed? What if the comma were missing after *peas*, as in "potatoes, peas and carrots." Would you prepare the peas and carrots separately or mixed?

In the second example, would the estate necessarily be split the same way if the comma after Charles were missing? For example:

>The estate was left to Robert, Rose, Charles *and* Sophie.

In fact, the above sentence is open for debate. Some could argue that the estate should be split only three ways, with Charles and Sophie splitting a third. Especially on legal documents, separate each entity (or separate individual) with a comma so that a debate does not ensue.

Placing the comma before the conjunction also removes other types of ambiguity; this comma rule is also referred to as the *Oxford comma*.

Another mistake is to separate *only two items* with a comma, especially when the items are long phrases (shown in italics below):

Incorrect: The <u>assistant</u> <u>provided</u> *a series of examples*, and *a good recap of the meeting*.

Corrected: The <u>assistant</u> <u>provided</u> *a series of examples* and *a good recap of the meeting*.

Complete the practice and then work on Rule 4: Comma Introductory, a rule that involves subordinating and adverbial conjunctions.

PRACTICE 4.2

Rule 3: Series (SER)

Instructions: Identify the sentence core and place commas where needed in the following sentences.

Incorrect: Jerry asked for squash peas and carrots.
Corrected: Jerry asked for squash, peas, and carrots. (SER)

1. We were assigned Conference Rooms A and B on the first floor.
2. Make sure that you bring your laptop phone and client list to the meeting.
3. You should call your manager arrange the meeting and submit your proposal.
4. Mitchell Helen and Sally conducted the workshop on culinary science.
5. They gave a workshop for Elaine Arlene Donald and Joanne on preparing cutting and storing vegetables.

Note: See page 359 for the key to the above exercise.

REVIEW POINT

As a refresher, here are the three types of conjunctions that play a role in punctuation, along with a few examples of each:

Coordinating conjunctions: *and, but, or, nor, so, yet*

Subordinating conjunctions: *if, after, while, when, as, as soon as, although, because*

Adverbial conjunctions: *however, therefore, for example, hence, as a result*

Conjunctions also play a role in creating a reader-friendly writing style because they signal the reader to key points and connections.

Rule 4: Comma Introductory (INTRO)

Place a comma after a word, phrase, or dependent clause that introduces an independent clause.

Since this rule is a bit complicated, let's break it down into the various parts: *word, phrase,* and *dependent clause.*

- In general, *word* refers to an adverbial conjunction such as *therefore, however,* and *consequently,* among others.

  However, I was not able to attend the conference.
  Therefore, we will convene the meeting in Boston this year.

- In general, *phrase* refers to a prepositional phrase, gerund phrase, or infinitive phrase.

  During that time, he spoke about the plan in detail.
  Leaving my bags at the airport, I took a taxi into the city.
  To arrive earlier, Michael rearranged his entire schedule.

- In general, a *dependent clause* begins with a subordinating conjunction, such as *since, because, although, while, if,* and so on.

  Although my calendar is full, we can meet this Friday morning.
  Before you arrive at my office, (you) call my assistant.
  Until I am available, you can use an extra office to work.

Writers mistakenly place a comma after a subordinating conjunction, for example:

Incorrect: *Although,* the information is timely, we cannot use it.
Corrected: *Although* the information is timely, we cannot use it.

Place the comma after the *dependent clause,* not after the subordinating conjunction.

PRACTICE 4.3

Rule 4: Introductory (INTRO)

Instructions: Identify the sentence core and then place commas where needed in the following sentences.

Incorrect: Although Mary flew to Boston she arrived a day late.

Corrected: Although <u>Mary</u> <u>flew</u> to Boston, <u>she</u> <u>arrived</u> late. (INTRO)

1. Because the letter arrived late we were not able to respond on time.
2. However we were given an extension.
3. Although the extra time came in handy we still felt pressured.
4. To get another extension George called their office.
5. Fortunately the office manager was agreeable to our request.

Note: See page 359 for the key to the above sentences.

REVIEW POINT

The subject and verb form the *sentence core*, the powerhouse of your sentence. Separating the subject and verb with only one comma creates a serious grammatical error. However, you can separate a subject and verb with a *set of commas*.

Rule 5: Nonrestrictive (NR)

Use commas to set off nonessential (nonrestrictive) elements.

The key to understanding this rule lies in the difference between the meaning of the words *restrictive* and *nonrestrictive*.

- *Restrictive information* is essential and should not be set off with commas.
- *Nonrestrictive information* is not essential and can be set off with commas.

Whenever you set off information between two commas, you are implying that the information *can be removed* without disturbing the structure or meaning of the sentence.

Nonrestrictive elements often come in the form of *who* or *which clauses*. Read the following two examples that illustrate this rule (*who* clauses are shown in italics):

> Alice Walker, *who is a prestigious author,* will be the keynote speaker.
>
> The woman *who is a prestigious author* will be the keynote speaker.

In the first example above, you would still know who the keynote speaker would be even if the *who* clause were removed:

> Alice Walker will be the keynote speaker.

However, in the second example, the meaning of the sentence would be unclear if the *who* clause were removed:

> The woman will be the keynote speaker. *Which woman?*

In fact, all commas that come in sets imply that the information set off by the commas can be removed; so here is another reminder of how to use commas with *essential* and *nonessential* elements:

- Essential information is *restrictive* and should not be set off with commas.
- Nonessential information is *nonrestrictive* and can be set off with commas.

Complete the following practice to test your understanding before moving on to Rule 6: Comma Parenthetical.

PRACTICE 4.4

Rule 5: Nonrestrictive (NR)

Instructions: Place commas where needed in the following sentences. The essential and nonessential clauses are shown in italics.

1. Our manager *who specializes in project grants* will assist you with this issue.
2. Tomas Phillips *who works only on weekends* will call you soon.
3. The paralegal *who researched this lawsuit* is not available.
4. Nick Richards *who is in a meeting until 3 p.m.* can answer your question.
5. Your new contract *which we mailed yesterday* should arrive by Friday.

Note: See page 359 for the key to the above sentences.

Rule 6: Parenthetical (PAR)

Use commas to set off a word or expression that interrupts the flow of a sentence.

This rule applies to adverbial conjunctions or other short phrases interjected into a sentence. By interrupting the flow of the sentence, a parenthetical expression places stress on the words that immediately precede or follow it. Parenthetical expressions should be set off with commas because they are nonessential and can be removed.

The following three examples show parenthetical expressions (shown in italics) set off with commas. Can you see how each could be removed, leaving the sentence complete and clear in meaning?

<u>Mr. Connors</u>, *however,* <u>arrived</u> after the opening ceremony.

<u>You can</u>, *therefore,* <u>place</u> your order after 5 p.m. today.

The <u>project</u>, *in my opinion,* <u>needs</u> improvement.

A common mistake occurs when a writer uses a semicolon in place of one of the commas, for example:

Incorrect: Ms. Philippe; in fact, approved the request last week.
Corrected: Ms. Philippe, in fact, approved the request last week.

Though a semicolon *can* precede an adverbial conjunction, that construction involves two sentences. In those cases, the adverbial conjunction functions as a bridge or a transition rather than an interrupter. (See Chapter 5, "Semicolons and Other Marks.")

Another common mistake occurs when a writer uses only one comma rather than a set of commas, for example:

Incorrect: Our sales representative, therefore will assist you at your convenience.
Corrected: Our sales representative, therefore, will assist you at your convenience.

Incorrect: Mr. Jones, however will plan this year's event.
Corrected: Mr. Jones, however, will plan this year's event.

The word *however* can be used as an adverb as well as an adverbial conjunction, as in the following:

> We will do the project *however* you prefer.

When using *however* as an adverb, do not set it off with commas.

Even though adverbial conjunctions are usually nonessential elements in terms of sentence structure, these conjunctions play an important role in writing style. Adverbial conjunctions provide vital clues to meaning, helping your reader identify key points.

After working on the practice below, work on Rule 7: Direct Address.

PRACTICE 4.5

Rule 6: Parenthetical (PAR)

Instructions: Identify the sentence core and then place commas where needed in the following sentences.

Incorrect:	Our contract however did not include delivery charges.
Corrected:	Our <u>contract</u>, however, <u>did</u> not <u>include</u> delivery charges. (PAR)

1. Customer service I believe can best assist you with this issue.
2. T. J. therefore will work this weekend in my place.
3. Our invoice unfortunately was submitted incorrectly.
4. The new contract in my opinion meets specifications.
5. Brown Company of course recommended us to a vendor.

Note: See page 360 for the key to the above sentences.

WRITING TIP   A Note about Style

Moving a parenthetical expression from the middle of a sentence to the beginning can improve its readability, for example:

Weak:	Our sales representative, therefore, will assist you.
Revised:	Therefore, our sales representative will assist you.

Weak:	Mr. Philippe, in fact, approved the request.
Revised:	In fact, Mr. Philippe approved the request.

Weak:	The project, in my opinion, needs improvement.
Revised:	In my opinion, the project needs improvement.

In addition, writers often interject a comment such as "I believe" or "I think" at the beginning of a sentence. By removing these kinds of parenthetical expressions, you improve the flow of the sentence.

Rule 7: Direct Address (DA)

Use commas to set off the name or title of a person addressed directly.

A direct address can appear anywhere in a sentence—at the beginning, middle, or end, as shown below:

>*Donald,* you can arrange the meeting in Dallas or Fort Worth.
>
>I gave the invitation to everyone in the department, *Marge.*
>
>Your instructions, *Professor,* were clear and to the point.

In each of the above examples, notice that the direct address is not the subject of the sentence.

Each of the following sentences also contains a direct address, but the subject of each sentence is implied. As you read each sentence, ask yourself, "*Who* is performing the action of the verb?"

>Thank you, *Astrid,* for speaking on my behalf.
>
>Feel free to call my office at your convenience, *David.*
>
>*Traci,* please assist me with the spring conference.

In the first sentence above, the implied subject is *I understood*; in the second and third, it is *you understood*:

>*I* thank you, Astrid, for speaking on my behalf.
>
>*You* feel free to call my office at your convenience, David.
>
>Traci, *you* please assist me with the spring conference.

In sentences that contain a direct address, the subject is often implied.

Complete the practice that follows before moving on to Comma Rule 8: Comma Appositive.

PRACTICE 4.6

Rule 7: Direct Address (DA)

Instructions: Identify the sentence core and then place commas where needed in the following sentences.

Incorrect: Bill please pay the delivery charges.
Corrected: Bill, (<u>you</u>) please <u>pay</u> the delivery charges. (DA)

1. Give your report to the auditor by Friday Marcel.
2. Jason do you have tickets for the game?
3. Doctor I would like to know the results of my tests.
4. Would you like to attend the banquet Alice?
5. Thank you for inviting me George.

Note: See page 360 for the key to the sentences above.

Rule 8: Appositive (AP)

Use commas to set off the restatement of a noun or pronoun.

With an appositive, an equivalency exists between the noun and its descriptor. In the examples below, the appositives are show in italics:

> <u>Caroline</u>, *my co-worker from Atlanta*, <u>requested</u> the date.
> <u>Mr. Johns</u>, *the building commissioner*, <u>refused</u> to give us a permit.

To check if the descriptor is an appositive, ask yourself questions such as the following:

> *Who is Caroline?* My co-worker from Atlanta.
> *Who is my co-worker from Atlanta?* Caroline.
>
> *Who is Mr. Johns?* The building commissioner.
> *Who is the building commissioner?* Mr. Johns.

When only one comma is used for an appositive, it changes the meaning of the sentence. Notice how the following sentences differ in meaning:

Incorrect: Josef, my former <u>boss gave</u> me the information.
Corrected: Josef, my former boss, <u>gave</u> me the information.

In the first sentence above, the subject shifts to "boss" because of Rule 1 which states, "Do not separate a subject and verb with only one comma." In the above example, leaving out the comma after "boss" turns *Josef* into a direct address, changing the meaning of the sentence. Also, grammar dictates that the real subject becomes "boss."

Appositives are not always nonrestrictive; an appositive can be restrictive, which means that the appositive is essential for clear meaning. For example, let's say that you have five brothers and one of them is named Charles, who is joining you for dinner.

Appositive: My brother, Charles, will join us for dinner.

Because of the commas, the above sentence translates to: *My brother will join us for dinner.* If you took "Charles" out of the above sentence, would the reader know which of the five brothers would join you for dinner? Thus, the above sentence is a **restricted appositive**, which would be punctuated as follows:

Restricted Appositive: My brother Charles will join us for dinner.

A restricted appositive, as illustrated by the sentence above, should not be set off with commas. For practice, complete the following exercise.

PRACTICE 4.7
Rule 8: Appositive (AP)
Instructions: Identify the sentence core and then place commas where needed in the following sentences.

1. Jacob Seinfeld our associate director decided to hire Williams.
2. Janet Sparacino my best friend applied for a job here.

3. Jim Martinez the registrar approved your request.
4. The department chair Dr. George Schmidt received your transcript.
5. The director asked Clair my sister to join us for dinner.

Note: See page 360 for the key to the above sentences.

Rule 9: Addresses and Dates (AD)

Use commas to set off the parts of addresses and dates.

The term *set off* means that commas are placed on both sides of the part of the address or date. For example, notice how a comma is placed before and after *Massachusetts* and *California* as well as *August 15* and *Italy*:

> Boston, Massachusetts, is the best city to host the conference.
> Sally has worked in San Diego, California, for the past five years.
> On Wednesday, August 15, my friends in Rome, Italy, celebrated the *Ferragosta*.

Does it surprise you to learn that a comma is required *after* the state name when a city and state are written together? If so, you are not alone; the following mistake is common:

Incorrect: Dallas, Texas is a great city to start a new business.
Corrected: Dallas, Texas, is a great city to start a new business.

The same is true for dates; set off each part with commas:

Incorrect: Jerome listed August 15, 2005 as his start date.
Corrected: Jerome listed August 15, 2005, as his start date.

However, never separate the month and day with a comma:

Incorrect: September, 4, 2006 was the date on the application.
Corrected: September 4, 2006, was the date on the application.

PRACTICE 4.8

Rule 9: Addresses and Dates (AD)

Instructions: Identify the sentence core and then place commas where needed in the following sentences.

1. Send your application by Friday December 15 to my assistant.
2. San Antonio Texas has a River Walk and Conference Center.
3. Would you prefer to meet in Myrtle Minnesota or Des Moines Iowa?
4. Springfield Massachusetts continues to be my selection.
5. We traveled to Chicago Illinois on May 22 2010 for the workshop.

Note: See page 360 for the key to the above sentences.

Rule 10: Word Omitted (WO)

Use a comma for the omission of a word or words that play a structural role in sentences.

Though omitting words can be grammatically correct, some omitted words can also create a gap.

And Omitted. When two adjectives modify the same noun, they should be separated by *and*; if the word *and* is omitted, separate the adjectives with a comma, for example:

Mr. Adams presented the long *and* boring report to the board.
Mr. Adams presented the long, boring report to the board.

That Omitted. The word *that* sometimes functions as a conjunction. When the omission of *that* breaks the flow of a sentence, use a comma to fill in the gap, for example:

The problem is *that* the current situation is quite grim.
The problem is, the current situation is quite grim.

Repetitive Words Omitted. Sometimes words are omitted when their restatement would be obvious, for example:

Tuesday's meeting is scheduled for 4 p.m.; Monday's, for 10 a.m.

PRACTICE 4.9

Rule 10: Words Omitted (WO)

Instructions: Place commas where needed in the following sentences.

1. The president shared two intriguing confidential reports.
2. The photo shoot is on Tuesday at 5 p.m. on Wednesday at 6 p.m.
3. The problem is some of the results are not yet known.
4. Leave the materials with Ann at the Westin with Sue at the Hilton.
5. Silvana presented a short exciting PowerPoint on Italy.

Note: See page 360 for the key to the above sentences.

Rule 11: Direct Quotation (DQ)

Use commas to set off a direct quotation within a sentence.

A direct quotation is a person's exact words. In comparison, an indirect quotation does not give a speaker's exact words and would *not* be set off with commas.

Direct Quotation:	Gabrielle said, "I have a 9 o'clock appointment," and then she left abruptly.
Indirect Quotation:	Gabrielle said that she had a 9 o'clock appointment, and then she left abruptly.
Direct Quotation:	Dr. Gorman asked, "Is the environment experiencing global warming at a faster rate than previously predicted?"
Indirect Quotation:	Dr. Gorman asked whether the environment is experiencing global warming at a faster rate than previously predicted.

As an exception, a short quotation built into the flow of a sentence does not need to be set off with commas.

Short Quotations: Marian shouted "Help!" as she fell forward.

My boss told me "Do not sweat the small stuff" before he let me go.

The advice "Give the project your best this time" sounded patronizing rather than encouraging.

In direct quotations, the first word of the quotation is capitalized. In addition, here are the rules for using punctuation with quotation marks:

- For commas and periods, place quotation marks on the outside.
- For semicolons and colons, place quotation marks on the inside.
- For exclamation points and question marks, place quotation marks based on meaning, either on the outside or inside.

The above guidelines are based on *closed punctuation*, which is the standard used in the United States. For practice, complete the following exercise.

PRACTICE 4.10

Rule 11: Direct Quotation (DQ)

Instructions: Place commas where needed in the following sentences.

Incorrect: Someone screamed help before the siren went off.
Corrected: Someone screamed "Help!" before the siren went off. (DQ)

1. Patrick shouted get back! before debris fell on us.
2. As Tyler stated all children can learn if they can find an interest.
3. My father warned me when you choose an insurance company, find one with good customer service.
4. As I started the race, Sharon yelled go for the gold.
5. Lenny said to me keep your confidence and you will do well.

Note: See page 361 for the key to the above sentences.

Rule 12: Contrasting Expression or Afterthought (CEA)

Use a comma to separate a contrasting expression or afterthought from the main clause.

A contrasting expression or afterthought adds an interesting twist to writing style. The contrasting expression catches the reader's attention, for example:

> Go ahead and put the property on the market, if you can.
>
> I asked for the information to process the sale, not to lose it.
>
> My cousin Buddy, not my brother Chuck, drove me to the airport.

The CEA comma makes your comments stand out and gives your writing a more conversational flow.

PRACTICE 4.11

Rule 12: Contrasting Expression or Afterthought (CEA)

Instructions: Identify the sentence core, and place commas where needed.

Incorrect: Our contractor charged for delivery not the packing.

Corrected: Our <u>contractor</u> <u>charged</u> for delivery, not the packing. (CEA)

1. You will find the manuscript in John's office not in Bob's.
2. Marcus secured the contract but only after negotiating for hours.
3. Chair the budget committee if you prefer.
4. Lester rather than Dan received the award.
5. Work to achieve your dreams not to run away from your fears.

Note: See page 361 for the key to the above sentences.

Recap

Below is a list of the comma rules. You will find additional practice worksheets at www.commasrule.com. Practice is the key to success. *Now go for it!*

Comma Rules

Rule 1: The Sentence Core Rules
Do not separate a subject and verb with only one comma.

Rule 2: Conjunction (CONJ)
Use a comma to separate two independent clauses when they are joined by a coordinating conjunction (and, but, or, nor, for, so, yet).

Rule 3: Series (SER)
Use a comma to separate three or more items in a series.

Rule 4: Introductory (INTRO)
Place a comma after a word, phrase, or dependent clause that introduces an independent clause.

Rule 5: Nonrestrictive (NR)
Use commas to set off nonessential (nonrestrictive) words and phrases.

Rule 6: Parenthetical (PAR)
Use commas to set off a word or expression that interrupts the flow of a sentence.

Rule 7: Direct Address (DA)
Use commas to set off the name or title of a person addressed directly.

Rule 8: Appositive (AP)
Use commas to set off the restatement of a noun or pronoun.

Rule 9: Addresses and Dates (AD)
Use commas to set off the parts of addresses and dates.

Rule 10: Word Omitted (WO)
Use a comma for the omission of a word or words that play a structural role in sentences.

Rule 11: Direct Quotation (DQ)
Use commas to set off direct quotations within a sentence.

Rule 12: Contrasting Expression or Afterthought (CEA)
Use a comma to separate a contrasting expression or afterthought.

Writing Workshop

Topic A: Leaving a Legacy

Write about your responses to the following questions:

1. How old do you believe you will live to be?
2. Imagining that you are that age and looking back on your life, what do you want to be able to say about the legacy of your life?
3. What might you do with your remaining time between now and then so that when you look back on your life you have no regrets about how you lived it?

Topic B: A Message in a Bottle

One of the most wonderful gifts that you can give or receive is a letter. Just ask anyone who has suddenly lost a loved one, with only letters left behind as a reminder.

Who needs to hear from you? Write your letter, and then decide whether or not to send it. In fact, you may choose to write to someone who is no longer in your life—even someone who has passed on.

Finally, write a letter to yourself. Pretend that you are your own best friend and give yourself words of encouragement for the journey ahead. Put the letter in a safe place, or ask a friend to hold on to it and mail it to you when you are not expecting it.

Editing Workshop

Draft

Instructions: Proofread the following, correcting the punctuation. The revision is on the next page.

Georgia Jones is the employee of the month for July. Georgia, has been with our company for five years, Georgia's duties consist of assisting clients; maintaining records and filling orders. In addition, to her daily workload Georgia exemplifies a model team player, she is always available to support our department and her strong work ethic encourages others to succeed. George works productively efficiently and enthusiastically.

Finally I would like to point out that Georgia has a great sense of humor, join me in congratulating, Georgia, in this honor.

Revision

How many of the 13 punctuation errors were you able to correct?

> Georgia Jones is the employee of the month for July. Georgia has been with our company for five years. Georgia's duties consist of assisting clients, maintaining records, and filling orders. In addition to her daily workload, Georgia exemplifies a model team player. She is always available to support our department, and her strong work ethic encourages others to succeed. Georgia works productively, efficiently, and enthusiastically. Finally, Georgia has a great sense of humor.
>
> Join me in congratulating Georgia in this honor.

5

Semicolons, Dashes, and Ellipses

Most people find commas a necessity, sprinkling them throughout their writing even when unsure about how to use them correctly. It does not work that way with semicolons, however. Many people develop an aversion to using semicolons, hoping to avoid them.

The truth is, you can avoid using semicolons. However, if you do not use semicolons, you are sometimes likely to put a comma where a semicolon belongs, creating a serious grammatical error.

While semicolons are not similar to commas, they are similar to periods. Most of the time, the following rule of thumb will work for you:

> Use a semicolon in place of a period.

In other words, if you cannot use a period, you probably should not use a semicolon either.

If you never need to use a semicolon, why use one? Though you may not yet realize it, punctuation speaks to your reader in subtle, yet powerful, ways. Here are two things to consider about the semicolon:

1. The semicolon whispers to your reader that two sentences share a key idea.
2. The semicolon alerts readers to slight shades of meaning, helping them see connections and draw relationships.

In addition, once you use semicolons correctly, you are likely to use them more often just for the thrill of it! OK, so *thrill* might be a bit of a stretch;

however, the more serious you become about writing, the more you will enjoy using the less common punctuation marks, such as semicolons, dashes, and ellipses.

These marks give you choices and options; but more important, they give your voice a fingerprint and add momentum to your message.

The Semicolon

Here are three basic semicolon rules that you will learn in this chapter:

1. *Semicolon No Conjunction*: use a semicolon to separate two independent clauses that are joined without a conjunction.
2. *Semicolon Bridge:* place a semicolon before and a comma after an adverbial conjunction that acts as a bridge between two independent clauses.
3. *Semicolon Because of Comma:* when a clause needs major and minor separations, use semicolons for major breaks and commas for minor breaks.

Before working on each of the semicolon rules that follow, write a sentence or two using a semicolon.

Rule 1: Semicolon No Conjunction (NC)

Use a semicolon to separate two independent clauses that are joined without a conjunction.

This semicolon rule closely relates to the comma conjunction (CONJ) rule, which states "place a comma after a coordinating conjunction when it connects two independent clauses." When a conjunction is not present, the two independent clauses need to be separated by a period or a semicolon, for example:

Comma Conjunction: Al <u>went</u> to the store, *but* he <u>forgot</u> to buy bread. (CONJ)

Semicolon No Conjunction: Al <u>went</u> to the store; he <u>forgot</u> to buy bread. (NC)

Period: Al <u>went</u> to the store. He <u>forgot</u> to buy bread.

Notice how each sentence has a slightly different effect based on how it is punctuated. Do you see how choppy the writing sounds in the example above which uses a period, thereby breaking up the sentences?

In general, avoid short, choppy sentences. One way to do this is to use a semicolon instead of a period. Apply the semicolon no conjunction (NC) rule when two sentences are closely related, especially when one or both sentences are short.

The examples and practice exercises in this book are designed to help you learn principles that lead to a better understanding of structure. Understanding structure provides a foundation that will help you improve your editing skills as well as your writing style. Before moving to the next semicolon rule, complete the practice exercise that follows.

PRACTICE 5.1
Rule 1: Semicolon No Conjunction (NC)
Instructions: Identify the sentence core of each major clause, and then place semicolons where needed in the following sentences.

Incorrect: Our proposal was too long, they want a revision by Friday.
Corrected: Our <u>proposal</u> <u>was</u> too long; they want a revision by Friday. (NC)

1. Miller will not approve our expense account she needs more documentation.
2. Ask Bryan for the report he said that he completed it yesterday.

3. Arrive on time to tomorrow's meeting bring both of your reports.
4. A laptop was left in the conference room Jason claimed it as his.
5. Recognize your mistakes offer apologies as needed.

Note: See page 361 for the key to the above sentences.

Rule 2: Semicolon Transition (TRANS)

Place a semicolon before and a comma after an adverbial conjunction that acts as a bridge between two independent clauses.

This semicolon rule corresponds to the comma parenthetical rule (PAR). Comma parenthetical applies when an adverbial conjunction interrupts an independent clause, for example:

Comma PAR: Bob, *however*, will determine the fees.

Instead, the semicolon transition rule involves two complete sentences, with an adverbial conjunction providing a bridge between the two:

Semicolon TRANS: Bob will determine the fees; *however*, he is open to suggestions.

For those who avoided semicolons prior to working on this chapter, here is how you might have incorrectly punctuated the above sentence:

Incorrect: Bob will determine the fees, *however*, he is open to suggestions.

The above example is a run-on sentence, which results whenever a comma is placed where a semicolon (or period) belongs. A run-on is a serious grammatical error. Here are more examples of semicolon transition:

Lidia wrote the grant; *therefore*, she should be on the committee.
The grant was accepted; *as a result*, we will receive funding.
You should call their office; *however*, (you) do not leave a message.

Now that you have reviewed this rule, can you see how you may have needed to use a semicolon instead of a comma at times? Complete the exercise below before going on to the next semicolon rule.

PRACTICE 5.2

Rule 2: Semicolon Transition (TRANS)

Instructions: Identify the sentence core of each major clause and then place commas and semicolons where needed in the following sentences.

Incorrect: Our contract included delivery charges, however we were charged anyway.

Corrected: Our <u>contract included</u> delivery charges; however, we were charged anyway. (TRANS)

1. Carol suggested the topic fortunately Carlos agreed.
2. The project management team offered assistance however their time was limited.
3. Ken compiled the data therefore Mary crunched it.
4. The numbers turned out well as a result our new budget was accepted.
5. Roger ran in the marathon unfortunately he was unable to finish.

Note: See page 361 for the key to the above sentences.

Rule 3: Semicolon Because of Comma (BC)

When a clause needs major and minor separations, use semicolons for major breaks and commas for minor breaks.

This semicolon rule differs from the other two rules because it creates breaks *within* sentences rather than *between* sentences. As a result, this rule does not follow the "semicolon in place of period" rule of thumb that you learned earlier.

Since most sentences do not call for both major and minor breaks, the semicolon because of comma (BC) occurs less frequently than the other types of semicolons.

Apply this rule when listing a series of city and state names, for example:

Semicolon BC: Joni will travel to Dallas, Texas; Buffalo, New York; and Boston, Massachusetts.

Also apply this rule when listing a series of names and titles:

Semicolon BC: The committee members are Jeremy Smith, director of finance; Lorraine Kirk, assistant vice president; Carson Michaels, accountant; and Malory Williams, broker.

A more complicated example would include major and minor clauses within a sentence:

Semicolon BC: Millicent asked for a raise; and since she was a new employee, I sought Jackson's opinion.

Semicolon BC: Dr. Jones suggested the procedure; but I was unable to help, so he asked Dr. Ferretti.

PRACTICE 5.3
Rule 3: Semicolon Because of Commas (BC)

Instructions: Identify the sentence core of each main clause and then place commas and semicolons where needed in the following sentences.

Incorrect: We submitted our new proposal yesterday, and since our previous proposal was their top choice this one has a good chance of being adopted.

Corrected: We <u>submitted</u> our new proposal yesterday; and since our previous <u>proposal was</u> their top choice, this <u>one has</u> a good chance of being adopted. (BC)

1. Please include Rupert Adams CEO Madeline Story COO and Mark Coleman executive president.

80 *A Guide for Business Writing*

2. By next week I will have traveled to St. Louis Missouri Chicago Illinois and Burlington Iowa.
3. Mike applied for jobs in Honolulu Hawaii Sacramento California and Santa Fe New Mexico.
4. Your application arrived today but when I reviewed it information was missing.
5. You can resubmit your application today and since my office will review it you can call me tomorrow for the results.

Note: See page 362 for the key to the above sentences.

Now that you understand semicolons, you can add additional variety and depth by learning about the colon, the dash, and the ellipses. In fact, these less common marks of punctuation may seem like fun compared to the hard work you have already put in to improving your skills.

Next, you will work with the colon, which has unique and versatile functions.

The Colon

In general, the colon alerts readers that information will be illustrated, making the colon a strong mark of punctuation that commands attention.

If you have never used a colon in your writing, experiment using it after you read about it here.

Use the colon for the following purposes:

1. After salutations of business letters (and formal e-mail messages).
2. At the end of one sentence when the following sentence illustrates it.
3. At the end of a sentence to alert the reader that a list follows.
4. After words such as *Note* or *Caution*.

Illustrating Sentences. Using a colon to illustrate a complete sentence enhances your writing style, allowing you to convey your message in a slightly more emphatic way. For example:

> The colon is a strong mark of punctuation: a colon draws the reader's attention.
>
> Johnson Ecology accepted our proposal: we start on Monday.

In general, the first word of an independent clause following a colon should be in lower case. However, capitalize the first word if you are placing special emphasis on the second clause or the second clause presents a formal rule, as shown below:[1]

> Here is the principle that applies: Colons can be used in place of a period when the sentence that follows illustrates the one that precedes it.

When you use a colon to illustrate a sentence, use it sparingly or readers will tired of it, as they do with exclamation points.

Illustrating Lists or Words. To use the colon to illustrate a list of words or phrases, precede the colon with words such as *these, here, the following,* or *as follows*. For example:

> These are the materials to bring to the meeting: your annual report and current data.
>
> Bring the following identification: driver's license, social security card, and current utility bill.

However, do not use a colon after an *incomplete* sentence, for example:

Incorrect: This package includes: a stapler and 3-hole paper punch.
Corrected: This package includes a stapler and 3-hole paper punch.

Also notice that the colon can be used after *for example* to alert the reader that an example follows. In addition, use a colon after a word of caution or instruction, for example:

> Note: All meetings are cancelled on Friday.
>
> Caution: Do not use the staircase.

If a complete sentence follows *note* or *caution*, capitalize the first word, as shown above.

The Dash

The dash is the most versatile mark of punctuation, at times replacing the comma, the semicolon, the period, and even the colon. The dash adds energy, making information stand out.

Though the dash can be used in formal documents, the dash is most often used in informal communications. However, do not overuse the dash. When overused, the dash gives the impression that the writer is speaking in a choppy and haphazard fashion.

Here are some examples using the dash:

> Bob called on Friday—he said he'd arrive by noon today.
>
> Thanks—your package arrived right before our meeting.
>
> Feranda Wilson—our new executive VP—will host the event.

Though the dash is different from the hyphen, use the hyphen to create the dash.

Here are two ways to create a dash using hyphens:

1. Create an *em* dash by using hyphens without a space before, between, after them (as shown above), for example:

    Marie Claire invited us to the opening—I am so pleased!

2. Create an *en* dash by using two hyphens, but this time place a space before and after the hyphens, as follows:

   Marie Claire invited us to the opening – I am so pleased!

The *em* dash is the more traditional choice. However, check your company policy manual to see if the manual states a preference—some companies state a preference so that corporate communications remain consistent.

Once again, overusing dashes is similar to overusing colons or exclamation points. Writers enjoy using them, but readers tire of them easily. Thus, hold yourself back and use them sparingly. However, if you have never used a dash in your writing, try it. Dashes definitely add energy and are fun to use.

The Ellipses

Ellipses is the plural form for *ellipsis marks*. Ellipses indicate that information is missing, thereby removing an otherwise awkward gap.

In formal documents, ellipses allow writers to adapt quotations by leaving out less relevant information, making the main idea stand out. In informal documents, ellipses allow writers to jump from one idea to another without entirely completing their thoughts. Ellipses also allow the writer to convey a sense of uncertainty without coming right out and stating it.

- Ellipsis marks consist of three periods with a space before, between, and after each one, for example:

  This doesn't make sense to me . . . let me know what you think.

- Some software programs create ellipses when you space once, type three periods in a row, and then space once again, as follows:

  Vic was not pleased ... he will call back later.

Before using the automatic ellipses, check to make sure that it is acceptable practice within the domain you are submitting your work. In some domains, the unspaced, automatic ellipses are not acceptable.

Use a fourth period when the missing information is at the end of the sentence in a formal quotation, for example:

> "Don't aim at success—the more you aim at it and make it a target, the more you are going to miss it . . . . I want you to listen to what your conscience commands you to do and go on to carry it out to the best of your knowledge. Then you will live to see that in the long run—in the long run, I say!—success will follow you precisely because you had *forgotten* to think of it."[2]

As with dashes, use ellipsis marks sparingly for informal use. Whether for formal or informal use, display ellipsis marks correctly.

Writing Style: Punctuation and Flow

Punctuation helps create your writing style: punctuation packages your words, leading to a rhythm that affects the tone of your writing.

Writing generally does not flow well when it consists of short, choppy sentences. However, at times short, choppy sentences create a desired dramatic effect, as in the following:

Conan arrived late today. He resigned.

Most of the time, however, writing flows more effectively without the choppy effect that short sentences can create, which is one reason to use the semicolon. Consider the following example:

Jay offered the condo at a lower price; he needs to relocate.

In the above example, connecting the independent clauses with a semicolon does not necessarily reduce the choppy effect of the writing. A transitional word, such as a subordinate or an adverbial conjunction, can build a bridge between the "cause and the effect."

Here are some ways to use conjunctions to draw connections for the reader and eliminate choppy writing:

Jay offered the condo at a lower price *since* he needs to relocate.

Jay offered the condo at a lower price *because* he needs to relocate.

Jay offered the condo at a lower price; *unfortunately*, he needs to relocate.

In each example above, the conjunction smoothed out the flow of the writing. Most of the time, you use transitional words like these naturally. You can achieve a desired effect by using them consciously.

Now that you have reviewed commas and semicolons, experiment with punctuation and conjunctions and the effect they create. Now let's see how the same sentences sound using the colon, dash, and ellipses:

Jay offered the condo at a lower price: he needs to relocate.

Jay offered the condo at a lower price—he needs to relocate.

Jay offered the condo at a lower price . . . he needs to relocate.

What are the subtle ways each mark of punctuation changes the feeling or tone of the sentence?

Punctuation is one more tool to help you connect with your reader and get your message across; in fact, the way that you punctuate becomes part of your writing style, helping you to express your voice.

Recap

The semicolon along with the colon, the dash, and the ellipses can add variety and flair to your writing as long as you use them correctly . . . and as long as you do not overuse them.

- The semicolon is a strong mark of punctuation: in general, use a semicolon at grammatical breaks where you could also use a period.
- The dash emphasizes information; use the dash to add variety to your writing, but don't overuse it.
- Ellipses fill gaps and allow the writer to express uncertainty.

Semicolon Rules

Semicolon Rule 1: No Conjunction (NC)
Use a semicolon to separate two independent clauses that are joined without a conjunction.

Semicolon Rule 2: Transition (TRANS)
Use a semicolon before and a comma after an adverbial conjunction that bridges two independent clauses.

Semicolon Rule 3: Because of Comma (BC)
When a clause needs major and minor separations, use semicolons for major breaks and commas for minor breaks.

Writing Workshop

Topic: Life's Peak Experiences

Write about one or two work experiences (paid or unpaid) that had a deep impact on you.

Describe the situation, your contribution, the end result, and how it made you feel. What parts of that experience were energizing for you? Why?

Also write about one or two life experiences that had a deep impact on you. How did the experience change your views or way of thinking? How did it influence your relationships?

Editing Workshop

Draft

Instructions: Edit the following message, correcting punctuation errors. You may need to break up "sentences" or reword them. The revision is on the next page.

Hi Randy;

I was out of the office on Friday; so I am responding to your voice mail from last week.

You indicated that you are currently participating in our college reimbursement program and you were expecting to be reimbursed for your latest semester of graduate work. As the policy states—you will receive only 70 percent for graduate classes that do not relate directly to your current position, however, you will be reimbursed 100 percent for classes that do but the program reimburses for tuition only not books, fees, etc. …. not any other expenses you may incur.

Once you have your final grades submit a detailed invoice, both you and your supervisor must sign it.

If you have further questions please call me at 555-1212 ….. good luck with your coursework!!!

Best Regards

Jim

Revision

Were you able to find 14 errors?

Hi Randy,

Here's what you need to know about our college reimbursement policy.

The policy states that you will be reimbursed 70 percent for graduate classes that do not relate directly to your current position; however, you will be reimbursed 100 percent for classes that do. The program reimburses for tuition only, not books or fees or any other expenses you may incur.

Once you have your final grades, submit a detailed invoice. Both you and your supervisor must sign it.

If you have further questions, please call me at 555-1212. Good luck with your coursework!

Best regards,

Jim

End Notes

1. William A. Sabin, *The Gregg Reference Manual*, Tenth Edition, McGraw-Hill/Irwin, Burr Ridge, 2005, page 52.
2. Victor Frankl, *Man's Search for Meaning*, Beacon Press, Boston, 2006, page xiv-xv.

6

Verbs

Do you seek out strong verbs so that your writing has vigor? If your writing needs a boost, start by examining how you use verbs.

The verb drives the sentence, creating its core. If you are not using strong, decisive verbs, you have a great opportunity now to bring your writing to a higher level. As a part of speech, verbs are unique:

- Verbs create action.
- Verbs change time.

This chapter covers essential aspects of using verbs correctly, the first step in gaining control. The focus is on *verb parts* rather than verb tenses. Verb parts cause more problems for writers than verb tenses cause, and verb parts are less complicated to learn. This chapter also covers the –s form, linking verbs, and subjunctive mood.

Since this chapter is about using verbs correctly, Edited English is compared with local language. *Edited English* is formal English and is used in textbooks, on news casts, and in board rooms of major corporations. In contrast, *local language* is informal and used with family and friends.

No one speaks English perfectly, and no one writes English perfectly—that is not even a realistic goal. Instead, having the ability to switch codes gives you power because you gain control.

Start by taking the inventory of irregular verbs on page 105. Once you complete the inventory, if you feel this chapter is too basic, go on to the next chapter, which discusses active and passive voice.

Action Verbs

Use strong verbs to add power to your writing.

accelerate	edit	instruct	proceed
accept	empower	interpret	produce
adapt	encourage	introduce	promote
aid	energize	invent	propose
amplify	enhance	judge	provide
analyze	enlist	justify	rank
apply	establish	launch	rate
arrange	estimate	lead	rearrange
assemble	evaluate	learn	recognize
assist	examine	listen	reconcile
awaken	expand	maintain	reconstruct
break down	explain	modify	reinforce
build	extend	mold	relate
challenge	focus	monitor	reorganize
change	formulate	motivate	report
choose	fortify	negotiate	restore
compile	generalize	observe	review
complete	generate	operate	revise
compose	guide	orchestrate	rewrite
compute	heal	organize	score
construct	help	orient	seek
consult	hypothesize	originate	serve
convert	ignite	outline	simplify
coordinate	illustrate	participate	solve
counsel	implement	perform	stimulate
create	incorporate	persuade	summarize
demonstrate	increase	pinpoint	support
describe	influence	plan	synthesize
design	initiate	point out	teach
develop	inspect	prepare	train
devise	inspire	present	use
devote	install	preserve	widen
direct	institute	process	write

Verbs in Past Time

Let's start by going over some basic information about verbs in past time. Some of this information was covered in Chapter 2, "The Sentence Core," so this is partly a review.

1. All verbs have a base form: "to" plus a base form of a verb is called an *infinitive*; for example: *to see, to do, to be, to walk*.

2. All verbs have a *past tense* form and a *past participle* form:
   - A past tense form does *not* take a *helper verb* (also called an *auxiliary verb*).
   - A past participle form must be used with a helper verb.

Base	**Past Tense**	**Past Participle**
walk	walked	*have* walked
do	did	*have* done

3. Common helper verbs are *to have* (has, have, had), *to do* (do, does, did), and *to be* (am, is, are, was, were).

Based on the way the past tense is formed, verbs are broken down into two broad categories: *regular verbs* and *irregular verbs*. Let's work with regular verbs first and then work with irregular verbs.

Regular Verbs in Past Time

The vast majority of verbs are regular, which means that the past tense and past participle forms are both created by adding –ed to the base form, for example:

Base	**Past Tense**	**Past Participle**
walk	walked	*have* walked
file	filed	*has* filed
comment	commented	*had* commented
argue	argued	*have* argued

Though leaving off the −ed in past time is a pattern of choice in some local languages, use the −ed ending when you speak or write Edited English, for example:

Incorrect: We *walk* to the store yesterday after class.
Corrected: We *walked* to the store yesterday after class.

Incorrect: The committee *argue* all afternoon.
Corrected: The committee *argued* all afternoon.

Incorrect: After we *had serve* the meal, we gave awards.
Corrected: After we *had served* the meal, we gave awards.

If you leave off the −ed ending with past time regular verbs in your writing, check to see if you leave off the −ed ending in your speech also.

Notice your speech patterns: do you speak differently in informal situations with your friends than you do in more formal environments, such as a classroom or at work? If so, practice pronouncing the −ed ending so that you become fluent with it. Repetitive practice is key to language learning. Here are more examples:

Incorrect: The career counselor *review* my application.
Corrected: The career counselor *reviewed* my application.

Incorrect: Mark had *refer* to the incident when we spoke last week.
Corrected: Mark had *referred* to the incident when we spoke last week.

To gain extra practice with verbs, work on the exercise that follows.

PRACTICE 6.1
Regular Verbs in Past Time
Instructions: Change the following local language sentences to Edited English.

Incorrect: Our invitation receive a good response.
Corrected: Our invitation received a good response.

1. The coach misplace the roster before the game began.
2. My counselor suggest that I submit my resume.
3. Bart receive the award for most valuable player.
4. Last week, no one on our team want the schedule to change.
5. When Jonika suggest that we meet after school, everyone was pleased.

Note: See page 362 for the key to the above sentences.

Irregular Verbs in Past Time

Irregular verbs are used differently in local language than they are used in Edited English in two important ways.

First, in local language, an irregular past tense form is sometimes used *with* a helper, as in the following examples:

Local Language	**Edited English**
Lida *has wrote* the paper.	Lida *has written* the paper.
Bob *has spoke* to the director.	Bob *has spoken* to the director.
Alisha *has saw* that movie.	Alisha *has seen* that movie.

Second, in local language, an irregular past participle is sometimes used *without* a helper, as follows:

Local Language	**Edited English**
Lucas *seen* the paper.	Lucas *has seen* the paper.
Alisha *done* good work.	Alisha *has done* good work.
Marcus *drunk* the milk.	Marcus *has drunk* the milk.

Once again, common helping verbs are as follows :

    to be: am, is, are, was were
    to have: has, have, had
    to do: do, does, did

As you can see, irregular verbs create different problems for writers than regular verbs do. To use irregular verbs correctly in Edited English:

1. Know the past tense and past participle forms of each irregular verb.
2. When using the past tense form, do *not* use a helper verb.
3. When using the past participle, use a helper.

To understand which irregular verbs are troublesome for you, review the verb inventory that you took when you started this chapter. If you have not yet taken it, take it now—you will find it on page 105. Which verbs do you need to work on?

Write two or three sentences with each verb using the past tense form and the past participle form. Complete the practice exercise before reviewing the –s form, another troublesome category of verbs.

PRACTICE 6.2

Irregular Verbs in Past Time

Instructions: Correct the following sentences for verb usage.

Incorrect: Everyone in our department have went to the meeting.
Corrected: Everyone in our department has gone to the meeting.

1. We seen George the other day.
2. He done a great job helping the local food bank.
3. The town council had wrote a complimentary letter about him.
4. They brang up a good point.
5. Even though his budget was froze, George loaned them the resources they needed.

Note: See page 362 for the key to the above sentences.

The –S Form: Third Person Singular

In Edited English, all third person singular verbs in simple present tense end in an *s*. By referring to these verbs as –s form, you remain aware of their unique "spelling."

Leaving off the *s* in third person singular verbs is a pattern found in many local languages, for example:

Incorrect: Bob *don't* give the directions as well as he should.

Corrected: Bob *does not* (doesn't) give the directions as well as he should.

Incorrect: Martha *have* the right attitude about her job search.

Corrected: Martha *has* the right attitude about her job search.

Incorrect: My teacher *say* that the paper is due on Friday.

Correct: My teacher *says* that the paper is due on Friday.

After completing the practice exercise below, you will review linking verbs.

PRACTICE 6.3

The –S Form

Instructions: Change the following sentences from local language to Edited English by using the –s form.

Incorrect: Our contract state that delays are not acceptable.

Corrected: Our <u>contract</u> <u>states</u> that delays are not acceptable.

1. The coach say that we need to practice for one more hour.
2. Our team finish in first place every year.
3. Taylor choose the players for both teams.
4. The coach have enough good players already.
5. If the group listen carefully, they will learn the information.

Note: See page 362 for the key to the above sentences.

Linking Verbs

Though almost all verbs are action verbs, a handful of verbs are **state of being** or **linking verbs**. Here is a list of the 11 linking verbs:

> to be (am, is, are, was, were), appear,
> become, seem, *and at times* smell,
> taste, feel, sound, look, act, *and* grow

Action verbs are modified by adverbs. Action verbs transfer action from the subject to the object through the verb, as in "Jeremy threw the ball": **S→ V→ O.**

Action verbs:

The car runs *badly*.	(*badly* describes *how* the car runs)
When you presented, you did *well*.	(*well* modifies *did*)
The committee *finally* adjourned.	(*finally* modifies *adjourned*)
He choose *me* for the committee.	(*me* is an object)

Linking verbs are not modified. Linking verbs do not transfer action. Instead, linking verbs "link" the subject to its **subject complement** (SC): **S V$_L$ SC.**

Linking Verbs (State of Being Verbs):

I feel *bad*.	(*bad* modifies the subject *I*)
The cake tastes *good*.	(*good* describes the *cake*)
The decision appears *final*.	(*final* describes *decision*)
It was *I* who made the comment.	(*I* is a subject complement)

A **subject complement (SC)** modifies the subject, and thus a subject complement (also known as a *predicate nominative*) will be an adjective or a subjective case pronoun.

With a linking verb, think of an equivalency between the subject and its complement: **S = SC**

Here are three common mistakes related to verbs and modifiers:

1. Following linking verbs with adverbs, as in the following:
   Incorrect: I feel *badly*.
   Corrected: I feel *bad*.

2. Bobtailing adverbs that follow an action verb, as in the following:
   Incorrect: Drive *slow*.
   Corrected: Drive *slowly*.

3. Following action verbs with adjectives, as in:
   Incorrect: You did *good* on the report.
   Corrected: You did *well* on the report.

Because the adverb *well* can also be an adjective when referring to the state of one's health, both of the following statements are correct:

> I feel good.
>
> I feel well.

When in doubt, simply say, "I feel fine."

Subjunctive Mood

In addition to tense, verbs also express *mood*, which is a way of representing the writer's attitude toward a subject. Here are the possible moods that verbs can convey:

- **Indicative Mood:**   straight-forward, matter of fact
- **Imperative Mood:**   exclamatory
- **Subjunctive Mood:**   possibility, contrary to fact

Most writing, including this sentence, uses the indicative mood. The imperative mood is less common but easy to recognize. For example, look for words, phrases, or sentences that express emotion, ending in an exclamation mark: *Run Quickly! Don't go there!*

The subjunctive mood expresses improbability and often comes in the form of a *wish* or *possibility*. The subjunctive mood is also used in certain requests, demands, recommendations, and set phrases.

- For the **past subjunctive**, *to be* is always expressed as *were*, for example:

    If I *were* you . . . I *wish* I *were* . . . and so on.

- For the **present subjunctive**, the verb is expressed in the *infinitive* form, for example:

    It is critical that John *attend* the program.

Correct use of the subjunctive mood makes speech sound sophisticated.

Past Subjunctive

In a past subjunctive statement, the verb *to be* is always represented as *were*. Statements following the word *wish* would be written in the past subjunctive.

Local Language	**Edited English**
I *wish* I *was* the team leader.	I *wish* I *were* the team leader.
Bob *wishes* he *was* on vacation.	Bob *wishes* he *were* on vacation.
Barb *wishes* it *was* true.	Barb *wishes* it *were* true.

When a sentence begins with the word *if*, the statement that follows is often a *condition*, not a statement of fact. Conditional statements should also be made in the subjunctive mood.

Incorrect: *If* Bob *was* certain, he would go with us.
If Mary Lou *was* here, she would understand.
If I *was* you, I would not buy that jacket.

Corrected: *If* Bob *were* certain, he would go with us.
If Mary Lou *were* here, she would understand.
If I *were* you, I would not buy that jacket.

Now let's move from the past subjunctive to the present subjunctive.

Present Subjunctive

The present subjunctive occurs in *that* clauses following verbs that express requests, demands, recommendations, and set phrases. The present subjunctive is expressed by the infinitive form of the verb, regardless of the person or number of the subject, for example:

> The coach said that* it is essential that you be on time.
>
> It is urgent (that) your report be on time.
>
> Vinnie suggested (that) the team be invited to the opening.

*The word *that* is essential when the words *said* or *reported* precede it, thereby showing that a direct quote does not follow. However, the word *that* is implied even when removed.

PRACTICE 6.4
Subjunctive Mood

Instructions: Following sentences written in the subjunctive mood, correct verb usage.

Incorrect: I wish that I was in your position—I would accept the job.
Corrected: I wish that I *were* in your position—I would accept the new job.

1. The president insisted that Melba attends the reception.
2. Jacob wishes he was on this year's team.
3. If Dan was your team captain, would you support him?
4. The instructions require that the package is sent via UPS.
5. If I was you, I would run for office.

Note: See page 363 for the key to the above sentences.

Recap

As you see, verbs can be complicated. However, learning how to use verb parts correctly eliminates a great deal of the mystery about verbs.

- Regular verbs in past time end in *–ed*, but irregular verbs do not follow a pattern: *when in doubt, check the chart.*
- Past tense forms do not need a helper, but past participle forms need a helper.
- Third person singular verbs end in an *s*: the *–s* form.
- The subjunctive mood expresses possibility, not fact.
- For the past subjunctive, use *were*, as in "If I *were* you . . . ."
- For the present subjunctive, use the infinitive form of the verb.

Writing Workshop
Topic: What Is Self-Talk?

Words are powerful: they can inspire just as easily as they can discourage, discredit, and negate.

Self-talk consists of the messages that you give yourself on a constant basis. What do you say to yourself on a regular basis? Are your words positive or negative? Have you ever challenged the negative stories you tell yourself?

In her book, *Loving What Is: Four Questions That Can Change Your Life*, Byron Katie advises challenging negative thoughts.[1] Katie suggests that whenever you have a negative thought, ask yourself, "Is that true?" "Is that *really* true?"

If you cannot prove that a negative thought is true, let it go.

What are the messages that you give yourself on a regular basis? How can you use self-talk to make important changes in your life?

Editing Workshop

Draft

Instructions: Edit the following letter, paying special attention to verbs and punctuation. Feel free to cut unnecessary information.

On the next page is corrected copy and revised copy. After you make corrections, consider how you could improve the formatting by using bullet points to make key points stand out.

Dear Mary,

Thank you for opening two new checking account with us.

Enclose are some temporary checks for your individual account. Also enclose are the papers that you and your daughter need to sign for your joint account. As we discuss our office send new accounts to our regional office every week, therefore, wait until your daughter have signed her papers so you can send in all paperwork at one time in the enclose self addressed envelope.

If you have questions feel free to contact me at 555-1234.

Cordially

Sylvana Wright
Account Representative

Corrections only:

Dear Mary:

Thank you for opening two new checking account*s* with us.

Enclose*d* are some temporary checks for your individual account. Also enclose*d* are the papers that you and your daughter need to sign for your joint account. As we discusse*d,* our office send*s* new accounts to our regional office every week. *Therefore,* wait until your daughter ~~have~~ has signed her papers so you can send in all paperwork at one time in the enclosed self-addressed envelope.

Revision

> Dear Mary:
>
> Thank you for opening two new checking accounts with us.
>
> Enclosed are some temporary checks for your individual account.
>
> - Please sign the enclosed papers for your joint account.
> - Please have your daughter sign them also.
> - Return them in the enclosed, self-addressed envelope.
>
> If you have questions, feel free to contact me at 555-1234.
>
> Sincerely,
>
> Sylvana Wright
> Account Representative

Irregular Verb Inventory

Instructions: On the next page, fill in the past tense and past participle forms. With each past participle, make sure that you use a *helping verb*: use any form of *to be, to do,* or *to have.*

As a refresher, the various forms of *to be* are *am, is, are, was, were*; the forms of *to do* are *do, does, did*; and the forms of *to have* are *has, have, had.*

104 *A Guide for Business Writing*

IRREGULAR VERB INVENTORY

Base Form	Past Tense	Past Participle
arise	<u>arose</u>	<u>*has* arisen</u>
become	<u>became</u>	<u>*did* become</u>
break	<u>broke</u>	<u>*was* broken</u>
bring	_____	_____
buy	_____	_____
choose	_____	_____
do	_____	_____
drink	_____	_____
drive	_____	_____
eat	_____	_____
fly	_____	_____
forget	_____	_____
freeze	_____	_____
get	_____	_____
go	_____	_____
know	_____	_____
lend	_____	_____
prove	_____	_____
say	_____	_____
see	_____	_____
set	_____	_____
sink	_____	_____
sit	_____	_____
show	_____	_____
speak	_____	_____
stand	_____	_____
take	_____	_____
throw	_____	_____
wear	_____	_____
write	_____	_____

IRREGULAR VERB CHART

Base Form	Past Tense	Past Participle
arise	arose	arisen
become	became	become
break	broke	broken
bring	brought	brought
buy	bought	bought
choose	chose	chosen
dive	dived, dove	dived
do	did	done
draw	drew	drawn
drink	drank	drunk
drive	drove	driven
eat	ate	eaten
fall	fell	fallen
find	found	found
fly	flew	flown
forget	forgot	forgotten
freeze	froze	frozen
get	got	got, gotten
give	gave	given
go	went	gone
grow	grew	grown
know	knew	known
lend	lent	lent
lose	lost	lost
prove	proved	proved, proven
ride	rode	ridden
say	said	said
see	saw	seen
set	set	set
sink	sank	sunk
sit	sat	sat
show	showed	showed, shown
speak	spoke	spoken
stand	stood	stood
swim	swam	swum
take	took	taken
throw	threw	thrown
wear	wore	worn
write	wrote	written

STANDARD VERB TENSES

SIMPLE TENSE | DESCRIPTION

Past	spoke	an action that ended in the past
Present	speak	an action that exists or is repeated
Future	will speak	an action that will happen in the future

PROGRESSIVE TENSE

Past	was speaking	an action that was happening in the past
Present	am/is/are speaking	an action that is happening now
Future	will be speaking	an action that will happen in the future

PERFECT TENSE

Past (*Distant Past*)	had spoken	an action that ended before another action in the past
Present (*Recent Past*)	has/have spoken	an action that started in the past and was recently completed or is ongoing
Future	will have spoken	an action that will end before another future action or time

PERFECT PROGRESSIVE TENSE

Past	had been speaking	an action that happened in the past over time before another past action or time
Present	has/have been speaking	an action occurring over time that started in the past and continues into the present
Future	will have been speaking	an action in the future occurring over time before another future action or time

Based on the Irregular Verb Inventory, make a list below of the verbs that you intend to work on:

End Note

1. Byron Katie, *Loving What Is: Four Questions That Can Change Your Life*, Three Rivers Press, 2003.

7

Active Voice

Have you ever wondered how to turn passive, complicated writing into active writing that gets results? Active writing is clear, making it easier for readers to understand and respond, when necessary. In contrast, passive voice complicates meaning because the verb does not create action, which is its prescribed job in a sentence.

- With *active voice*, the verb performs action.
- With *passive voice*, the verb describes action.

Active voice makes writing clear and concise precisely because the various sentence parts play their designated roles: the verb performs action, and a real subject drives that action. With the passive voice, the real subject is more of a back-seat driver, if it is in the sentence at all. If this analogy does not mean anything to you right now, come back to it after you finish this chapter.

Though active voice is the preferred voice of business writing, passive voice fills important purposes. For example, the passive voice is perfect when a writer needs to be tactful. In addition, the passive voice is standard in scientific and academic writing because it seems to express objectivity and places the attention on the topic rather than the author.

However, passive voice creeps into all types of writing in which active voice would be the better fit. Writers use the passive voice unconsciously and out of habit for even simple communications, especially as they gain advanced degrees. In other words, you won't find many eighth graders writing in the passive voice, but you will find a most college students writing passively.

By graduate school, many writers use the passive voice without questioning its use. The same is true of corporate executives, unless the writer has experienced an "intervention."

Once writers start using the passive voice, they struggle to keep it. Because the passive voice becomes more prominent with more education, some writers think that they sound smarter: only smart people can produce complicated writing, right? But the truth is, the eighth grader writing in a crystal clear voice has a superior style to the corporate executive hiding behind layers of abstraction.

As Albert Einstein once said, "Everything should be made as simple as possible, but not simpler." In today's fast-paced world, complicated writing never sounds superior to simple, clear, concise writing. Readers prefer getting to the point quickly so that they can respond and move on.

As you let go of the passive voice, you may need to change the way that you think. Once you use active voice consistently, you will also see through the style of writers who cling to the passive voice for security.

Since real subjects play a deciding role in active voice, let's quickly review the difference between grammatical subjects and real subjects.

Grammatical Subjects Versus Real Subjects

Real subjects drive the action of verbs; however, as you know, the *real subject* (RS) of a sentence is not always its *grammatical subject* (GS).

- The *grammatical subject* precedes the verb.
- The *real subject* drives the action of the verb.

When the real subject precedes the verb, the real subject and grammatical subject are one and the same, for example:

> Jane's <u>manager</u> gave her a laptop.
>   GS/RS

In comparison, in the following sentence, the real subject *manager* is in the object position, and the grammatical subject is *Jane*:

> <u>Jane</u> was given a laptop by her <u>manager</u>.
> GS   RS

Since the real subject *manager* appears in the sentence (even though it is in the object position), the above example is *full passive*. In comparison, the following sentence has a grammatical subject, but not a real subject:

> A <u>laptop</u> was given to Jane.   *RS?*
>   GS

Who gave Jane the laptop? Based on the above sentence, we do not know. When a passive sentence does not contain a real subject, it is called a *truncated passive*.

Now let's go over active voice from the beginning.

Active Voice

The active voice is the most clear, direct, and concise way to phrase a sentence because each part of the sentence fills its prescribed role. However, active voice is one of those topics that is better explained through an example than through words. Here is a passive sentence:

Passive: The papers were sent to Sue by Bob.

In the sentence above, first identify the main verb, which is *sent*. Next, identify the real subject by asking who performed the action: *Who sent the papers? Bob did.* Finally, change the order in the sentence so that the real subject (Bob) is also the grammatical subject.

Active: Bob sent the papers to Sue.

Writers who are attached to the passive voice often argue that meaning changes when passive text is put into active voice. However, changing text from passive voice to active voice is an exercise in "translation"; the explicit meaning does not change.

However, because the tone can change, passive voice is preferred under specific circumstances which are discussed later in this chapter (Passive Voice, the Tactful Voice, page 113).

Here are the steps to change a sentence from passive voice to active voice:

1. Identify the main verb.
2. Identify the real subject by asking, *who performed the action of the verb?*
3. Place the real subject (along with modifying words) at the beginning of the sentence, which is the position of the grammatical subject.
4. Follow the real subject with the verb, *adjusting for agreement.*
5. Complete the sentence.

Using "shorthand," here is the process:

Step 1:	Main verb?
Step 2:	Real subject?
Steps 3 and 4:	Real subject + verb (*agreement and tense?*)
Step 5:	S – V – O.

Let's revise another sentence from passive voice to active voice.

    Passive: The merger was rejected by their new CEO.

Step 1: Main verb?	Rejected
Step 2: Real subject?	Their new CEO
Steps 3 and 4: Real subject + verb	Their new CEO rejected
Step 5: Complete sentence:	Their new CEO rejected the merger.

Here is the structure for the **active voice:**
    Who *did/does/will do* what.

Here is the structure for the **passive voice**:
    What *was done/is done/will be done* by whom.

Work on the following exercise to practice the active voice.

112 *A Guide for Business Writing*

PRACTICE 7.1

Instructions: Edit the following sentences from passive to active voice.

Incorrect: The instructions were given by Pat.
Corrected: Pat gave the instructions.

1. Sean was asked by his manager to lead the diversity team.
2. Phelps was given another chance by his coach to swim in the relay.
3. The holiday event was hosted by our department last year.
4. A new policy on reimbursement for travel expenses was implemented by our president.
5. The program was cancelled by the mayor due to lack of interest.

Note: See page 363 for the key to the above sentences.

Passive Voice, the Tactful Voice

In a passive sentence, the real subject does not need to be present; when situations call for tact, the passive voice is preferred over active voice.

Passive: A mistake was made on the August invoices.

Who made the mistake? Once again, an active sentence needs an actor or agent performing the action of its verb; however, a passive verb does not transfer action and does not an actor or agent. Here are a few more examples:

Passive: The check was not deposited in time to avert an overdraft.
The client was not consulted about the change.
Misinformation was given about that account.

You will use a truncated passive naturally in these situations. And, for these situations, the passive voice is not only a necessity, it is an asset.

While truncated passives play a vital role in writing, full passives that are used unnecessarily interfere with the quality and flow of writing.

Another element that complicates writing unnecessarily is the use of verbs in their nominal form. Nominalized verbs are often used in conjunction with the passive voice. After you work on the practice exercise below, you will work on getting rid of unnecessary nominalized verbs.

PRACTICE 7.2

Instructions: Edit the following sentences by changing passive voice to active voice. Then go back and determine which sentences would sound more tactful written in the passive voice.

Incorrect: Your account has been debited for the overdraft.

Corrected: We debited your account because of your overdraft. (Leave in the passive voice—it sounds more tactful.)

1. An error in invoicing was made on the Blackburn Account by Meyers last week.
2. If you wanted to avoid an overdraft, your check should have been deposited before 4 p.m.
3. For us to issue a refund, your receipt should have been enclosed with your return item.
4. Your order was sent to the wrong address and apologies are being made.
5. Your invoice needed to be paid before the first of the month to avoid penalties.

Note: See page 363 for the key to the above sentences.

Nominals

The word *nominal* refers to words that function as nouns. The actual term for a transforming a verb into a noun is *nominalization*.[1]

Would it surprise you to learn that most verbs have the potential to be used as nouns?

You've already worked with two forms of nominals: gerunds and infinitives.

- To form a gerund, add *ing* to the base form of a verb: *go* in its gerund form is *going*
- To form an infinitive, add *to* to the base form of a verb, as in *to go*.

As they are nominalized, some verbs change forms completely, following no specific pattern: the verb *analyze* turns into the noun *analysis* . . . the verb *fail* turns into the noun *failure* . . . and the verb *maintain* turns into the noun *maintenance*.

Many verbs, however, commonly turn into nouns by adding the suffix –*ment* or –*tion*. Here are some examples:

Verb	Nominal
accomplish	accomplishment
connect	connection
decide	decision
dedicate	dedication
develop	development
encourage	encouragement
evaluate	evaluation
facilitate	facilitation
institute	institutionalization
separate	separation
verify	verification

Nouns have no action and, for the most part, words originating as nouns cannot become verbs. When people turn nouns into verbs, the construction often sounds awkward, as in "Let's *lunch* together" or "Do you *lotto*?"

One word, however, has taken a unique place in English, and that word is *Google*. Google is a proper noun that also functions as a verb. Can you think of other proper nouns that also function as proper verbs?

Nominalization changes a verb's DNA, so to speak, taking action out of the verb. When writers use nominalizations unnecessarily, their writing becomes more complicated. However, just as passive voice at times adds value, nominalization can also add value when used effectively. And, let's be honest, isn't *nominalization* a word that you would rather avoid?

Here is an example of the verb *appreciate* and its nominalized form *appreciation*.

Nominalized: I want to express my *appreciation* for your help.
Active: I *appreciate* your help.

In the nominalized version above, the weak verb *want* replaces the strong verb *appreciate*. As well as stripping *appreciate* of its action, the nominalized version is more wordy. However, at times nominalizations work well, as in the following:

I value your *appreciation*.

Without the nominalization, the same sentiment might be expressed as follows:

When you appreciate my work, I value it.

Here is another example using the verb *commit* and its nominalized form *commitment*:

Nominalized: A *commitment* of resources for the disaster in New Orleans was made by our CEO at the annual meeting.
Active: At the annual meeting, our CEO *committed* resources for the disaster in New Orleans.

Once again, the more complicated writing is, the less effective it is. Use nominalized verbs purposefully, just as you would the passive voice.

When writers refuse to give up the passive voice, they may mistakenly believe that they sound sophisticated. Unfortunately, some writers fall into the same trap with nominalizations. Unnecessarily long four-syllable words do not improve the flow of writing. Follow Leonard da Vinci's advice, "Simplicity is the ultimate sophistication."

As an effective writer, make complex messages as *simple* as you can. Here is one more example that shows how the passive voice and nominalizations are used together:

Nominalized: *Encouragement* was given to me by my coach and teammates.

Passive: I *was encouraged* by my coach and teammates.

Active: My coach and teammates *encouraged* me.

The first sentence uses the nominalized form of the verb *encourage,* which is *encouragement.* In the second sentence, the nominal is removed, but the sentence is still passive. In the third sentence, *encourage* is an active verb in its past tense form.

Understanding these principles intellectually is much easier than actually applying them to your own writing. To achieve active writing, you need to be open minded and diligent. The more committed you are, the more you will improve.

PRACTICE 7.3

Instructions: Rewrite each sentence below by changing the nominal into an active verb.

Passive: The distribution of the product was made by Mary Lou.

Active: Mary Lou distributed the product.

1. The implementation of the dress policy was made official by management in August.
2. A suggestion was made by Jane that all new hires start on the first day of the month.

3. Information about that stock was given to us by our broker.
4. A discussion of the new account occurred at our last team meeting.
5. An announcement about the merger was made by our president before the deal was final.

Note: See page 363 for the key to the above sentences.

Style, Tone, and Meaning

Some writers argue that changing a sentence from passive voice to active voice changes its meaning. Shifting voice does not necessarily change the meaning, but it does change the tone. When all actors are present in a sentence, changing from passive voice to active voice is an exercise in *translation*.

Active voice is direct and clear. Passive voice is indirect and abstract to the point that the person performing the action does not even need to be present:

Passive: The problem will be solved.
Passive: A solution will be developed.

Who is solving the problem? Who is developing a solution? The passive voice allows people to say things without taking responsibility for their actions. In addition, with passive voice, writers do not connect with their own words in the way that they must with active voice, for example:

Passive: A discussion of the issue ensued at length before an acceptable compromise could be established.

Once again, *who discussed the issue?* By adding "people" to the mix, the sentence becomes much more reader-friendly.

Active: We discussed the issue at length before we reached a compromise.

Though passive voice sounds more formal, today's culture no longer supports that distant formality. Change is difficult. Changing your style of writing is difficult. Breaking out of an academic or a corporate mold takes courage and commitment.

If you start writing in the active voice, your associates will appreciate your clear, direct writing style that saves them time and energy.

Style and Process

Your writing style will not change overnight. Editing involves working on individual sentences to improve their structure. Commit time and energy to applying these principles as you edit, and you will see a striking difference in your writing style.

Even though you now have some good editing tools in your writing toolkit, you still may be trying to get your words down "right" as you compose. The *first and final draft* approach does not work: effective writing takes shape as you edit, not as you compose.

If you try to write the perfect sentence as you compose, you are sabotaging your writing. As you write, you need freedom to put ideas on the page in the way that they take shape in your mind. If you interfere with that process, writing is much more challenging for you than it needs to be.

The next chapter covers parallel structure, another topic that ranks high along with the active voice in making your writing effective.

Recap

Changing from passive voice to active voice improves the quality and readability of writing, but does not necessarily change meaning.

➢ Active voice is clear, concise, and direct.
➢ Passive voice is complicated and abstract but perfect for situations that call for tact.
➢ Nominalization takes action out of verbs and complicates writing.
➢ Active voice is the preferred voice of business communications.

Stay vigilant in your quest to write actively: active voice brings writing to life.

Writing Workshop

Topic: Lessons Learned

If you had your life to do all over again, what advice would you give to your younger, less experienced self?

What important life lessons have you learned? To refresh your memory, take out a photo of yourself when you were ten or twenty years younger than you are now.

> What memories does the photo awaken?
>
> What insights bubble up?
>
> What kinds of advice would you give to that more naïve version of yourself?

Write a letter to the young person in the photo. If you haven't already done so, you may want to consider beginning your memoir, writing about one experience at a time.

Editing Workshop

Draft

Instructions: As you revise the letter below, cut information and revise passive sentences to active voice.

Also, could this letter benefit from using bullet points to make the needed actions clearer for the reader? The revision is on the next page.

Dear Helen,

Every five years, an update is made on all active accounts by our data processing unit. The procedure is simple. The data on file is sent out to clients such as yourself so that changes can be made with a minimum of inconvenience. Please find enclosed your data form.

As your information is reviewed, any necessary changes should be made and initialed. Once all information has been updated, your signature is needed on the line provided.

Finally, please find enclosed a postage paid, self-addressed envelope so that the updated and signed form can be returned directly to our data processing unit.

Let me convey my appreciation for your prompt attention to this account revision.

Sincerely yours,

Mitchell Szewczyk
Account Executive

Revision

If you think the revision benefits from using bullets to make requested action stand out, review Chapter 13, Paragraphing and Formatting Basics, and Chapter 14, Formatting Letters, Memos, and E-Mail.

Dear Helen:

Every five years, our data processing unit updates their records on all active accounts.

Your current data form is enclosed so that you can update your information.

- Please initial any changes that you make.

- Sign the bottom of the form and return it in the enclosed self-addressed envelope.

We value your business and appreciate your prompt attention to this update.

Sincerely,

Mitchell Szewczyk
Account Executive

End Note

1. Joseph M. Williams, Style: Toward Clarity and Grace, The University of Chicago Press, Chicago, 1990.

122 A Guide for Business Writing

8

Parallel Structure

When writing sounds choppy, check to see if it lacks parallel structure. Parallel structure means that similar sentence elements are expressed in the same grammatical form; that is, noun for noun, verb for verb, phrase for phrase, and clause for clause.

- Parallel structure gives writing balance, rhythm, and flow.
- Parallel structure enhances understanding.

As you have seen with the active voice, readers appreciate writing that is clear and easy to understand. In sentences, shifts in parallel structure often occur with the following:

- Gerunds and Infinitives
- Active and Passive Voice
- Verb Tense

Also check for parallel structure when using bullet points to create lists, when using correlating conjunctions, and when making comparisons. This chapter covers each of these topics.

Throughout the centuries, speakers and writers have used parallelism in a variety of ways to draw attention to their point. On a broad level, consider the parallel features of Dr. Martin Luther King's speech, *I Have a Dream*. King's repetition not only built up listeners' expectations but also added an indelible rhythm to his speech. When you listen to an especially effective speech, consider if the speaker uses parallel repetition to draw you in.

Thus, on a macro level, parallel structure involves using repetitive phrases or sentences to draw in readers and build their expectations. On a micro level, parallel structure involves putting similar sentence elements in the same grammatical form. At all levels, parallel structure creates rhythm and flow.

Let's get to work on the smaller elements of parallel structure that affect your writing on a daily basis.

Noun for Noun

Writers have various ways of shifting structure when using nouns, thereby losing parallel structure.

Inconsistent:	You deserve *rest, relaxation,* and *weather that is warm.*
Parallel:	You deserve *rest, relaxation,* and *warm weather.*
Inconsistent:	During summers, I worked as *a secretary, assistant cashier,* and *did tutoring.*
Parallel:	During summers, I worked as *a secretary, an assistant cashier,* and *a tutor.*

Another common way to lose parallel structure is to shift from infinitives to gerunds. Infinitives and gerunds are nominals, so they function as nouns, not as verbs.

- An infinitive is the base form of the verb plus *to*, as in *to see, to go,* and *to keep.*
- A gerund is the base form of the verb plus *ing*, as in *seeing, going,* and *keeping.*

For parallel structure, the key to using gerunds and infinitives is using one or the other, but not both.

Inconsistent:	My favorite activities are *to jog, swimming,* and *going to the park and golfing.*
Parallel:	My favorite activities are *jogging, swimming,* and *golfing.*

When you create a list, apply parallel structure to the way that you display your items. Here is an inconsistent list:

Goals for tomorrow:
1. New computer software acquisition.
2. Making an appointment with HR consultant
3. Time for doing program report

To make the above list parallel, start each item with an infinitive form *or* a gerund form. If you choose to use infinitives, drop the "to" and simply use the *base form* of the verb (which is actually the same as an active verb in the "you" viewpoint).

Base Form:
1. Buy new computer software.
2. Make an appointment with HR consultant.
3. Plan time for program report.

Gerunds:
1. Buying new computer software.
2. Making an appointment with HR consultant.
3. Planning time for program report.

Complete the exercise below for practice putting lists in parallel form.

PRACTICE 8.1

Instructions: Make the following list parallel by using infinitives (active voice) or gerunds.

Weak: Group Assessment for Management Training
Revised: Assessing Groups for Management Training

- Creation of High Performance Teams
- Development of Effective Communication Skills
- Effective Job Performance Coaching

Chapter 8: Parallel Structure **125**

- Conflict Resolution
- Recruitment and Retention of Managers
- Personality Differences in the Workplace Valued
- Climate Assessment in Change Efforts

Note: See page 364 for the key to the above sentences.

Adjective for Adjective

With lists of adjectives, writers sometimes drift from an adjective into a phrase or clause. When you see yourself making that kind of shift, edit out the inconsistency.

Inconsistent: Marguerite is *nice, pretty,* and *has a lot of talent.*
Parallel: Marguerite is *nice, pretty,* and *talented.*

Inconsistent: The program is *short, intense,* and *many people like it.*
Parallel: The program is *short, intense,* and *popular.*

Phrase for Phrase

When using prepositional phrases, check for parallel agreement. For example, the lead-in preposition may not fit the phrases that follow it:

Inconsistent: I am disappointed *about the situation* and *the people* who caused it.

Parallel: I am disappointed *about the situation* and *with the people* who caused it.

You may also find a prepositional phrase followed by another type of structure, such as a dependent clause, as shown below:

Inconsistent: Our company applauds them *for their dedication* and *because they are passionate about* their cause.

Parallel: Our company applauds them *for their dedication to* and *for their passion about* their cause.

Clause for Clause

Another way to lose parallel structure is to shift voice from passive to active, or vice versa:

Inconsistent: Bob received his brother's old car because a new car was bought by his brother. (active-passive)

Parallel: Bob received his brother's old car because his brother bought a new car. (active-active)

Inconsistent: We ran out of money in our budget, so that project was dropped. (active-passive)

Parallel: We ran out of money in our budget, so we dropped that project. (active-active)

PRACTICE 8.2

Instructions: Edit the following sentences for parallel structure.

Incorrect: You request is being considered; in the meantime, we hope that you will remain a loyal customer.

Corrected: We are considering your request; in the meantime, we hope that you will remain a loyal customer.

1. My manager asked me to attend the annual meeting, and arriving early on Friday was required.
2. My family will join me in Florida, and reservations will be made for them by my assistant.
3. Everyone is excited about the trip, but little free time has been planned for me to join them in sight-seeing activities.
4. If my schedule can be adjusted, I will join them in some fun activities.
5. My boss approved the extra time, so now my travel arrangements must be changed.

Note: See page 364 for the key to the above sentences.

Tense for Tense

Do not shift verb tense unnecessarily. Stay in present tense *or* past tense unless the meaning of the sentence demands that you change tenses.

Inconsistent: Tim *tells* me last week that the competition *was* over.
Parallel: Tim *told* me last week that the competition *was* over.

Inconsistent: Management *says* that our team won.
Parallel: Management *said* that our team won.

The following exercises gives you practice using verb tense consistently.

PRACTICE 8.3

Instructions: The following sentences shift tense unnecessarily. Change the verbs, making tenses consistent.

Incorrect: My manager tells me on Thursday afternoon that I needed to cancel the retreat on Friday, so what was I to do?

Corrected: My manager told me on Thursday afternoon that I needed to cancel the retreat on Friday, so what was I to do?

1. The message is not clear and needed to be changed.
2. My boss says that their account has been closed for some time now.
3. The new computers arrive today, so then I had to install them.
4. Yesterday my co-worker tells me that was supposed to attend the budget meeting.
5. First Mary says that she wants the position then she didn't.

Note: See page 364 for the key to the above sentences.

Correlative Conjunctions

Here are common pairs of correlative conjunctions—notice that the second word in the pair is a coordinating conjunction:

either . . . or
neither . . . nor
both . . . and
not . . . but
not only . . . but also
whether . . . or

When you use correlative conjunctions, follow the second part of the correlative with the same structure as the first part, for example:

Inconsistent: We will *not only* upgrade your account *but also* are providing monthly reports.

Parallel: We *not only* will upgrade your account *but also* will provide monthly reports.

Parallel: We will *not only* upgrade your account *but also* provide monthly reports.

PRACTICE 8.4

Instructions: Edit the following sentences for parallel structure.

Incorrect: Whether you choose not to attend or are planning to be there, the meeting will go on.

Corrected: Whether you choose not to attend or plan to be there, the meeting will go on.

1. My boss not only asked me to complete the report but also presenting it at the meeting was required.
2. I both plan to visit Rome and seeing the ancient ruins.
3. Our team neither focused on winning the game nor show good team spirit.

4. Your motivation both will help you to achieve success and getting what you want in life.
5. The new jerseys have not only been received by me, but now I must pass them out.

Note: She page 365 for the key to the above sentences.

Recap

Parallel structure comes in all shapes and forms. Developing a keen eye for similar sentence elements takes time and commitment. As you focus attention on parallel structure, you will begin to see connections that you did not previously see.

- Put similar sentence elements in the same grammatical form: noun for noun, phrase for phrase, clause for clause, and so on.
- Do not shift verb tense unnecessarily.
- Start bulleted lists with infinitives (which are the same as active verbs in the "you" viewpoint) or gerunds (the *ing* form of the verb).
- Pay special attention to parallel structure when using correlative conjunctions.

Writing Workshop

Topic: About Work

Write your response to the following questions:

1. Why do you want to work? Identify the reasons other than to earn money.

2. What are your expectations of work? Is work something to be suffered through and endured, or should your job be more than that? Why?

3. Describe your dream job. If you had no constraints (money, family, or geography requirements), what work would you love to do?

Editing Workshop

Draft

Instructions: Work on the following bulleted list, making the items parallel. You will find the revision on the next page.

At the Leadership Institute, you will work on:

- A review and understanding of state-of-the-art leadership qualities
- The development of strategies to improve productivity
- Best practices for training programs are identified and applied
- Creation of a personal network for problem solving
- Gain insight into the processes that create effective teams
- Acquisition of tools for managing training programs

Revision

Notice that one of the revisions below uses gerunds and the other uses active verbs (which are actually the same as verbs in their infinitive form).

At the Leadership Workshop, you will work on the following:

- Understanding state-of-the-art leadership qualities.
- Developing strategies to improve productivity.
- Identifying and applying best practices for training programs.
- Creating a personal network for problem solving.
- Gaining insights into the processes that create effective teams.
- Acquiring tools for managing training programs.

Or:

At the Leadership Workshop, you will:

- Review state-of-the-art leadership qualities.
- Develop strategies to improve productivity.
- Identify and apply best practices for training programs.
- Create a personal network for problem solving.
- Gain insights into the processes that create effective teams.
- Acquire tools for managing training programs.

9

Pronouns

Most people aren't aware of the mistakes that they make with pronouns, so keep an open mind as you go through this chapter. You see, you may be feeling quite confident as you err in your use of common pronouns; for example, is it "between you and *I*" or "between you and *me*"? Should you give the report to "John and *myself*" or "John and *me*" or "John and *I*?

When using pronouns, people have a tendency to *hypercorrect*, using a formal-sounding pronoun when a less formal-sounding pronoun would be correct. Examples of hypercorrections would include using *I* as an object instead of *me* or perhaps using *myself* when either *I* or *me* would have been correct.

Unsure speakers pick up incorrect pronoun use unconsciously, almost the way they would pick up a virus. Eventually, the incorrect usage sounds correct. Until you are certain that you are using pronouns according to the way that they *function* in a sentence, stop basing decisions on how they *sound*. Eventually, the correct patterns will sound correct, and then you will have sound and principle on your side.

Changing patterns of speech is challenging. Repetition is key. Once you identify a pattern that you need to change, repeat the correct pattern until it sounds right to you. Learning just a few basic principles in this way will help you gain control and confidence.

You start this chapter by reviewing personal pronouns, which are broken into four cases: *subjective, objective, possessive,* and *reflexive.* Then you work with *who, whom,* and *that,* pronouns that can be confusing but that become simple with only a bit of instruction.

As you know, a pronoun is a word that is used in place of a noun or another pronoun. The following chart categorizes personal pronouns based on how they function in a sentence. In other words, subjective pronouns function as subjects of verbs; objective pronouns function as objects of verbs, prepositions, infinitives, and so on.

Personal Pronouns: Four Cases

	Subjective	Objective	Possessive	Reflexive
Singular				
1st Person	I	me	my, mine	myself
2nd Person	you	you	your, yours	yourself
3rd Person	he	him	his	himself
	she	her	hers	herself
	it	it	its	itself
Plural				
1st Person	we	us	our, ours	ourselves
2nd Person	you	you	your, yours	yourselves
3rd Person	they	them	their, theirs	themselves

Here is a summary of the role each case plays in a sentence:

- *Subjective case* pronouns function as *subjects* of verbs, and thus a subjective case pronoun is used as the subject of a sentence.
- *Objective case* pronouns function as *objects*, usually of verbs or prepositions.
- *Possessive case* pronouns *show possession* of nouns or other pronouns.
- *Reflexive case* pronouns, also known as *intensive* case pronouns, reflect back to *subjective case pronouns*.

Subjects Versus Objects

The big divide in pronoun use lies between subjective case and objective case. Once you gain control of subjects and objects, other elements of pronoun use fall naturally into place. Therefore, at the core of pronoun use, here is the question you need to answer:

Does the pronoun function as a *subject* or an *object*?

You have worked with the sentence core and should be familiar with the difference between subjects and objects. However, old habits die hard. Since subjective case pronouns sound more formal than objective case pronouns, you may be using *I* as an object when *me* would be correct. Another example would be using *he* as an object when *him* would be correct. The choice becomes more challenging when a pronoun is part of a pair, such as *Jim and I* or *Jim and me*.

So that you can check your use of pronouns, you are given some choices between Edited English and local language. As you will recall, Edited English is formal usage and local language is informal. Make your choice before looking at the explanation below each set. The first set is below; which of the following sounds correct to you?

Choice 1: Bill asked Mike and *I* to assist him.
Choice 2: Bill asked Mike and *me* to assist him.

In the above example, the pronoun is in the object position. One way to test this example is to take "Mike" out of the sentence. For example, would you ever say "Bill asked *I* to assist him"? Choice 2 is Edited English; Choice 1 is local language.

Choice 1: Her manager and *her* went to the game last Friday.
Choice 2: Her manager and *she* went to the game last Friday.

In the above example, the pronoun is in the subject position. Once again, take "Her manager" out of the sentence. While "Her manager and *her*" might sound correct, "*Her* went to the game" clearly sounds wrong. Choice 2 is Edited English; Choice 1 is local language.

Some writers substitute a reflexive case pronoun in place of a subjective case or objective case pronoun, as in the following local language sentences:

> George and *myself* went to the game last Friday.
> Bill asked Mike and *myself* to assist him.
> Sue and *yourself* can work on the project.

Use a reflexive case pronoun only when you are referring to a subjective case pronoun or noun that is already part of the sentence. To test the above, take the "other person" out of the sentence. Would you ever say any of the following?

> ~~George and~~ myself went to the game last Friday.
> Bill asked ~~Mike and~~ myself to assist him.
> ~~Sue and~~ yourself can work on the project.

Stop using reflexive case pronouns until you are sure that you are using them correctly, as in the following Edited English examples:

> *I* will do the work *myself*.
> *You* can complete the project *yourself*, if you have the time.
> *Susan* referred to *herself* as the person in charge of hiring.
> The *dog* bit *itself* on the foot, mistaking his foot for a bone!

As these examples show, pronoun usage is most difficult when the pronoun is part of a pairing. If a pronoun is part of a pair, check for correct usage by using the following substitutions:

1. Use *I* if you could substitute *we*:

    Sam and *I* went to the game: *We* went to the game.

2. Use *me* if you could substitute *us*:

    Sally asked *Juan and me* for help: Sally asked *us* for help.

3. Use *he* or *she* if you could substitute *they*:

    Martin and he finished the project: *they* finished the project.

4. Use *him* or *her* if you could substitute *them*:

   Melissa encouraged *LaTika and her* to go: Melissa encouraged *them*.

As shown above, another way to check for formal usage would be to simplify the sentence, taking out the other person and then testing for sound. Using examples from above, here is how you would test pronouns based on sound:

Incorrect:	Sam and *me* went to the game.
Simplified:	~~Sam and~~ *me* went to the game.
Corrected:	Sam and *I* went to the game.
Incorrect:	Sally asked Juan and *I* for help.
Simplified:	Sally asked ~~Juan and~~ *I* for help.
Corrected:	Sally asked Juan and *me* for help.
Incorrect:	Martin and *him* finished the project.
Simplified:	~~Martin and~~ *him* finished the project.
Corrected:	Martin and *he* finished the project.
Incorrect:	Melissa encouraged LaTika and she to go.
Simplified:	Melissa encouraged ~~LaTika and~~ she to go.
Corrected:	Melissa encouraged LaTika and *her* to go.

> **Writing tip**
> **Rule of Thumb Substitution:**
> - If you can substitute *we* for a pair, use *I*.
> - If you can substitute *us*, use *me*.

PRACTICE 9.1

Instructions: Edit the following sentences for formal pronoun usage.

Incorrect:	My manager and me are both going to the conference.
Corrected:	My manager and *I* are both going to the conference.

1. If you can't reach the office, feel free to call myself.
2. The attendant asked Claudia and I to move to the back.
3. Fred and him collected for the local charity drive.
4. Her manager and her have two more reports to complete.
5. That committee is co-chaired by Jim and I.

Note: See page 365 for the key to the above sentences.

Pronouns Following *Between*

When a pronoun follows *between*, oftentimes the local language version sounds "more correct" than Edited English. Which of the following sounds correct to you?

Choice 1: Between you and *I*, we have too much work.
Choice 2: Between you and *me*, we have too much work.

Remember the saying, "What is the object of the preposition?" The word *between* is a preposition, so an object would follow it. The Edited English answer is Choice 2: when a pronoun follows *between*, use the objective case; in this example, *me*.

Which of the following sounds correct to you?

Choice 1: Milton split the project between *he* and *I*.
Choice 2: Milton split the project between *him* and *I*.
Choice 3: Milton split the project between *him* and *me*.

Once again, follow the preposition *between* with the objective case, so Choice 3 is correct.

Here are more examples using the objective case after *between*.

Incorrect: You can split the project between *Bob* and *I*.
Corrected: You can split the project between *Bob* and *me*.
You can split the project between *us*.

138 *A Guide for Business Writing*

Incorrect: That issue should remain between *yourself* and *I*.
Correct: That issue should remain between *you* and *me*.
  That issue should remain between *us*.

PRACTICE 9.2

Instructions: Edit the following sentences for formal pronoun usage.

Incorrect: The issue should remain between you and I.
Corrected: The issue should remain between you and me.

1. Mark said to split the data sheets between you and I.
2. The problem has nothing to do with me—it's between you and he.
3. The decision is between Bob and yourself.
4. You can split the work between Margaret and I so that it gets done on time.
5. Between Bob and myself, we have our work cut out for us.

Note: See page 365 for the key to the above sentences.

Pronouns Following *Than*

Most of the time, speakers follow the word *than* with an objective case pronoun without giving any thought to their phrasing. However, the word *than* is a conjunction and may need to be followed by a subject and a verb. Which of the following sounds correct to you?

Choice 1: Paco is taller than *me*.
Choice 2: Paco is taller than *I*.

In the above example, the verb is implied, making the objective case pronoun sound correct even though it is not Edited English. Choice 2 is Edited English. The statement actually reads, "Paco is taller than I (am tall)."

If you prefer to be correct without sounding too formal, do not use implied verbs. Instead, always state the verb at the end of a sentence. Here are more examples:

Incorrect: Mark shoots hoops better than *me*.
Corrected: Mark shoots hoops better than *I do*.

Incorrect: Our department has more work than *them*.
Corrected: Our department has more work than *they do*.

Incorrect: Mitchell has more time than *me*.
Corrected: Mitchell has more time than *I have*.

Incorrect: Arun runs faster than *me*.
Corrected: Arun runs faster than *I run*.

When you use *than* in a comparison, do not automatically follow it with an objective case pronoun. Instead, check to see if you need to follow it with a subject and a verb.

PRACTICE 9.3

Instructions: Edit the following sentences for formal pronoun usage.

Incorrect: Your department has more time than us.
Corrected: Your department has more time and our's (or "our department" or "we do").

1. Willow has more time than me.
2. The other team has more resources than us.
3. Bob has a nicer car than me.
4. Massimo should get the job if he is more competent than me.
5. I'm taller than him.

Note: See page 365 for the key to the above sentences.

Who, Whom, and That

Most people feel a bit of anxiety about using the pronoun *whom* because they are unsure about how to use it correctly. As a result, the objective case pronoun *whom* is becoming somewhat extinct.

However, *whom* is not that difficult to master once you clearly know the difference between *I* and *me*. You see, the difference between *who* and *whom* is the same as the difference between *I* and *me*: *who* is a subject and *whom* is an object.

As you work on these pronouns, realize that the pronoun *whom* is leaving the American vocabulary. Drop your trepidation about using *whom* correctly; the more relevant and urgent issue is to avoid misusing *that*. Let's take a look at how to use each pronoun correctly.

1. Use *who* as the subject of a clause or a sentence.

   Who gave you the report?

   Who said that the program starts now?

2. Use *whom* as an object of a verb, a preposition, an infinitive, or other verb phrase.

   To *whom* are you referring?

   You are referring to *whom*?

3. Use *that* when referring to things, not people.

   The yellow car is the one *that* is broken.

   Not: Mary is the person *that* spoke first.

4. Use *who* as a subject complement of a linking verb such as *to be* (*is, are, was,* or *were*).

   Who do you want *to be* when you grow up?

   You want *to be who* when you grow up?

When you are having difficulty choosing among the relative pronouns *who*, *whom*, and *that*, use *who* as your "default" pronoun:

> When in doubt, use *who*.

Here is why:

1. *Whom* is falling out of use: only a small fraction of the population use *whom* correctly.
2. *Whom* is highly formal and sounds out of place for most conversations, even when used correctly.
3. *Whom* sounds strange when used incorrectly: *Whom* goes there?

To improve your speech as well as your writing, focus on pronouncing your words clearly.

Local Language:	*Whoja* go to lunch with?
Edited English:	*Who* did you go to lunch with?
Formal English:	With *whom* did you go to lunch?

Do the following exercise to gain practice with *who*, *whom*, and *that*.

PRACTICE 9.4

Instructions: In the following sentences, cross out the pronoun that would be incorrect usage in Edited English.

Incorrect:	(Who, Whom) gave the you go ahead on the project?
Corrected:	(Who, ~~Whom~~) gave you the go ahead on the project?

1. (Who, Whom) wrote the monthly report?
2. (Who, Whom) are you going to the meeting with?
3. Is Alleso the person (who, whom, that) spoke with you?
4. The doctor (who, whom, that) saw you yesterday is not available.
5. Every person (who, whom, that) arrives late will be turned away.

Note: See page 366 for the key to the above sentences.

Indefinite Pronouns

Indefinite pronouns are words that replace nouns without specifying the noun they are replacing. To use an indefinite pronoun correctly, first determine whether it is *singular* or *plural*.

Singular Indefinite Pronouns:

another	everybody	no one
anyone	everyone	nothing
anybody	everything	somebody
each	neither	someone
either	nobody	something

Singular indefinite pronouns take singular verbs and singular antecedents:

>*Every* situation *calls* for a different response.
>
>*Neither* of the girls *works* here.
>
>*Someone* leaves *his* or *her* locker ajar every day.

Plural Indefinite Pronouns:

>both, few, many, others, several

Plural indefinite pronouns take plural verbs and plural antecedents:

>*Many* (of the participants) *were* unprepared for *their exams*.
>
>*Several* (people) *arrive* daily to update *their accounts*.

Indefinite Pronouns, Singular or Plural:

>all, none, any, some, more, most

Indefinite pronouns that can be singular or plural are generally followed by a prepositional phrase that contains a noun. If the noun is singular, then the pronoun is singular. If the noun is plural, then the pronoun is plural. Here are examples:

>*None* of the cake *was* eaten.
>
>*None* of the cookies *were* gone.

All of the paint *has* spilled.
All of the brushes *are* spoiled.

Some of the participants forgot *their* paperwork.
Some of the paperwork *is* not available.

Do the following exercise to practice using indefinite pronouns.

PRACTICE 9.5

Instructions: Edit the following sentences for formal pronoun usage.

Incorrect: Someone leaves their computer on every day.
Corrected: Someone leaves his or her computer on every day.

1. Neither of the proposals are ready to send out.
2. None of our stores opens early on Saturday.
3. Everyone should make their own reservations.
4. Some of the papers lists the correct date.
5. All of our assignment have been completed on time.

Note: See page 366 for the key to the above sentences.

Recap

To eliminate most errors, stay aware of the difference between subjective and objective case pronouns.

- Subjective case pronouns function as subjects of verbs.
- Objective case pronouns function as objects of verbs, prepositions, infinitives, and so on.
- Reflexive case pronouns refer back to a subjective case pronoun or noun; for example: *I* will do the work *myself*.
- The pronoun *who* functions as a subject; *whom*, as an object.
- When referring to people, use *who*; to objects, use *that*.
- When in doubt, choose *who*.

Writing Workshop

Topic: Reflective Writing

Writing is a form of meditation. Once you start writing about a topic, your mind continues to explore it even when you are not actively putting words on the page. Below are two quotes; what does each mean to you?

You can't depend on your eyes when your imagination is out of focus.

--Mark Twain

The house you live in is your mind. Your own integrity—don't worry about the rest of it.   --Ralph W. Tyler

What is your favorite quote? What does it mean to you? Jot down your ideas. Notice if you continue to think about your quote after you finish writing about it.

Editing Workshop

Draft

Instructions: Edit the following message, paying special attention to pronoun use. The revision is on the next page.

Hi Rudolfo,

Juliana and myself are concerned that we will not have enough time to complete our end-of-month inventory. Between she and I we have a total of 45 hours to devote to it.

Some of our assistants has had their over-time canceled and that is part of the problem. Last month, none of our workers was cut so we had double the time for inventory.

We are entering a high-volume sales period and this situation can quickly turn into a mess, Juliana is more concerned than me. She feels that if human resources was to hear from yourself, they would be more inclined to extend over-time hours. If that was the case her and I could turn this situation around.

Let me know what you think by Friday if possible.

Best, Randy

Revision

The first message below is a *correction* of the original message, the second a *revision*.

Correction:

> Hi Rudolfo,
>
> Juliana and ~~myself~~ *I* are concerned that we will not have enough time to complete our end-of-month inventory. Between ~~she and I~~ *her and me,* we have a total of 45 hours to devote to it.
>
> Some of our assistants ~~has~~ *have* had their over-time canceled, and that is part of the problem. Last month, none of our workers ~~was~~ *were* cut, so we had double the time for inventory.
>
> We are entering a high-volume sales period, and this situation can quickly turn into a mess. Juliana is more concerned than ~~me~~ *I am.* She feels that if human resources ~~was~~ *were* to hear from ~~yourself~~, they would be more inclined to extend over-time hours. If that ~~was~~ *were* the case, ~~her~~ *she* and I could turn this situation around.
>
> Let me know what you think by Friday, if possible.
>
> Randy

Revision:

> Hi Rudolfo,
>
> We are entering a high-volume sales period, and we are short staffed.
>
> So that we have enough time to complete our end-of-month inventory, would you be willing to request that human resources extend our over-time hours?
>
> Thanks for your help and let me know what you think.
>
> All the best,
>
> Randy

10

Point of View

Pronouns are a core element of everything that you write; so regardless of what you write, you will struggle with pronouns until you find your comfort zone with them. Finding your comfort zone with pronouns entails using them consciously and consistently.

The various types of writing—academic, scientific, creative, and business—employ pronouns differently, resulting in distinctive types of voices. Although this book stresses business writing, comments about each domain are included here to provide a vantage point.

In most academic and scientific text, writers do not directly express their own point of view. In fact, readers do not expect to hear the writer's point of view, until possibly the end of a paper. The writer, instead, focuses on summarizing research and arguing a position or explores problems in the quest of reaching new levels of insight. That is partly why some academic and scientific writers employ the passive voice. The idea is that passive voice highlights the findings rather than the person conducting the research or writing the article. Thus, academic and scientific writers do not typically use pronouns to speak from their own voice.

Creative writers, on the other hand, provide intricate details and vivid pictures to ignite their readers' imaginations. With creative writing, writers strive to develop a strong, clear voice that engages their readers and brings them into an experience of their stories. Active voice achieves this end well. Active voice requires real subjects, which means that pronouns are an integral part of creative writing.

Business writing, on the other hand, does not thrive on detail but does rely on a writer's voice to engage its readers. With business writing, context defines the various players and the "script," which means that pronouns, along with the active voice, play a big role in business writing.

When business writers try to avoid speaking from their own voice, their only choice is a passive and complicated style, which makes readers suffer unnecessarily.

As you work through this chapter, reflect on how pronouns contribute to a writer's voice and help create the tone of a document. First, let's work on a topic that involves using pronouns correctly and consistently, the first step in the process of using pronouns effectively.

Pronoun and Antecedent Agreement

Pronouns are used in place of nouns and other pronouns, and the words that pronouns refer to are known as *antecedents*. In the following example, *managers* is the antecedent of *they* and *their*.

> All *managers* said that *they* would submit *their* quarterly reports before the 30th of the month.

Pronouns must agree in number and gender with their antecedents. Many antecedents are not gender specific, such as *person, doctor, engineer, lawyer, teacher*, and so on, which creates a problem. When writers use singular antecedents that are gender neutral, English does not provide choices that allow writing to flow naturally. Instead, writers must use combinations of pronouns, such as *he/she* or *him/her*. For example, the antecedent "broker" is gender neutral.

> When a *broker* performs *his* or *her* duties, *he* or *she* must remain attentive to *his* or *her* clients.

When using singular antecedents, writers are prone to make errors with the pronouns. For example, many writers would have erred on the above sentence by writing it as follows:

> When *a broker* performs *their* duties, *they* must remain attentive to *their* clients.

To avoid the awkwardness of using singular pronouns (such as *he or she* or *his or her*) with singular antecedents and simultaneously avoid the type of error shown above, use plural antecedents.

> When *brokers* perform *their* duties *they* must remain attentive to *their* clients.

Here are a few more examples:

Incorrect: When a *pilot* flies, *they* need to stay focused.
Corrected: When a *pilot* flies, *he* or *she* needs to stay focused.
Corrected: When *pilots* fly, *they* need to stay focused.

Incorrect: Every *member* should bring *their* own *laptop*.
Corrected: Every *member* should bring *his* or *her* own *laptop*.
Corrected: All *members* should bring *their* own *laptops*.

Notice in the above example that *laptops* becomes plural right along with *team members*. Consistency and agreement apply to all related elements.

Another issue arises in sentences that contain more than one antecedent. When two or more antecedents appear in a sentence, pronoun reference can be unclear. For example, in the following sentence, which person does the pronoun *she* refer to?

> *Sue* and *Martha* completed their report by Tuesday so that *she* could present the findings in a conference on Thursday.

At those times when meaning is unclear, restate the antecedent rather than using a pronoun:

> *Sue* and *Martha* completed their report by Tuesday so that *Martha* could present the findings in a conference on Thursday.

Here is another example:

Incorrect: Charley said that John should be on his team because he would be available during his training.

Corrected: Charley said that John should be on his team because Charley would be available during John's training.

Complete the following exercises for pronoun-antecedent agreement.

PRACTICE 10.1

Instructions: Correct the following sentences for pronoun-antecedent agreement.

Incorrect: Ask a friend for their help only when you really need it.
Corrected: Ask friends for their help only when you really need it.

1. When an employee calls in sick, they should give a reason.
2. When a server does not relate well to their clients, they need more training.
3. A nurse is going beyond their job description when they assist a patient's guests.
4. A flight controller's job is challenging because they work long hours under difficult conditions.
5. When a customer does not have a receipt, they not should necessarily to return an item easily.

Note: See page 366 for the key to the above sentences.

Point of View and Consistency

In most types of writing, you must address the issue of point of view. Point of view, or pronoun viewpoint, can emanate from first, second, or third person, singular or plural.

	Singular	**Plural**
First Person	I	We
Second Person	You	You
Third Person	A person	People

Here are examples of the various viewpoints:

> When *I* speak, *I* must pay attention to *my* audience.
>
> When *you* speak, *you* must pay attention to *your* audience.
>
> When a *person* speaks, *he* or *she* must pay attention to *his* or *her* audience.
>
> When *we* speak, *we* must pay attention to *our* audience.
>
> When *people* speak, *they* must pay attention to *their* audience.

Though the *one* viewpoint is not common in the United States, other English-speaking countries commonly use the *one* viewpoint, for example:

> When *one* speaks, *one* must pay attention to *one's* audience.

An error many writers make, however, is to use the pronoun *one* when they are unsure, for example:

Incorrect: *I* think *one* should write daily because *you* improve *your* skills.

Incorrect: If *one* arrives on time, *they* will receive good service.

As you compose, let yourself write freely. However, when you edit, screen your work thoroughly for correct usage, consistency, and agreement. Do not shift point of view within sentences or even entire paragraphs. Here is how the above sentences could be written:

Correct: *I* should write daily because *I* will improve *my* skills.

Correct: If *you* arrive on time, *you* will receive good service.

Here are more examples of shifting point of view:

Incorrect: *I* like to swim because it's good for *you*.

Corrected: *I* like to swim because it's good for *me*.

Incorrect: *An employee* should follow the rules so that *you* treat *your* customers fairly.

Corrected: *An employee* should follow the rules so that *he* or *she* treats *his* or *her* customers fairly.

Even though the above sentence is correct, notice how tedious it is to present it in third person singular. Better choices would be making the antecedent plural or using the *you* viewpoint:

Correct: *Employees* should follow the rules so that *they* treat *their* customers fairly.

Correct: (*You* should) Follow the rules so that *you* treat *your* customers fairly.

Point of view helps you adapt your topic for your audience. Once you select a point of view, the key is using it consistently. Edit individual sentences and individual paragraphs for consistency; at times, you will even need to edit entire documents for consistency.

Point of View and Voice

An important way for business writers to engage their readers is to write from their own viewpoint, which means using the personal pronoun *I*. Therefore, when you write from your own experience, use the *I* point of view.

***I* Viewpoint:** *I* will turn in the paperwork on Friday.

If you were to choose not to write from the *I* viewpoint, you would need to write passively:

Passive: The paperwork will be turned in on Friday.

However, just as writers use the passive voice unnecessarily, they also use the *I* viewpoint unnecessarily. For example, at times writers automatically use the *I* viewpoint when the *you* viewpoint would be a more effective choice. The *you* viewpoint engages the reader directly, keeping the focus on the reader and the reader's needs.

***I* Viewpoint:**   I appreciate that you were able to help with the Baker account.

***You* Viewpoint**:   You helped me significantly when you assisted with the Baker account.

Choose the *you* viewpoint over the *I* viewpoint when feasible to do so. (You will also work on the *you* viewpoint in Chapter 11, "Tone.")

An extension of the *I* viewpoint is the *editorial we*. Business writers use the *we* viewpoint to stress that they represent their company, as in the following:

***We* Viewpoint**:   *We* appreciate your business—please let *us* know if there is anything *we* can do to make your stay comfortable.

Now let's shift from business writing to academic writing. Academic writing depends more heavily on the *third person point of view*. When summarizing a research article, start your summary by stating the author's first and last name and the title of the article. Then use the author's *last name* throughout your summary as you speak from the author's viewpoint.

In addition to speaking from the author's viewpoint, speak from a third-person (the topic) viewpoint as you summarize points about the topic (however, do not speak from your own viewpoint until possibly the conclusion), for example:

> In *Janet Barnes'* article, "An Internet Dilemma," *she* argues that the Internet can distract its users, ultimately creating stress and lost time. *Barnes* specifically identifies students as being at risk for getting sidetracked and losing focus.
>
> The *Internet* has many uses, ranging from pursuing personal interests to being an academic research vehicle; and *Barnes'* argument highlights how sites such as Facebook can actually interfere with student learning and their doing research on the Internet.

When summarizing anyone's writing, use your own words. Cut and paste plagiarism does nothing to improve your skills and may jeopardize your academic or professional career.

Gain practice using pronouns by doing the following exercise.

PRACTICE 10.2

Instructions: Edit the following paragraph, screening for pronoun consistency.

> I enjoy working on team projects because you learn so much from your teammates. A team member needs to be helpful because they never know when they will need assistance from his or her colleagues. When you are on a team, every member needs to carry their weight. That is, teammates who do not do his or her share of the work can be a burden to the team and jeopardize their project.
>
> If a team member stays motivated, you are more valuable to the team. I always strive to do my best because you never know when you will need to count on your team members.

Note: See page 366 for the key to the above exercise.

Recap

By using pronouns correctly and consistently, you ensure that documents are professional and reader-friendly.

- For business writing, using the *I* viewpoint is generally superior to using the passive voice.
- For business writing, writers use the *editorial we* to convey that they are acting on behalf of their company.
- Pronouns must agree in number and gender with their antecedents and in number with any items of possession.
- One key to using pronouns consistently with their antecedents is to use plural antecedents.

Writing Workshop

Topic: Change Your Thoughts, Change Your World

Do you agree with Norman Vincent Peale when he said, "Change your thoughts, and you change your world"?

For the next day or so, notice your thoughts, paying special attention to the ones that give you energy. Jot down 10 positive thoughts as well as 10 negative thoughts.

Are you able to challenge your negative thoughts? Do you notice that writing about your thoughts helps transform them?

Editing Workshop

Draft

Instructions: Edit the following message, paying special attention to pronoun use. You will find the revision on the next page.

Hey Mick,

Sandro and myself attended a meeting the other day at the Training Institute, and both him and me are interested in their program.

There director said that if you sign up for their manager's program, you can get a 20 percent discount on a series of management seminars. One seminar teaches you how to write more professional, which both myself and Sandro could use. I was interested in knowing if human resources reimburses you for this program, as me and Sandro are interested in signing up.

If you have info on our company's policy please pass it on.

Cheerio,

J. J.

Revision

Each of the following revisions uses pronouns correctly.

Hi Mick,

Do you have any information on our company's reimbursement policy?

Sandro and I attended a meeting the other day at the Training Institute, and he and I are both interested in their program.

If I sign up for their manager's program, I can get a 20 percent discount on a series of management seminars. One seminar teaches professional writing, which Sandro and I both could use.

I was interested in knowing if human resources would reimburse me for this program.

Thanks.

Jake

Jake Jackson
Sales Representative
Eastern Division

Or:

Mick,

Sandro and I attended a meeting the other day at the Training Institute, and we are both interested in their program.

If I sign up for their manager's program, I can get a 20 percent discount. It includes a seminar on professional writing.

Does this program qualify for tuition reimbursement? Sandro and I are both interested.

All the best,

Jake

---

156 A Guide for Business Writing

11

Conciseness

When you write, do you ever have magical moments? You know the ones—when you can sit down and write what you mean without effort.

Most of the time, writing does not work that way. Even seasoned writers struggle with their words until their *thoughts* become clear, and those are the real magical moments—the insights, the clarity, the next step revealed. After you have those insights, you may be ready to shift from composing to editing.

Adapt your expectations so they are in line with the reality of the writing process, and writing will not disappoint you. Writing develops your thinking: compose fearlessly until you understand your point. Then edit your writing so that you say what you mean in the simplest, most concise way.

To get rid of the clutter in your writing, you may need to change some ways of thinking, giving up some security blankets. This chapter shows you how to make the painful cuts, and here is the principle to follow:

Less is more.

If you find yourself in a mire of words, remember the following:

1. Simple words and short messages convey information more effectively than complex words and long messages.
2. Using big, four-syllable words is *not* a sign of intelligence.

Get rid of empty information as well as artificial and abstract language. As Mark Twain once said,

"The more you explain it, the more I don't understand it."

Before looking at the kinds of words to cut, let's briefly review process and structure.

Compose to Learn—Edit to Clarify

Creating a concise message is a function of editing—not composing. Wordiness is essential in the composing process because writers learn their message as their ideas unfold on the page. Trying to figure out the message *before* beginning to write can lead to procrastination and frustration: start writing, and you will begin to solve the problem at hand.

Use mind maps to capture your ideas, use page maps to organize them and create a visual map, and last but not least:

> Compose fearlessly—edit ruthlessly.

As a wise writer once said, "If I had more time, this would have been shorter." The first step in cutting excess comes after you have clear insight into your purpose.

Put Purpose First

When you are composing, you will eventually reach an *aha* moment—you know, often the last sentence or two that you write as you convey a key point. Those are the moments of insight when you say to yourself, "Wow, that's what I was trying to say! Now I can stop writing."

Those *light-bulb* experiences are the best moments of writing, making the struggle worthwhile. Once you know your key point, follow these steps:

1. Highlight your key point.
2. Move it to the beginning of your message.
3. Cut all unnecessary information.

Deadwood comes in various categories—let's start with the smaller details before identifying bigger chunks of information to cut.

Eliminate Redundant Pairings

Some redundant pairings have been passed on for centuries, such as *various and sundry* and *first and foremost*. Do you even know what *sundry* means? And if you list something *first*, isn't it also *foremost*?

Though redundant pairings seem to fit together like bookends, you need only one of the words; and when you use both, you are automatically and unconsciously . . . oops, is that a redundant pairing?

For the following pairings, which word would you cut? Cover the revised words as you go through the original list.

Original	**Revised**
and so on and so forth	and so on
any and all	any *or* all
basic and fundamental	basic
each and every	each *or* every
fair and equitable	fair
first and foremost	first
full and complete	complete
if and when	if *or* when
hopes and desires	hopes
hope and trust	trust
issues and concerns	issues
more and more	more
null and void	void
questions and problems	questions
true and accurate	accurate
this day and age	today
thoughts and ideas	thoughts *or* ideas

In fact, it's a good idea to check all pairings for redundancy, including compound subjects and compound verbs (see pages 30-31).

Also cut unnecessary verb add ons:

Verb Add ons	Revised
add up	add
add together	add
advance forward	advance
continue on	continue
combine together	combine
refer back	refer
repeat again	repeat
rise up	rise

Cut Redundant Modifiers

Some words simply do not need to be modified. For example, have you ever wondered about *free gifts*? If gifts are not free, are they still gifts? What about *terrible tragedies* and *advance reservations*? Aren't all tragedies terrible and all reservations made in advance?

Redundant modifiers come in all shapes and sizes. Once again, cover the revised words as you work through the originals.

Original	Revised
advance warning	warning
close proximity	close
cold temperature	cold
combine together	combine
completely demolished	demolished
completely eliminate	eliminate
completely finish	finish
difficult dilemma	dilemma
each individual	each
end result	result
exactly identical	identical
final outcome	outcome

160 *A Guide for Business Writing*

foreign imports	imports
frozen ice	frozen, ice
future plans	plans
general public	public
honest truth	truth
most perfect	perfect
new breakthrough	breakthrough
one hundred percent true	true
past memories	memories
personal beliefs	beliefs
sudden crisis	crisis
true facts	facts
tuna fish	tuna
unexpected surprise	surprise
very unique	unique
12 noon/12 midnight	noon *or* midnight

Get practice by cutting unnecessary words in the following exercise.

PRACTICE 11.1

Instructions: Edit the following sentences to remove empty information, redundancy, and outdated expressions.

Wordy: First and foremost, please realize that you are an important and valued client.

Revised: ~~First, please realize that~~ You are a valued client.

1. We hope and trust that as a valued customer you find our services helpful and worthwhile.

2. Our new breakthrough in design makes our laptop even more perfect than it was before.

Chapter 11: Conciseness **161**

3. The final outcome of this project depends on each individual employee doing his or her best.

4. Before you finish this step to go on to the next step in the process, please review and examine all the items in your shopping cart.

5. We want you to be absolutely certain that you have not ordered multiple items that are exactly alike.

Note: See page 367 for the key to the above sentences.

Cut Vague Nouns

If you use vague nouns as a lead in to your point, cut them. For example, nouns such as *area, factor, manner, situation, topic,* and even *purpose* are often fillers during the composing phase. Say what you mean and be specific.

Wordy:	My field of study is the area of sociology.
Revised:	I am studying sociology.
Wordy:	I have found myself in a situation in which I am forced to make a decision.
Revised:	I am forced to make a decision.
Wordy:	The topic that I have chosen to write about is gender differences.
Revised:	Gender differences answer common questions about miscommunication . . .
Wordy:	The purpose of my paper is to explore climate change.
Revised:	Climate change affects all living species . . .

Can you think of any vague nouns that you use?

Eliminate the Obvious

Isn't *round* a shape and *red* a color? Go through the list below, cutting the obvious. As a 14th century Franciscan monk named William of Ockham is credited for saying, "Plurality should not be posited without necessity." Go through the list below cutting the obvious, as illustrated by the first few:

audible ~~to the ear~~	of an uncertain condition
brief ~~in duration~~	period of time
bright ~~in color~~	rate of speed
consensus of opinion	red in color
dull in appearance	re-elected for another term
extreme in degree	round in shape
filled to capacity	soft to the touch
heavy in weight	unusual in nature
honest in character	visible to the eye

In fact, when you find yourself using the following phrases, simply delete them and get right to your point:

all things considered	in a manner of speaking
as a matter of fact	I wish to take this opportunity
as far as I am concerned	my purpose for writing is
for the most part	the point I am trying to make
for the purpose of	what I am trying to say is that
in my opinion	what I want to make clear is

Update Outdated Phrases

Outdated phrases are like viruses—they invade writing like contagious bugs, jumping from one person's writing to another. Even if someone you respect still uses these outdated phrases, be confident and eliminate them from your writing. (And yes, some of them, such as *per*, are difficult habits to give up!)

Once again, to turn this into a learning activity, cover the right column that shows current use as you work through the outdated column.

Outdated	**Current**
as per our discussion	as we discussed
as per your request	as you requested
at all times	always
at the present time	now, today
at your earliest convenience	*give a specific date*
attached please find	attached is
due to the fact that	because
during the time that	while
every seven days	weekly
gave a report to the effect	reported
gave assistance to	helped
in the event that	if
in a situation in which	when
in almost every instance	usually
in the near future	soon
in receipt of	*instead say,* "Thank you for . . ."
in reference to	about
is of the opinion that	believes
I wish to thank you	*don't wish and thank*
may I suggest	*don't ask permission to suggest*
prior to	before
subsequent to	after
sufficient number of	enough
thank you in advance	thank you
thank you again	*one thank you is sufficient*
the manner in which	how
this day and age	today
with regard to	about or concerning

By the way, thanking someone *in advance* can put off some people because it sounds a bit presumptuous; it also conveys that you may not say *thank you* after the fact, which is when people would appreciate hearing it.

164   *A Guide for Business Writing*

PRACTICE 11.2

Instructions: Remove redundancy and outdated expressions from the following sentences.

Wordy: As per our conversation, George is of the opinion that we should take the contract.

Revised: As we discussed, George believes we should take the contract.

1. Attached please find the papers that you requested.

2. You have our complete and absolute confidence, and we appreciate and value our business alliance.

3. As per our discussion, the new policy should be received and reviewed this week.

4. You can completely eliminate any questions or problems by sending your agenda early in advance of the meeting.

5. I would like to thank you in advance for your cooperation, support, and assistance.

Note: See page 367 for the key to the above sentences.

Avoid Legalese

At one time, attorneys filled their writing with "legalese." However, today even attorneys avoid using the following terms.

Legalese	**Revised**
as stated heretofore	as stated
aforementioned	as mentioned
concerning the matter of	concerning
enclosed herewith please find	enclosed is
enclosed herein	enclosed is
notwithstanding	without
pursuant to	regarding

the writer/the undersigned	use *I* or *me*
until such time as	until

In fact, attorneys are not required to use legalize but do so out of choice. To judge if a phrase is outdated, read your writing aloud: *If you wouldn't say it that way, don't write it that way.*

Use Simple Language

Some people think that using complicated words rather than simple ones make them "sound smart." However, savvy writers choose simple words. As Leonardo da Vinci advised, "Simplicity is the ultimate sophistication."

Outdated	**Revised**
apprise	inform
ascertain	find out
cognizant of	aware of
contingent upon	dependent on
deem	think
endeavor	try
facilitate	help
implement	start, begin
initiate	begin
is desirous of	wants
methodology	method
prior to	before
render	make, give
render assistance	assist
referred to as	called
termination	end
transpire	happen
transmit	send
utilization	use

Instead of saying this:	**Say this:**
We *utilize* that vendor.	We *use* that vendor.
I am *cognizant* of the change.	I am *aware* of the change.
We *endeavor* to sell the best product.	We *try* to sell the best product.
Prior to working at Macy's . . .	*Before* working at Macy's . . .

Revise the sentences below to get practice.

PRACTICE 11.3

Instructions: Simplify the following sentences.

1. We are utilizing that product, and they are cognizant of our choice.
2. Subsequent to the merger, we have endeavored to compromise.
3. As per your request, the inclusion of that information in the report is being made.
4. If the merger is contingent upon our utilization of their facilities, we should endeavor to change locations
5. If you are cognizant of their objections, endeavor to make changes.

Note: See page 367 for the key to the above sentences.

Modify Sparingly

With creative writing, detail supports the reader's experience; with business writing, unnecessary detail creates frustration. Two kinds of modifiers that creep into writing are **hedges** and **emphatics**.

- *Hedges* are words that writers use to qualify a statement; use them only when they are necessary, for example:

    This principle is ~~kind of~~ important if you are writing a textbook.

- *Emphatics* are words that writers use to stress a point, but the emphatic has the opposite effect, for example:

    The meeting is ~~very~~ important, and you ~~really~~ need to be there.

Here are some common *hedges* to avoid:

kind of, sort of, rarely, hardly, at times, tend, sometimes, maybe, may be, perhaps, in my opinion, more or less, possibly, probably, seemingly, to a certain extent, supposedly, usually, often, almost always

Here are some common *emphatics*; use them sparingly:

very, most, many, often, really, literally, virtually, usually, certainly, inevitably, as you can plainly see, as everyone is aware, as you know, always, each and every time, totally, it is quite clear that, as you may already know, absolutely, undoubtedly, first and foremost

Example with hedges and emphatics:
For the most part, trust is best established from the beginning and *really* difficult to regain once breached. *First and foremost,* assume that *each and every* communication *may* have the potential to build trust as well as the potential to destroy trust.

Example *without* hedges or emphatics:
Trust is best established from the beginning and difficult to regain once breached. Always assume that every communication has the potential to build trust as well as the potential to destroy trust.

Avoid Fillers

The words *just* and *like* are not modifiers--they are known as *fillers*. These words creep into casual speech and writing.

Incorrect:	He *like* gave me a great recommendation.
Corrected:	He gave me a great recommendation.
Incorrect:	She *like just* told me the correct information yesterday.
Corrected:	She told me the correct information yesterday.

In fact, job interviewers discount applicants who use fillers such as *like* and *just* in their speech. *Can you see how cutting a few select words makes a difference?*

Modify Correctly

When you use modifying phrases, place the modifying phrase close to the noun it modifies.

Misplaced modifier: Bert is the person across the room *in the navy pinstriped suit*.

Corrected: Bert is the person *in the navy pinstriped suit* across the room.

Modifying phrases take as their subject the noun closest to them. What does the following sentence actually say?

Dangling modifier: While walking into the conference room, Jill's cell phone starting ringing loudly.

Corrected: As Jill walked into the conference room, her cell phone started ringing loudly.

PRACTICE 11.4

Instructions: Revise the following for use of modifiers.

Incorrect: My boss like told me to go to the office at 9 a.m. in Oak Brook.

Corrected: My boss told me to go to the Oak Brook office at 9 a.m.

1. While giving her report, a phone began to ring in Joanie's briefcase.
2. In my opinion, you should feel really certain what the true facts are before you sign the contract.
3. Can you confirm that it is totally true that they might possibly back out of their agreement?
4. You should speak to my friend who specializes in energy conservation from college.
5. I would kind of like for you to speak to the person who really knows a lot about this topic, literally.

Note: See page 368 for the key to the above sentences.

Edit Out Background Thinking

As you compose your message, you may go down many different lines of thought to get to your main point. Everything leading up to your main point could be background thinking. Background thinking gives unnecessary details that lead you to your point. As you read the following, identify information that you can cut:

> After we spoke, I continued to think about the situation in which we find ourselves. Not that long ago, the economy was strong and we were looking for different ways to invest our profits. Now, with the sudden change in the economy, we are faced with uncertainty—many of our clients will be tightening their belts and looking for ways to avoid buying our product. Here's my point: we can go right on using the same methods to sell our product, or we can look for new, innovative approaches—something we've never tried before. I think we should open up a contest among our sales reps to see what they can come up with. What do you think?

Note that background thinking is different from explaining an issue or giving evidence to support a point. *Note*: See Endnote 1, page 174, for a possible revision of the above paragraph.

Leave Out Feelings and Opinions

Making a key point different from sharing your feelings in the hopes of getting your reader to change his or her mind.

Once again, you may find that writing about your opinions helps you get to your key points, but they usually aren't relevant once you find your key point.

If you find yourself rambling off the point, that is a cue to start cutting. Also, be cautious when using phrases such as *I believe*, *I think*, and *I feel*. Unless you use them on purpose to affect the tone, they are simply *I* statements that merit deletion.

Also, do not tell your reader *how* to interpret your message; these added comments may give the reader the impression that you are unsure of your message or that you lack confidence. Thus, remove phrases or sentences that tell your readers *how you think* they will react. As you read the following, identify information that you can cut:

> I received your message suggesting that we cut this summer's sales meeting by one day. I know you're not going to be pleased with my reaction, but I'm already feeling stressed out trying to fit in everything that I have planned with my staff. In fact, they are all enthused about the meetings and getting prepared for them. It would be a major letdown for me to have to tell them that we now have to cut 20 percent of everything that we have planned. So if you go forward with this idea, don't expect me to support it. Sure, it's a good idea to try to cut the budget, but this isn't the road to take.

Don't presume that big words or lengthy phrases will impress your readers. Keep your writing simple and to the point. *Note:* See Endnote 2, page 174, for a possible revision of the paragraphs above.)

Recap

When you can simplify or cut words, do it.

➢ Put purpose first, and you will have a clear idea of what to cut.
➢ Get rid of your background thinking and your opinions.
➢ Modify sparingly, paying special attention to hedges and emphatics.
➢ Be direct and say what you mean.
➢ Remember, give yourself freedom to compose—cut when you edit and revise.

Writing Workshop

Topic: Focus on Your Strengths

Traditionally, assessments focus on weaknesses as much as strengths, with the idea that working on weaknesses makes a person more effective.

However, in his book *Go Put Your Strengths to Work*, Marcus Buckingham turns that approach upside down.[3]

Write a short self-assessment identifying your strengths:

- What qualities do you have that assist you in being successful?
- What have you accomplished that makes you feel good about yourself?
- What situations have you turned around, making something good come from something challenging?
- What are the good things in your life and how can you expand them?

By focusing on what you like and spending more time doing it, you will achieve better results and enjoy life more in the process.

Editing Workshop

Draft

Instructions: Edit the following message, paying special attention to cutting redundant and outdated information. The revision is on the next page.

Jaclyn,

Per my voicemail I will need more information in order to troubleshoot the problem that needs to be addressed immediately. And yes, you are contacting the right person—I should be able to help. As you said in your message earlier today, Carrie Thompson cannot log on to her account. I realize this is a serious issue because she travels a lot and not having access to her account can be frustrating. So once I am able to talk with her, I'm confident that I can get her back up and running. How can I reach Carrie?

You can also tell Carrie she can contact me directly by phone at 555-222-1212. Hope you are having a great day—talk to you soon.

Matteo

Revision

> Jaclyn,
>
> Thank you for letting me know about Carrie's problem logging on to her account.
>
> Is there a way for me to reach Carrie directly? If you wish, you can have her call me at 555-222-1212.
>
> Hope you are having a great day—talk to you soon.
>
> Matteo

End Notes

1. Background Thinking Revised: Since the market has changed, we need some fresh ideas. What do you think about opening up a contest among our sales reps to see what they can come up with?
2. Feelings / Opinions Revised: Trying to cut the budget is a great idea. Would you be able to meet anytime soon to discuss this?
3. Buckingham, Marcus, *Go Put Your Strengths to Work*, Free Press, 2007.

12

Tone

Tone reflects the emotions of writing: tone is not as much about *what* you say as about *how* you say it. Tone also seeps out through *micro-messages: the messages hidden between the lines.* At times, the unspoken micro-message has more impact on tone than the spoken message.

Tone can either build up a relationship or tear it down. Keep your mind open to the fact that just as there are two sides to every story, there are two sides to tone:

> Tone is just as much about the way that a reader *interprets* a message as it is about the way that a writer *conveys* a message.

Have you ever received a message that sounded accusatory or negative on first read? Did your reaction change after you read the message again a day or so latter?

Do your feelings affect the way that you interpret a message? Do you tend to question someone's tone when you feel good about yourself and feel good about life in general? *Or,* are you more likely to question someone's tone when you are having a bad day? You see, it is easy to read too much into the written word; and when that happens, problems spring forth.

Chapter 15, "Best Practices for E-Mail," also covers tone. However, before getting into the details of creating a professional tone, let's look at the umbrella under which tone resides: *professional relationships.* In fact, all professional writing is done within the context of a relationship.

Client Relationships and Trust

Clients want accurate, timely information, but they also want to feel respected. When you build your clients' confidence that you are acting in their best interests, you enhance more than communication—you enhance trust.

That is why an underlying purpose of all business communication is to strengthen relationships, both with internal clients and with external clients. When you have a good relationship with someone, you probably give that person the *benefit of the doubt*—correct? Giving a colleague the benefit of the doubt helps you avoid blame games, which is what a lot of the problems surrounding tone are about.

Trust is best established from the beginning and difficult to regain once breached. Always assume that every communication has the potential to build trust as well as the potential to destroy trust.

Any negative message that you send may feel like a good emotional release at the moment, but you will live with the guilt as well as other repercussions, possibly for a long time. If they are honest, though, most people will admit to having sent at least one flaming e-mail and regretting it. Releasing emotions inappropriately through e-mail is simply a bumpy part of the learning curve, so do not beat yourself up too badly over it.

To avoid negative complications, one principle that people base their actions on is the *Golden Rule:*

> Do unto others as *you* would have them do unto *you.*

The Golden Rule works most of the time. However, what about the situations when the other person sees the world through different lenses than you do? To count for diversity, the *Platinum Rule* trumps the Golden Rule:

> Do unto others as *they* would have you do unto *them.*

The Platinum Rule tells us that people view the world differently, having different understandings and different styles. When you work with people from different cultures or different generations, you cannot use your own baseline of experience to judge how they will react. For example, if you are from the United States and you are working with colleagues from Japan or

India or Great Britain, you have different traditions and protocols. The same is true with people from different generations within the same country.

Something that you do quite naturally with colleagues from your own generation could be quite offensive to a business associate who is much older or much younger than you are.

In preparation for understanding diversity, let's examine how unspoken messages may be just as important as the spoken ones.

Micro-Messages

Though the words you choose and the way that you shape them create a tone, your *unspoken* messages also affect your tone. In chapter 1, you reviewed the concept of *micro-messages*, the messages "hidden between the lines." Micro-messages have just as much potential to harm a relationship as the written word.

Suppose that someone sends you an e-mail, and you simply do not respond to it? What message does that convey to the sender? Or, what if you send someone a message and copy that person's manager? If the message complimented the recipient, it could mean that you were being positive and supportive. However, if the message were pointing out an error, your Cc to the manager could be interpreted as criticism.

As you read about diversity, realize that many issues are created by micro-messages: the ones that you send as well as the ones that you infer as you interpret someone else's messages.

Now let's take a look at diversity.

Diversity: A Catalyst for Misunderstanding

Not so long ago, gender was a hot diversity topic. Now the workplace abounds with all sorts of differences, with generational and cultural differences ranking at the top of the list along with gender.

Different generations have different communication expectations and, at times, problems occur as a result. In general, people do not create problems on purpose. If you look closely enough, when a person acts difficult, hurt feelings lie below the surface.

When someone is being difficult, try not to take it personally. Otherwise, you may end up acting difficult too. You see, hurt feelings and anger are somewhat contagious. Only by containing the negativity can you keep from spreading it around.

In the professional arena, what kinds of experiences lead to hurt feelings? One is unfulfilled expectations that are tied to generational, cultural, and personality differences—let's see how.

Generational Diversity

Since sources vary, here is roughly how the various generations break down:

- Veterans and Silent Generation, born 1925 to 1945
- Baby Boomers, born 1945 to 1964
- Generation X, born 1964 to 1980
- Generation Y or Millenniums, born 1980 to 2000

Have you noticed generational differences in the way people communicate and use technology? Let's take a look those differences.

> *Veterans* and *Boomers* use e-mail effectively, but at times prefer phone calls and face-to-face communication.

Veterans and Boomers are known for not saying what is on their minds, but instead *they tend to make people guess*. Veterans and Boomers grew up in an era in which politeness and protocol kept communications running smoothly.

In fact, many base their decisions on protocol, not necessarily how they feel at the moment: Veterans, and Boomers to a lesser extent, were taught that their feelings were not relevant when it comes to business, but getting the job done was.

If a personal problem arises with a Veteran or Boomer, take it seriously and deal with it proactively: most of the time you can melt the problem by showing some attention to the issue and respect for the person.

178 *A Guide for Business Writing*

When a Boomer acts suspiciously, often the real the message the Boomer is trying to give is "Respect me, and I'll be nice."

Gen Xers prefer e-mail and instant messages.

In contrast to Boomers, Gen Xers do not make you guess, *they tell it like it is*. Listen to what they have to say and stay connected. Once they speak their minds, you and the Gen Xers should both move on.

Gen Xers are not only technically savvy, they use technology to stay connected with friends and family. Gen Xers also play an important role: they bridge communication between Boomers and Nexters, buffering communication so that misunderstandings are averted.

Nexters prefer text messaging, instant messaging, and blogging.

Nexters are unique in that *they ask for what they want*. They are more assertive than older generations in the way they communicate. Though Nexters do not make you guess or wait for you to ask them what is going on; when they speak up, older generations can interpret the way they communicate as disrespectful and abrupt.

On the job, Nexters expect the newest technology, and they use it constantly to stay connected with friends and family. When Nexters ask for information, they are more interested in getting their answer quickly than in being treated politely. In contrast, when a Boomer makes a request, the Boomer expects to be treated with respect. If a Veteran's requests are ignored or treated abruptly, expect a reaction.

Communication is like a dance, and each generation dances differently, resulting in a slightly different tone. Know your client's dance, and respect individual styles—how people communicate contributes to who they are as human beings.

Do not read too much into the meaning behind the style, and you will have fewer obstacles to building effective business relationships.

Cultural Diversity

Cultures differ in important ways, and one dimension is **context**, the unspoken cultural norms and rituals.

Think of a culture as being either **low context** or **high context**. In low context cultures, people interact with few rituals—communication is somewhat informal and not very structured. In contrast, in high context cultures, people follow shared protocol which defines how they will interact. Communication is more structured and more formal.

- People from *low context cultures*, such as the U.S., are direct and get right to the point.

In low context cultures, communication can be highly personal, even with strangers. However, in business environments, people from low context cultures get right down to business, quickly dismissing small talk. Getting down to business too quickly can put off people from high context cultures:

- People from *high context cultures*, such as Japan, South America, India, and some parts of Europe, prefer to follow formal protocol, especially in the beginning.

In high context cultures, communication is generally impersonal and includes a lot of small talk before getting down to business. Anything too personal can be highly offensive.

To adapt to cultural diversity, neither judge nor be easily offended. Be patient and give the other person the benefit of the doubt. In fact, authenticity is the best solution in diverse environments. Sincerity, humility, and a considerate attitude can take you a long way in global communications.

Once again, think of communication as a dance. By mirroring the other's behavior and letting the other person take the lead, and you are likely to step on fewer toes.

Personal Diversity: *Thinkers* and *Feelers*

Along the wide spectrum of ways that personalities differ is the *thinker-feeler* category. The Meyers-Briggs Type Indicator (MBTI) scores that difference: If you score high on either *thinking* or *feeling*, your writing style will reflect your personality type.

- *Thinkers* tend to get right to the point and make little or no effort to connect with the reader as one human to another.
- *Feelers* tend to place more emphasis on connecting to the reader than to the information they are conveying.

While thinkers tend to be abrupt, feelers tend to include fluff in their writing. While thinkers resist using fluff and niceties, feelers seem compelled to say things such as "have a great day" and "thank you," even when not called for.

Extreme Feeler message:

Hi Ashby,

Thanks for checking in with me about the dates for the conference. You are right, the date is April 15. Please let me know if you need more information—I'm always here to help.

Hope your day is going well, and I'll talk to you later.

Thanks again.

Beth

Extreme Thinker message:

Yes.

Balanced message:

Hi Ashby,

You are correct—the date for the conference is April 15.

If you need more information, let me know.

Have a great day.

Beth

Chapter 12: Tone

Though neither approach is right or wrong, a balanced approach is more effective and easy to achieve with minimum effort. To find more balance, first accept diversity in other people's communication styles by dropping any judgment. Next, be open to adjusting your own style.

If you are a *thinker*, one change that you can make is to use a salutation and closing. If you are really brave, you can add a comment such as "have a great day." If you are a *feeler*, stay to the point and limit your niceties. Do not say "thank you" more than once per message, and say "thank you" only when someone has actually done something for you.

What specific steps can you take to adjust to your readers?

Analytic Versus Global Learners

Whether you thrive on detail or prefer only the bottom line relates in part to your learning style.[1]

- *Global learners* prefer the big picture, and details can frustrate them.
- *Analytic learners* thrive on the details that lead to the big picture.

Can you tell by the above descriptions which type of learner you are? If not, do some Internet research on *learning styles*. Knowing your learning style validates your unique approach and aids you in making effective choices. More importantly, however, knowing the difference between analytic and global learners gives you one more tool to adapt your writing for your audience.

If you are analytic, you include a great amount of detail in your writing. Because you appreciate the detail, you may have difficulty understanding how your reader may find the detail distracting. You see, global learners easily become frustrated by too much detail, especially when they cannot see where the detail is leading.

Learning styles, like other elements of diversity, are somewhat programmed into our DNA, making change difficult but not impossible. The first step is to be aware of your own style and then to understand the needs of your polar opposite.

And once again, the time to shape your writing for your audience is when you edit, not when you compose. If you cling to detail, expect to have difficulty cutting, but do it anyway.

The *You* Viewpoint

The *you* viewpoint keeps the focus on your reader, and thus improves the tone of your document. The *you* viewpoint also helps the reader stay connected.

As you compose, you may find that you begin many of your sentences with the personal pronoun "I," writing sentences such as the following:

Weak: *I* am writing you to ask a few questions related to the Becker account.

When you edit, shift to the *you* viewpoint:

Revised: Could *you* help answer a few questions about the Becker account?

The *I* viewpoint is effective and even necessary at times, so don't try to eliminate every sentence that begins with *I*. Here are more examples:

***I* Viewpoint:** I appreciate the job you did on the Olson account.
I would like to invite you to our next team meeting.

***You* Viewpoint:** You did a great job on the Olson account.
Would you be able to attend our next team meeting?

At one time, writing experts discouraged business writers from starting sentences with the personal pronoun *I*. As a result, writers overused the passive voice. As the active voice became established as the voice of business, the *I* viewpoint again became appropriate. Hence, when you can appropriately shift to the *you* viewpoint, do so.

PRACTICE 12.1

Instructions: Revise the following sentences to the *you* viewpoint.

Weak: I hope that you will be able to attend the workshop.
Revised: Please consider attending the workshop.

1. I would like to know if I am able to assist you with the Baker project.
2. I am sending you paperwork that needs to completed and returned to me by Friday so that you are officially on our payroll.
3. I am hoping that I have made it clear that your dedication to the project is exemplary.
4. I am interested in hearing what you think about the merger.
5. I was hoping to find out of this project interests you.

Note: See page 368 for the key to the above sentences.

A Positive Focus

Everyone appreciates positive words; even subtle comments add energy. To stay positive, focus on what will go right if procedures are followed rather than on what will go wrong if they are not followed.

In fact, even valuable services can sound threatening if stated in the negative. For example:

Negative: If I don't hear from you within a week, I'll assume you are not interested.
Positive: If you are interested, please contact me within the next week.

Another way to improve tone is to avoid the word *not*:

Negative: You cannot take time off until you complete the project.
Positive: Once you complete the project, you can take time off.

Whenever you edit a sentence so that you state the same message without the word *not*, the tone sounds more positive.

PRACTICE 12.2

Instructions: Revise the following sentences so that they are written in the affirmative.

Weak: You are not well prepared for your presentation.

Revised: You will do a better job if you are more prepared.

1. We cannot change your health insurance until you make your request in writing.
2. When you do not respond negatively, no one else does either.
3. By not asking the question, you have no chance of getting an answer.
4. If you plan to apply for the job, don't put off turning in your application.
5. The longer you wait, the less likely you will be considered for the job.

Note: See page 368 for the key to the above sentences.

Clear, Accurate Language

Slang, jargon, and abbreviations affect tone on many levels, often having a negative effect.

E-mail is not the same communication medium as text messaging. When business professionals write e-mail messages as if they are text messages, they are giving their readers a multitude of micro-messages. Now that you know more about generational differences, how do you think Veterans or Boomers interpret the tone of a message full of text message abbreviations?

To respect your audience, also avoid colloquial phrases such as "bite the bullet" and "written in sand," which can be challenging for people from diverse cultures to understand.

How do you feel when you don't understand something? Isn't it normal to feel confused or left out?

Beyond avoiding jargon and clichés, also avoid telling jokes and using sarcasm. You have no idea how your reader will respond, and you have no idea to whom your reader may forward your message.

Even traditional abbreviations that come in the form of acronyms or initialisms can be difficult for new employees to understand. By the way, an acronym is an abbreviation that can be spoken as if it is a word, such as AARP or MADD; an initialism consists of using the first letter of each word, such as NBC for National Broadcasting Company.

When you work with new employees, limit shortcuts. If you must use an abbreviation, put the full name in parentheses immediately following it, as follows:

> The Accounts Receivable Department (ARD) will answer your request. Although the ARD is closed for the holidays, you will be able to reach them after December 26.

Or, you can use a less traditional format, putting the full name in parentheses following the abbreviation:

> The ARD (Accounts Receivable Department) will answer your request . . . .

The point is, the first time that you use any acronym or initialism in your writing, spell out the words in full. You will save your reader time and frustration. Everything that you do to make your message easier for your reader improves tone.

Apologies Necessary

If you get into a situation that calls for an apology, you can dissolve hurt feelings by apologizing quickly and humbly. Going into detail might make the situation worse, so simply say that you are sorry.

Don't say: I'm really sorry that you feel slighted that I couldn't call you sooner, but I was so busy and had a thousand people pulling me from different directions—your call was on my priority list, but I couldn't get to it until now.

Do Say: I apologize for not getting back to you sooner; thank you for being patient. What can I do now to assist you?

If you feel emotional, your words will convey your feelings as well as your ideas. In other words, you can state your message perfectly, but still create problems. When someone writes with emotion, first try to understand what provoked the person's actions; then wait until you gain a clear perspective *before* you respond.

Before being defensive, ask yourself:

Did I make a mistake? How can I apologize without sounding self-deprecating?

Don't say: I'm sorry things didn't work out; but quite frankly, Jeremy was supposed to be the one who handled your account. He called in sick at the last minute, so I did the best I could under very difficult circumstances.

Do Say: I apologize for the delay. We were short staffed. I appreciate working with you, so please let me know if there is anything I can do now to assist you.

Before going on the offensive, consider the following:

What provoked this person's actions? Could something serious be going on, such as sickness or death or something tragic?

Don't say: I sent you a message two days ago and have yet to receive a response. I know that you carry around a Blackberry, so I can only assume that you've received my message. Can you please take the time to answer my question!

Do Say: Did you receive my request for information the other day? I was hoping to receive a response by Friday because I need to include the figures in a report that's due. If you can't respond by then, please let me know if someone else can help.

If you receive one of the previous messages, respond quickly; however:

Don't respond: I'm handling 50 accounts and yours is only one of them.

Do Respond: Sorry about the delay. I've been in meetings for three days. You will receive the information before Friday. Thank you for your patience.

When a message strikes you the wrong way, the best approach is to clarify the message. Though a *fight or flight response* is a normal response to conflict, remain objective and do not put anything in writing until you are clear headed and feel confident.

Think about it: when you feel good about yourself, you are likely to deal well with any kind of challenge that comes your way. In contrast, when you feel that you are being "beaten up by the world," you are likely to be defensive or even go on the offensive, reaping devastating results. Make important decisions only when you feel confident.

Bad News Messages

Once in a while, everyone needs to convey news the reader does not expect or would prefer not receiving. A bad news message is one of the few times when you need to include details *and* when you need to give those details before stating your purpose.*

By giving the details first, you give the reader an opportunity to understand the *why* of the unwelcome decision. Therefore, explain logic, rationale, and background details before getting to the key point. If you get right to the point, the reader is likely to have an immediate negative reaction and may not even read the logic behind the decision.

The two messages that follow are alike except for the placement of the bad news. Read both messages and identify the change. Does the subtle change in structure create a shift in tone?

Note: A bad news message is also known as an *indirect message*. For more information, please see pages 214-215.

188 *A Guide for Business Writing*

Message 1: Direct Bad News Message

Dear Sam:

Your request for a leave of absence has been denied.

The policy manual states that only employees who have worked with our company for a minimum of one year are eligible for a leave of absence. Even so, I checked with human resources to find out if an exception could be made for you. HR didn't think so, but they took the extra effort to contact corporate. Corporate confirmed that an exception could not be made because they receive many requests every year. If they made exceptions, the policy could be challenged legally.

I wish there were something else we could do for you. Please keep me apprised of your situation.

Best regards,

Alesso

Message 2: Indirect Bad News Message

Dear Sam:

Here's information in response to your request for a leave of absence.

The policy manual states that only employees who have worked with our company for a minimum of one year are eligible for a leave of absence.

Even so, I checked with human resources to find out if an exception could be made for you. HR didn't think so, but they took the extra effort to contact corporate. Corporate confirmed that an exception could not be made because they receive many requests every year. If they made exceptions, the policy could be challenged legally.

Therefore, your request for a leave of absence has been denied. I wish there were something else we could do for you. Please keep me apprised of your situation.

Best regards,

Alesso

Bad news is best shared in person. However, when you must share bad news in writing, you show respect for the reader by taking the time to structure the message using an *indirect* approach (see pages 214-215).

Recap

This chapter included several principles to help you make more effective writing decisions. However, the only way to become a better writer is to write more, using writing as a problem-solving tool. The more you write, the better your skills will become, with or without a writing coach.

Here are some of the key points stressed in this chapter:

- Tone has two sides: the way a writer conveys a message as well as the way a reader interprets it.
- The Platinum Rule tells us, "Do unto others as *they* would have you do unto them."
- Generational and cultural diversity affect communication.
- The *you* viewpoint connects effectively with readers and makes them the focal point.
- When you write, focus on what will go right if procedures are followed rather than on what will go wrong if they are not.
- When conveying bad news, give details first and purpose last.

An underlying purpose of business writing is to build client relationships. Keeping the tone of your messages positive is an important element in building effective relationships.

Writing Workshop

Journal Topic: A Positive Focus

In this chapter you learned how to write in the affirmative. List some negative statements that you make to yourself daily, for example:

> "My house is a mess."
> "I don't eat the right foods and feel lousy."
> "I have gained weight, and my clothes don't fit right."

Do those nagging thoughts sound like the words of a victim or someone ready to take action?

Rather than use your words to drain your energy, focus instead on the affirmative, for example:

> "When I clean my house, I feel good. I will work on one project today so that I feel more in control of my surroundings."
>
> "I will prepare some healthy snacks so I have them when I am hungry." Or, "I will stay focused on making right decisions about food rather than easy decisions."
>
> "I am a kind person and deserve to feel good about myself."

Write five to ten negative statements and their affirmative equivalents. Do this daily until you focus your thinking on the positive.

According to Leonardo da Vinci, "Inaction weakens the vigors of the mind . . . action strengthens the essence of creation." Take action and then see how you feel.

Editing Workshop

Draft

Instructions: Edit the following message by paying special attention to the tone of the message. The revision is on the next page.

Notice to Employees:

Anyone who does not turn their paperwork in by Friday at 4 p.m. will not have met this month's payroll deadline. As a result, you may not receive your paycheck on time but instead may experience a delay.

In addition, receiving paperwork after the deadline has gotten out of hand and is creating additional work for the staff. If the payroll department continues to receive late paperwork at the current rate, we will be forced to administer some sort of penalty, such as postponing payment until the next pay period.

Revision

The following revision is realistic and at the same time focuses on positive outcomes.

Notice to Employees:

To meet this month's payroll deadline, please turn in your paperwork by Friday at 4:30 p.m. Meeting the deadline will ensure that you receive your paycheck on time; in fact, we can only guarantee paychecks on time for paperwork that is submitted on time.

Please make special efforts to meet our deadline so that we can continue giving you the prompt, efficient service to which you are accustomed.

13

Paragraphing and Formatting Basics

Regardless of what you write, your aim is to make your ideas easily accessible to your reader. Paragraphs play a vital role in that aim: paragraphs break information into manageable chunks, helping readers digest information.

Academic writing is different from business writing. At times, when professionals transition from academic writing to business writing, their paragraphs tend to be long. In fact, business readers dread seeing a series of sentences that seem to go on forever with no breaks. So if you haven't yet focused on how you create paragraph breaks, now you can.

While there is no recipe to write a paragraph, a few guidelines are helpful. For example, a paragraph can be as short as a sentence or two or as long as seven or eight sentences. Every paragraph has one sentence that seems to capture its essence, and that is its *topic sentence*. The rest of the paragraph flows from that topic sentence, creating a *topic string*. When the topic changes, so does the paragraph.

Not all paragraphs are equal. For instance, paragraphing for e-mail is different from paragraphing for hard copy. One difference is that e-mail is somewhat conversational and paragraphs tend to be short.

This chapter also covers other principles to make key ideas accessible, for example:

- Old to new information flow
- Side headings
- Formatting features, such as bullet points, numbering, bold, and italics

Let's start by reviewing how to produce cohesive, coherent paragraphs.

Paragraphs

Effective paragraphs are *cohesive* and *coherent*.

- *Cohesive* paragraphs develop only *one main idea* or *key point*.
- *Coherent* paragraphs develop the main idea through a *logical flow of ideas*.

Many writers are able to insert paragraph breaks as they compose. However, if paragraph breaks do not appear naturally to you as you write, work on them when you edit. Eventually, you will hear when a new topic springs from your writing. When you reach that point, writing will feel more satisfying.

The first step in editing a paragraph so that it is cohesive is to identify its topic sentence. The next step is ensuring that each sentence in the paragraph develops the topic, creating a topic string.

- A *topic sentence* gives an overview of the paragraph; a topic sentence is broad and general.
- A *topic string* is a series of sentences that develop the main idea of the topic sentence. Each sentence extends the controlling idea, giving specifics that illustrate the main idea of the topic sentence.

Here is a step-by-step process for editing paragraphs:

1. Identify your topic sentence. Select the sentence that best captures the broader, more general topic that the rest of the paragraph develops through specifics.
2. Bring your topic sentence to the beginning of the paragraph.
3. Screen each the remainder of sentences in the paragraph to make sure that it develops some element of the topic sentence.
4. Cut sentences that do not fit or use them to start a new paragraph.

Take a look at the draft paragraph that follows, which seems to ramble because it changes topics.

As you read the paragraph, ask yourself the following questions:

- Which sentence or sentences seem to capture a main topic?
- Which sentences seem off topic?
- Which sentences seem to belong in a different paragraph?

Draft:

> I believe editing is important, and I even knew an editor once. But I never knew how to edit before, and I was always confused about how to improve my writing. Editing improves the quality of writing. Before I didn't take the time to edit, now I do because I know how to make corrections and how to how to revise a document. When you edit, correct errors in grammar and punctuation and try to improve the flow of the writing. Change passive sentences to active voice, if you can. Editing also involves putting the purpose up front and then cutting what doesn't belong. When I read papers that are not edited well, I can tell because the writer jumps from one topic to another. Poorly written documents also seem to ramble on and on without paragraph breaks, so make an effort to add paragraph breaks. Take time to edit, and you will see an improvement in your final document.

Edited Version 1

The following version focuses on editing, taking the writer's experience out of the piece:

> Editing improves the quality of writing. When you edit, correct errors in grammar and punctuation and try to improve the flow of the writing. Put the purpose up front and then cut what doesn't belong. Change passive sentences to active voice, and make an effort to add paragraph breaks. If you take time to edit, you will see an improvement in your final document.

Edited Version 2

Version 2 takes the writer's point of view. Notice how the voice shifts to the *I* viewpoint:

> I believe editing is important. Before I didn't take the time to edit, now I do because I know how to correct and revise a document. When I edit, I correct errors in grammar and punctuation and improve the flow of the writing. I change passive sentences to active voice, if I can. I also put the purpose up front and then cut what doesn't belong.
>
> When I read papers that are not edited well, I can tell because the writer jumps from one topic to another. Poorly written documents also seem to ramble on without paragraph breaks. When I take time to edit, I see an improvement in my final document.

For a paragraph to be coherent, ideas must flow logically; writing should not seem chaotic and full of disjointed ideas. However, as you compose, disjointed ideas seem to make sense. To correct disjointed writing, step away from your work so that you can evaluate your writing objectively.

Do you write on a computer? The way that your writing sounds when read on the screen is different from the way that it will sound when read from hard copy. For important documents, print out a copy and read it so that you can see final changes that you need to make. Have a peer read it: ask for honest feedback, as that is the only kind of feedback that will help you make your writing stronger. Keep an open mind and ask for specific changes that you can make to upgrade your writing.

Principles of information flow can also assist you in understanding how to adjust your writing so that it is reader friendly. Let's take a look at how to apply them.

Information Flow

Information flow—the order in which you present ideas—affects the quality of your writing. Let's start by breaking information into three broad categories:

- *Old Information*: familiar information.
- *New Information*: unfamiliar information.
- *Empty Information*: irrelevant information.

Writing that flows well tends to mix old information effectively with new information, with the familiar introducing the unfamiliar.[1]

- Old information tends to be more global, and new information tends to be more specific.
- Old information is an anchor for new information, which extends the reader's knowledge.

Right now, information flow may be a new concept. Work with this concept until you get a feel for identifying the difference between old and new information. In the following examples, old information is italicized:

New to *old* information flow:

The national budget crisis will be *the topic of our next meeting.*

A new construction project has begun *at the corner of State and Lake.*

Chocolate, sardines, and goat's milk are on *my shopping list.*

Can you see how the beginning of each of the above sentences sounds abrupt? For example, doesn't "chocolate, sardines, and goat's milk" sound abrupt in comparison to "my shopping list"? Now let's look at these same sentences reversing the information flow.

***Old* to new information flow:**

At our next meeting, we will discuss the national budget crisis.

At the corner of State and Lake, a new construction project has begun.

My shopping list includes chocolate, sardines, and goat's milk.

Even in these short, simple sentences, can you see how the information flow affects readability? Do you find that the sentences beginning with the familiar, anchoring information are a bit easier to understand?

As you edit your paragraphs, cut sentences that contain only old, redundant information. If you find a sentence that contains all new information, it will sound abrupt and out of place because it shows a gap in the way you are developing your topic.

Next, you work on other formatting tools and techniques, starting with structuring an e-mail message. Even short e-mail messages can often benefit from editing for information flow. But first, complete the exercise below so that you get some practice applying this principle.

PRACTICE 13.1

Instructions: In the following sentences, adjust the information flow so that familiar information precedes unfamiliar information.

Weak: Gaining at least five new clients before August is my goal.

Revised: My goal is to gain at least five new clients before August.

1. A change in consumer spending patterns is one reason the economy has shifted.
2. Outsourcing jobs to third-world countries is a topic you might consider for the next paper.
3. The applicant who graduated from Indiana University Northwest has been hired as the department's new assistant.
4. A budget revision that needs to be completed by next week is the topic of today's meeting.
5. Please consider the cost as well as the time required to make the revisions as you complete your report.

Note: See page 368 for the key to the above sentences.

E-Mail Messages

A paragraph in an e-mail is different from a paragraph in other types of documents. Therefore, when you write e-mail messages, do not try to write cohesive, coherent paragraphs.

A paragraph in an e-mail can consist of one sentence or two to three sentences. If you find yourself writing paragraphs much longer than that, edit your writing or see if you can do some cutting.

E-mail are best when they are short—about one screen in length. Limit most messages to one main issue. By breaking your message into short paragraphs, you are making it easier for your readers to understand what you need so that they can respond more efficiently to your requests.

Begin your message by connecting with the reader on a personal level by using the recipient's name. Then, put the most important information at the beginning of the message, getting right to the point. By putting purpose up front, you will more easily see what to cut. (See Chapter 15, "E-Mail Guidelines," for more information.)

Now let's take a look using side headings, which are also an excellent formatting element for longer e-mail messages.

Side Headings

To add white space to your documents, consider using side headings.

Side headings add visual appeal. Simply take the key point from a paragraph or section, and use it as a side heading. By doing so, you make the key point instantly visible to your reader, making the reader familiar with your topic at first glance.

Though you are used to seeing side headings in books (such as this one) and longer documents that are broken into sections, you may not have considered using side headings in e-mail or business letters.

Be brave: experiment using side headings. After your first attempt or two, you will be pleased with the visual appeal that side headings add to your documents, even short documents.

Remember the composing tools you learned in Chapter 1? Create a mind map and then use the information to create a page map. If you have not yet tried that idea, try it the next time you write. You may find that side headings are also useful in personal documents, such as journals.

Beyond side headings, how do you make your ideas stand out? Consider using boldface, underlining, and italics, but use them only according to standards.

Formatting Features and Marks

Formatting features include **bold**, underscore, and *italics*; special marks include parentheses and quotation marks.

- *Bold*: Put words or **key ideas** in boldface type to make them stand out.
- *Underscore*: Stress key words by underscoring them; however, the preferred method to stress words is bold or italics.*
- *Italics*: Stress *words* or *give definitions*; display *book titles* or *foreign terms* in italics.
- *Quotation Marks*: Enclose direct quotes, intentionally misused words, and slang as well as technical terms presented for the first time in quotation marks.

  Do not use quotation marks to make words stand out, as readers assume the opposite meaning, as in "That's a 'good' idea." (Use single quotation marks within double quotation marks.)
- *Parentheses:* Put parentheses around information that gives a brief explanation or that does not directly relate to your topic. Also put parentheses around a paraphrase or an abbreviation.
- *Caps:* Follow traditional capitalization guidelines; do not use all capital letters (all caps) to make words stand out.

Within a document, be consistent in the way that you display these features and marks. Since the bold and underscore features provide a similar purpose, use one or the other, not both at once.

**Note*: Underscoring was the only option on a typewriter keyboard, but electronic communication gives writers options that only a professional printer had in the past. Do not use underscoring to stress words; instead, use bold or italics.

Bullet Points and Numbering

Have you ever written an e-mail that included three questions; but when you received your response, only two questions were answered with one being ignored? Next time, consider numbering your questions, leaving one line of white space between each question.

Bullet points and numbering are strong visual cues. They not only make key points instantly visible for your reader, they also organize and prioritize your key points.

- For items of equal importance, use bullet points.
- For items with different degrees of value, use numbers, listing the most important items first.
- For a series of questions or a list of tasks, use numbers.

Display bullet points in parallel structure: noun for noun, verb for verb, phrase for phrase. For example, if you start with an active verb, start every item in the list with an active verb in the same tense. If you present your information in complete sentences or short phrases, end your bulleted or numbered points with a period.

For bullets or numbered items, you have a variety of different styles from which to choose. Stay consistent with the bullet or numbering style throughout your document, and shift from one style to another only if you have a special purpose for changing styles; for example, use a larger bullet for major points and a smaller bullet for minor points.

By numbering questions in an e-mail, you are making it easier for your reader to give you a complete response, which in turn aids you in getting your job done.

Spacing

The next chapter gives you official spacing guidelines for letters and other business documents.

However, many are not up to date about how many spaces to leave after a period. For example, you may have learned to space twice after a period, but now the recommendation is to space only once. That's right: space one time after a period, *not two*.

Here's why: printing presses have variable spacing, and printers have always left only one space after a period. However, most typewriters did not have variable spacing, so typists were instructed to space two times after a period and a colon. Since computer software provides variable spacing, the style for spacing is back to where it started.

Thus, try to train yourself to leave only one space after a period, and you will be following state-of-the-art spacing guidelines!

Recap

Here are some of the key points stressed in this chapter:

- Screen your paragraphs to ensure that they are cohesive and coherent.
- Make sure that your topic sentence gives a broad, general overview of your paragraph.
- Develop a topic string from the topic sentence; change paragraphs when you change topics.
- Use special features such as bold typeface, underscoring, and italics to make key ideas stand out.
- Use bullets so that your key ideas are instantly visible.
- Use numbering to make it easier for your recipient to respond to a series of questions or complete a list of tasks.
- Add side headings to give your reader instant access to key points.
- Space once after a period, not twice.

As you experiment using these tools to enhance the visual appeal of your documents, you will soon use them with confidence and ease.

Writing Workshop

Topic: Joy Journal

As Meister Eckhart, a 13th century Dominican friar, philosopher, and mystic once said, "If the only prayer you ever say in your entire life is thank you, it will be enough."

When you hear the word *joy*, what types of words or images pop into your mind? Do you think that if you took the time to reflect upon and acknowledge the good parts of your life that it could have an impact on your health and well being (or the well being of others)?

To start a joy journal, set aside 5 minutes daily to list the things in your life that you appreciate and that bring you joy.

Editing Workshop

Draft

Instructions: As you edit the following message, pay attention to formatting. The revision is on the next page.

Jesse,

April 12, June 7, and September 27 are the dates for the training sessions in Washington, D.C. Two flip charts, markers, and name tents are the only supplies that will be needed. A u-shape is how the room should be set up. Fifteen participants will be attending, so that's how many set-ups that will be needed. Muffins and coffee have been ordered for breakfast; sandwiches, chips, soft drinks, and cookies have been ordered for lunch. Invoices have been prepared and should be received by participants by next week. Should participants be contacted by myself before the training?

Best,

Diana

Revision

Notice the use of white space as well as numbering to make key points stand out. Did you change passive sentences to active voice? Were there any other corrections you made?

By the way, your revision does not need to match the one below to meet an excellent standard.

Jesse,

The dates for the training sessions in Washington, D.C., are April 12, June 7, and September 27.

Here is what we need for the training:

1. Two flip charts, markers, and name tents.
2. U-shaped room.
3. Set-ups for 15 participants.

For breakfast, participants will have muffins and coffee; for lunch, sandwiches, chips, soft drinks, and cookies.

The invoices are prepared, and participants will receive them next week.

Should I contact participants before the training?

All the best,

Diana

Diana Gatto
Training Associate
WTK Training
312-555-1212

End Note

1. Joseph M. Williams, Style: Toward Clarity and Grace, The University of Chicago Press, Chicago, 1990.

14

Visual Persuasion:
Formatting Letters, Memos, and E-Mail

Do you realize that readers evaluate your documents at first glance? In fact, documents are formatted their best when key points are instantly visible.[1]

Right now, you may be spending extraordinary efforts to craft your message while still overlooking the obvious: the overall appearance of your document on the page. Now that you understand formatting basics, use what you know to shape all types of business documents so that your readers have easy access to your ideas.

When you use formatting effectively, readers find your document credible, appealing, and easy to understand. Formatting is a form of *visual persuasion:* think of formatting as an element of your writing style.

- *Formatting speaks to your reader* at a glance, and correct formatting gives your document credibility.
- *Formatting gives visual cues* to aid the reader in understanding the content.

In this chapter, you review formatting for business letters, e-mail messages, and faxes. As you have seen, formatting involves the use of bullets, bolding, italics, and side margins.

Another critical element of all business documents is *white space*, the unused portions of the page. To present an effective finished product, all elements must work together harmoniously.

White Space and Balance

The term *white space* refers the unused areas of your document, such as top and side margins and spacing between lines. Official guidelines dictate a range of minimum to maximum spacing to leave between parts. After you learn official guidelines for spacing, which are reviewed in the following pages, you will develop a trained eye for document placement.

White space gives your readers' eyes a place to rest and delineates the various parts of your document. White space also gives readers a place to make notes and comments. White space controls the way your document looks at a glance. Therefore, before you consider any document complete, ask yourself the following questions:

- Does this document look balanced, appealing, and professional?
- Is too much information crowded into too little space?
- Does the document look lop-sided or does it look as if it is surrounded by a *picture frame* of white space?

Documents should look balanced, with top and bottom margins being roughly equal; side margins should be somewhat equivalent. The easiest mistake to make is to leave too little space at the top of a document, resulting in too much empty space at the bottom. A professional rule of thumb is to aim for a picture-framed effect.

Use the **Print Preview** feature that is part of the **Print** option to examine how your document looks before you print it. Next you will review basic guidelines for these documents:

- Business Letter
- E-Mail
- Fax

However, before reviewing formatting and white space guidelines for these business documents, you will review how to adjust the paragraph settings on your computer. Otherwise, spacing guidelines will not display correctly correct.

Computer Settings

To format your documents professionally, adjust your computer settings to the correct starting point. The following instructions guide you in adjusting your paragraphs settings and margin settings for Microsoft Word:

1. Go to the **Home** tab (located at the upper left corner of your screen).
2. Open the **Paragraph** tab by clicking on the arrow.
3. At **Indents and Spacing**, find **Spacing**.
4. Set **Before** and **After** at **0**.
5. Set **Line spacing** at **Single**.
6. Click **OK**, so that you are back at the **Home** tab.
7. At the **Home** tab, set your font at Times New Roman, Size 12.
8. Finally, go to the **Page Layout** tab, click on **Margins**, and then select **normal**.

In short:

1. Home → Paragraph → Spacing → Before and After → 0
2. Home → Paragraph → Line Spacing → Single
3. Page Layout → Margins → Normal

Once you become an expert, you can experiment with various font types and sizes. Until then, follow the guidelines here closely, as they will keep you from making mistakes that are confusing to correct.

Letters

- Start most letters 2 to 2.5 inches from the top the page. Most software is set to have a 1 inch default top margin. (If you are using a 12-point font, 1 inch of vertical spacing results from spacing down 6 times.)

- If you are using a company letterhead, space down at least 3 times before typing the date. (If you are writing a personal letter, create your own letterhead modeled after the one in the example or be creative).

- Use the default margins for most letters, which are 1 inch.

- For short or long letters, add or delete vertical space before the dateline, between the date and address, and between the closing and the signature line; you can also adjust your margins.

- Double space (DS) between most parts or ↓ 2.

- Do not justify right margins on business correspondence.

Business Letters

1. *Letterhead.* Corporate letterhead contains the name, address, phone number, fax number, web address, and company logo; many individuals design their own letterhead.
2. *Dateline.* The date appears at least 3 lines below the letterhead and no more than 2.5 inches from the top of the page.
3. *Inside Address.* The inside address contains the name of the recipient, his or her title, the company name and address. Use two-letter state abbreviations, but avoid using other types of abbreviations in addresses.
4. *Salutation.* The traditional greeting for letters starts with *Dear*, as in "Dear Mr. Jones" or "Dear George"; follow the salutation with a colon, *not* a comma (and never a semicolon).
5. *Body.* The text of your message should be single spaced with 1 blank line between paragraphs; block paragraphs (do not indent them).
6. *Closing.* A common closing is "Sincerely."
7. *Writer's Signature Block.* The writer's name is typed along with a title, when used.
8. *Reference Initials.* If the typist is different from the writer, indicate the typist's initials.
9. *File Name Notation.* This code indicates where a document is stored. When used, file names often have three components: a name, a dot used as a separator, and an extension consisting of 1 to 3 characters.
10. *Enclosure Notation.* This notation alerts the recipient (and reminds the writer) that something is enclosed with the letter.
11. *Delivery Notation.* This notation indicates that a letter was sent in a special way, such as UPS, FedEx, Express, and so on.
12. *Copy Notation.* A "cc" notation (courtesy copy) indicates to whom copies of the letter are being sent.
13. *Postscript.* A post script is an afterthought; represent the post script with or without periods and with or without a colon; however, use capital letters (PS, P.S., or PS:).

Figure 14.1 | Blocked Letter Format

As you review the letter below, notice the recommended vertical spacing. Also notice that all lines are blocked at the left for efficiency, producing a clean, uncluttered style.

Young Communication[1]
180 North Michigan
Chicago, IL 60611
youngcommunication.com   ↓ 3+

July 11, 2011[2]   ↓ 4

Mr. Michael Scott [3]
Top Notch Consultants, Inc.
333 West Hill Street
Los Angeles, CA 90210   ↓ 2   (DS: double spacing leaves 1 blank line)

Dear Mr. Scott: [4]   ↓ 2

In the first paragraph, connect with your reader. If you are writing a direct message, state your main point in the first paragraph. [5]

In the body of your letter include details about your purpose.

- Use bullets or numbering to make key points instantly visible.
- Follow the salutation of a business letter with a colon.
- Double space (DS) between most parts.

In the last paragraph, define *action needed* or next steps. Also invite the reader to contact you by including your phone number and Web address.

Sincerely,[6]   ↓ 4

Robert Young [7]
Instructional Designer   ↓ 2

djy[8]
scott.711[9]
Enclosure [10]
By UPS[11]
cc: Reggie Jones [12]   ↓ 2

PS Before you print your letter, use the print preview function to make sure that margins are balanced, creating a picture-framed effect. [13]

Chapter 14: Formatting Letters, Memos, and E-Mail   **209**

E-Mail Messages

For the body of an e-mail, double space (DS) after the salutation, between paragraphs, and before your closing. By spacing down two times, you leave one blank line of white space. Here are some points to consider.

- When you expect recipients to take action based on information in your message, list their names in the *To* section, not the *Cc* section.

Reserve Cc use for when you copy a message to someone but do not expect the recipient to take action. With messages that you are forwarding, add a note at the top of the message stating expected action from recipients.

- Use an accurate **subject line** and update it as needed.

As your conversation evolves, update the subject line to reflect new information. Also, include due dates in the subject line to alert the reader to needed action.

- Use a **greeting,** even if it is as simple as the recipient's name.

Greetings personalize messages and engage the reader. When you write to several people, use a greeting such as "Hello, team," "Hi everyone," or "Good day." When you write to one person, use the person's name followed by a comma; if you wish, also use *Hi* or *Hello*. If the e-mail is formal, use *Dear*.

- Keep the message to about one screen in length.

If your message is long and detailed, consider phoning. Though e-mail may be a convenient way to communicate, consider other channels when communication becomes complicated or relationships become strained.

- Use a simple **closing.**

An e-mail is not as formal as a business letter, so you can use an informal closing such as "Best regards," "All the best," "Enjoy your day," or "Take care," among others.

For professional messages, include a sign-off that lists your company name, address, phone number, and other relevant contact information.

Figure 14.2 | E-Mail Formatting

Notice the use of white space in the e-mail message below. White space is an element of visual persuasion because it aids the reader in understanding your message.

To: Michael Scott
Cc:
Subject: Policy Manual Update

Hi Mike,   ↓ 2

It was great speaking with you this morning—here's the information you were looking for: ↓ 2 *(DS between paragraphs)*

1. Follow standard rules for capitalization. (The personal pronoun "I" is always capitalized!)

2. Avoid using abbreviations. (E-mail messages should not be written as if they are text messages; e-mail are professional communications.)

E-mail messages can be used in litigation. Therefore, advise employees *not* to send messages if they have any doubts. When they feel unsure about their message, they should either save the message as a draft or make a phone call.

I look forward to hearing from you soon. ↓ 2

Best regards,   ↓ 2

Bob   ↓ 2

Robert Young   *(Create your automatic sign-off)*
Young Communication
180 North Michigan Avenue
Chicago, IL 60611
Phone: 312-555-1212
Fax: 312-555-1234

Fax Cover Sheet Format

When faxing information, create a cover sheet, as shown below. Send your fax cover sheet with your document to ensure that everyone on the receiving end clearly understands who sent the fax, who should receive the fax, and the number of total pages to expect.

Figure 14.3 | Fax Cover Sheet

If your company does not have a formal fax cover sheet, create your own using the format below.

FAX COVER SHEET

TO:	Betty Francis	**FAX:**	800-555-9215
FROM:	Don Draper	**PHONE:**	888-555-9242
FAX:	888-555-9243		

* 3 Pages Follow *

Betty, attached is the real estate contract for the property in Long Grove. The closing is next Friday at 10 a.m. Please call me if you have questions.

I look forward to seeing you there.

D. D.

---

212 *A Guide for Business Writing*

Business Letters: Connect – Tell – Act

The business letter is an excellent vehicle to build business relationships. Your letters represent you and your company and may be the only image your client has of your company.

Though it may sound basic, all letters should contain an *intro*, *body*, and *conclusion*. You can organize most letters successfully by applying the following structure:

- In the *introduction*, **connect** with the reader as one human being communicating with another. Connect your purpose to the reader's needs and interests; be friendly rather than stiff and abstract.

- In the *body*, **tell** your reader details, explanations, and facts. Summarize and highlight information supporting your purpose.

- In the *closing*, state the **action needed** or next steps. Express good will; invite the reader to contact you for more information.

To simplify the structure, think of the direct message as a diamond:

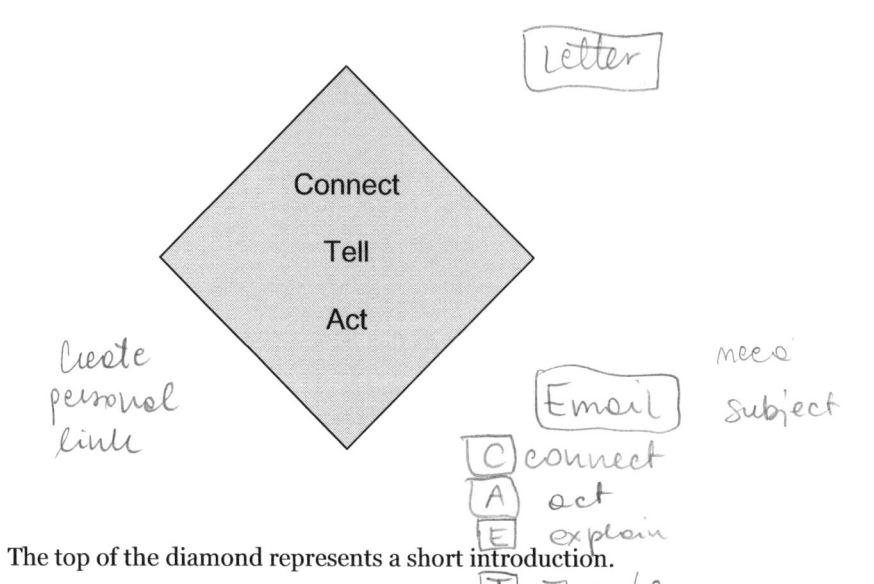

Diamond diagram labeled:
- Connect
- Tell
- Act

Handwritten annotations:
- Letter
- Create personal link
- Email — need subject
- [C] connect
- [A] act
- [E] explain
- [T] Thanks

- The top of the diamond represents a short introduction.
- The middle, the bulk of the information.
- And the bottom, a short closing that includes action needed.

When you write a letter, you also need to determine whether you will communicate information using a **direct approach** or an **indirect approach**.

The Direct Message

Most letters take a direct approach by putting the purpose and main point in the first paragraph. Once readers understand the purpose, supporting information in the body confirms and expands their understanding of your message.

The bulk of the letter is in the body, which can consist of one paragraph (or as many paragraphs as it takes to convey your message). Give as many details as necessary, but do not stray from the principle *less is more*.

The closing in a direct message is usually short; the closing states the action or the next steps that you intend to take or that you request your reader to take. The closing also expresses good will and opens the door for additional communication.

The Indirect Message

Some letters purposely take an indirect approach. When conveying unexpected or bad news, first explain the rationale before stating your main point or decision. This approach equips the reader to accept the bad or unexpected news by understanding the logic behind it. The indirect approach is tactful and shows respect for the reader.

In the introduction, state the purpose in a general way. Then give enough explanation so that the rationale leading to the news makes sense to the reader (or as much sense as possible). State your main point or bad news toward the end of the body or possibly in the conclusion.

The indirect message is also known as the *bad news message* (see pages 188-189.)

Direct Message	Indirect or Bad News Message
Connect with the reader	Connect with the reader
State purpose/get to the point	State general purpose
Give supporting details	Give supporting details
Close with desired actions or next steps	State outcome or conclusion
	Close with cordial words (and next steps if they apply)

As in the direct message, the closing paragraph of an indirect message lets your reader know that he or she may contact you or someone else for additional information.

Recap

Here are some of the points stressed in this chapter:

➢ Ensure that you leave an appropriate amount of white space between each part of every document.

➢ Follow the salutation of a business letter with a colon (:), not a comma and especially not a semicolon (;).

➢ Structure business letters so that you include an *intro*, a *body*, and a *conclusion*. In other words, even when you write short letters, aim for three paragraphs.

➢ Adjust your computer settings so that spacing guidelines make sense.

➢ Create a letterhead for your personal business documents.

➢ Use the **Print Preview** option to make sure your business letters look balanced on the page with a picture-framed effect.

As you experiment using these tools to enhance the visual appeal of your documents, you will become more confident and use them with ease.

Writing Workshop

Topic: Purpose Statement

Just as companies have mission statements that reflect their core values and purpose, you can write your own *purpose statement*.

Purpose answers the deep questions of life, such as "Who am I?," "Why am I here?," "What am I meant to do?," "How do I lead a life that is meaningful?"

Purpose is uncovered over time. The first step in writing your purpose statement is to read through some of your writings that you completed in previous exercises, *looking for themes about your passionate concerns, deep interests, and natural talents.*

Make notes about what you notice, and follow these steps:

1. Based on your notes, write several different drafts of a purpose statement. Begin each sentence with "My purpose is to . . ." (an action verb will follow, such as "my purpose is to design . . .") Simply let the words flow and do not be concerned about writing coherent sentences. You will have an opportunity to edit later.
2. Over the period of a few days, reread your purpose statement drafts, noticing how they feel to you. Notice any words or phrases or clauses that are emotionally appealing. Read the drafts out loud. Take note of any words or phrases that quicken your heart when you hear them.
3. Write a new draft of your purpose statement, incorporating the words that you emotionally connected with in Step 2.
4. Share your revised draft with a friend or partner to get feedback.

Use the prompts below to begin your purpose statement:

In my life, I am most proud of . . .

The things I value most in life are . . .

The most important of these is . . .

Each day I contribute to others by . . .

In the future, I hope my successes will include . . .

To achieve these goals, I plan to . . .

The most important thing in the world to me is . . .

Your purpose statement will change over time; so if this exercise gives you insight, you may consider repeating it in the future.

Editing Workshop

Draft

Instructions: Edit the following message paying special attention to formatting. In fact, consider whether you can use bullets or numbering to enhance your revision.

Hey Tasha, account #2345 needs a credit of $250 dollars. Originally a deposit for 125.00 was made on 2/24 but on 2-25 the Customer received a Debit rather than a credit. The customer, hasnt been credited yet even though we ensured her that her Account would be brought up to date by 2-28.

If you can get back to me on this issue ASAP i would appreciate it.

Best Regards,

Silvia

Revision

Hi Tasha,

Account No. 2345 needs a credit of $250.

- On February 24 the customer deposited $125.
- On February 25, the customer received a debit rather than a credit.

The customer hasn't been credited yet, even though we assured her that her account would be brought up to date by February 28.

Please let me know when you have made the correction so that I can follow up with the customer.

Thanks for your help.

Silvia

End Note

1. Jane Curry, Curry Young Consultants, www.curryyoung.com; Curry Young specializes in training as well as speech and business writing.

15

Persuasive Communication

When you write to persuade, you write to prompt understanding and action. Persuasion affects the way people feel, think, and act.

You may now think that most of your persuasive writing will relate to **formal persuasion**, which is getting a stranger to adopt an idea, product, or service; but that kind of persuasion in business is rare. More common is the persuasion you will use daily to persuade your co-workers, which is **informal persuasion.**

- *Informal persuasion* is an everyday activity and shown in the way you interact with coworkers and clients.
- *Formal persuasion* is used in customer letters and proposals as well as formal presentations to clients and co-workers.

Persuasion is a two-way street: effective persuasive writing demands that you understand the concerns, positions, and needs of your audience. Without this understanding, you cannot successfully persuade anyone to take action, whether that action is buying your products and services or accepting your ideas and solutions.

Avoid the common mistake of assuming that clients are interested in you, your years of experience, or the size of your company. Your clients are interested in how you can help them achieve *their* goals.

Many suggest that if your audience has a negative bias, you use an indirect approach. Perhaps there are highly political circumstances in which an indirect approach may still be the best. However, most business people are so busy and so stressed that they will be more receptive if you don't beat around the bush: they want the facts straight and the explanation without frills.

Being straight forward, however, doesn't mean forgetting good manners. Sometimes you will need to persuade in subtle ways, such as offering an apology or making a complaint. Persuasion includes acknowledging and correcting your mistakes. Persuasion also includes making your expectations clear so that others can correct their own mistakes

Persuasion isn't coaxing, encouraging, or trying to get individuals to do something they don't want to do. Persuasion is finding meaningful benefits and developing creative solutions.

Persuasion is a process, not an event—each contact that you have with a client builds understanding and thus enhances trust. Therefore, keep your focus on the fact that communicating is about building relationships, not simply conveying information.

The Process of Persuasion

Persuasion is all around you in small and large ways. You persuade others and they persuade you even when you are not aware of it. Think about your family and friends. When have you tried to affect someone's decision—for example, deciding where to go to eat, which movie to see, where to go on vacation, or whether to buy a new car?

Persuasion relates to what you can do for others; persuasion involves demonstrating that you will use everything within your power and expertise to get the job done—to serve others in reaching *their* goals.

In getting the job done, you must always remember that persuasion is an *interactive process*: what you offer must intertwine with what others need and want. In each situation, your focus is on solving your *client's* problems. Because persuasion affects how someone thinks, acts or feels, persuasion involves change. All change, good or bad, relates to *resistance*. Identifying resistance and working with it in a constructive way is an important element of persuasion.

The Role of Trust in Informal Persuasion

Informal persuasion takes many forms, both written and social. A critical element of persuasion is building good rapport that leads to relationships based on trust.

What are some specific strategies to build relationships? Politically and culturally accepted methods change as the corporate culture changes. At one time, the best way to build business relationships was to invite clients out to lunch; people commonly joked about the *2-martini business luncheon.* Now busy executives don't have time for leisurely lunches and, in most circles, having a martini on company time is *not* acceptable.

The business world is now more competitive than ever, with most jobs requiring more and more. One way to establish a deeper trust with clients is to have *briefer, more frequent contact,* such as periodic phone conferences. Compared to on-site meetings or luncheons, short phone meetings command a minimal time commitment. One busy trade executive contacts clients to set up a convenient time for a phone conference, saying that he has information on the changing market. Rarely does a client turn him down because he proves in each meeting that his information is in fact valuable.

Another way to build good rapport is to show that you appreciate what others do for you. Clients feel your sincerity by your doing something as simple as sending out a thank-you note. One successful consulting partnership makes it a point to send out two handwritten thank-you notes a week. By acknowledging those who support and assist them, they show that they genuinely appreciate efforts on their behalf.

With customers, you are using persuasion informally when you call or send an e-mail for updates on progress and satisfaction. With co-workers, you are using persuasion informally when you present ideas at a team meeting, linking them to team and corporate objectives. These informal persuasive touches help strengthen your relationships with your clients, and this leads to deeper *trust*: the central quality of a successful business relationship.

Guidelines for Informal Persuasion

To be persuasive, you must establish good rapport. A friendly, reliable business relationship with a predictable track record does more to persuade than a well-written letter or e-mail.

Let's start by examining a few basic guidelines that apply to the process of persuasion.

1. *Know as much about your client as you do the idea, product, or service that you are "selling."*

    - What is your client's mission?
    - What are your client's needs and objectives?
    - Do you have common clients, interests, or friends?

When you present ideas, show how your proposal benefits individuals and supports corporate objectives. Show your clients how your proposal will:

- Solve or alleviate a current problem.
- Increase productivity, efficiency, or effectiveness.
- Motivate employees to do their best or work together cooperatively.

2. *Understand all aspects and implications of your proposal's ideas, products, or services.*

    - How much time and money will it save?
    - Why is it better or different from what was tried before?
    - What are the short- and long-term effects of adopting your proposal?
    - What are the consequences of *not* adopting your proposal?

Before you bring your proposal to a decision maker (even if that is your own manager), familiarize yourself with all aspects of it.

Discussing your ideas with a peer helps you to anticipate difficult questions; developing your thoughts on paper helps you to organize your proposal logically and effectively.

3. *Develop trust.* You build trust daily through your words and actions. Look beyond your own needs and focus on the needs of others: show respect for superiors and subordinates. You cannot force trust; trust takes time to build.

- Do you respect others and listen to their ideas?
- Are you objective, fair, and consistent in managing relationships?
- Who supports your efforts and trusts your recommendations?
- Are you accountable for your words and actions?

Your daily actions contribute more to your credibility than your education, experience, and training.

One successful consulting firm operates under the philosophy, *We promise our clients everything, and then we deliver more than we promise.*

4. *Understand resistance.* Resistance can tug at decision makers from many sources; consider the following:

   - Do they have a belief, assumption, or bias holding them back?
   - Is there a lack of trust in you, your product, or your proposal?
   - Is the cost or time-frame prohibitive?
   - Are the decision makers attached to a less effective product?
   - Are other priorities creating conflicts? Are "politics" involved?

Use communication to uncover resistance, and then remain flexible and open-minded with the attitude that *every problem has a solution.*

Unless decision makers ask for details, prioritize and simplify the information you include. For example, sometimes decision makers can't act because proposals don't reflect the most fundamental courtesies, such as *brevity*.

For instance, one large, national commercial real estate corporation sent out an RFP (request for proposal) for a large project and received five proposals: four were an inch and a half thick. The winning proposal was three pages long. The firm's senior vice president remarked, "I didn't even read the long ones. I just didn't have time."

You can counter resistance by producing evidence that your product or service has benefits that exceed the client's reservations. For example, if the client objects to the cost, show how much money your product or services will save in the long-run. If the concern is that the product is good but not needed, *show how much more effective operations will be if it is adopted.* If decision-makers are attached to a product due to habit, *demonstrate how easy it is to adjust to yours.*

Sometimes these kinds of antidotes help dissolve resistance and move the process forward. However, real reasons for resistance are not easily uncovered, and you won't always have a solution to counteract it. By seeing the situation clearly and then developing an honest response, you know you have done your best regardless of whether you get the business.

Client Relationships

Establishing good working relationships with co-workers and clients contributes to your success in persuading. To some extent, you redefine your relationships each day.

When you take the time to smile and acknowledge others, they notice. When you treat colleagues with respect and kindness, they treat you well in return. When you go out of your way for team members, they remember your consideration. In turn, when you ask others to consider your suggestions, they measure your proposals in part by the way they feel about you.

Listening to the needs of others and responding effectively earns you respect, which translates to power.

- Establish rapport and trust with *everyone* with whom you work.
- Understand your clients' needs and interests and respond to them.
- Be aware of resistance and embrace it.
- Be accountable for your words, actions, and commitments.

Formal Persuasion

With formal persuasion, you need to go through various stages to adapt your product or service to your client.

Regardless of your proposal, the final adoption is unlikely to be exactly as you initially present it. Remember that persuasion is a process, and change is an integral part of the process. As you learn more about your client's needs, adapt your proposal to meet those needs.

Dismiss an *all or nothing* mind set. Most resources are negotiable; create a compromise and embrace change to make the transaction flow smoothly. By adapting your proposal, you can sometimes turn an initial rejection into a "win-win" situation.

Purpose

One way to increase the likelihood that your client will respond to your proposal is to have a clearer understanding of your own mission. You can define your purpose by keeping service to others at the core of your operations. Explain how your product or idea fits into the larger picture.

For example, by offering employees on-the-job training, a company helps its people become more productive. In the process, employees may also become more loyal and less likely to seek jobs elsewhere. Thus, training improves not only skills and morale but also retention. In the long-run, the company saves money and has more control over quality; these are some of the deeper purposes served through training.

Audience

Persuading—or selling—can create anxiety. One of your primary responsibilities is to ensure that your client, that is, your audience, feels at ease and confident that you have his or her best interests in mind.

For example, you can have the best product in the world, but *if you don't know your clients, you can't link your proposal to their needs.* Analyze your client's needs and interests and adapt your proposal to ensure you've put your client's needs first. Once you put your client's needs first, you will alleviate your anxiety as well.

To understand your audience, answer these questions:

- Who is the key decision maker?
- What are you client's needs, objectives, interests, and mission?
- How do your client's objectives mesh with your proposal?

You'll respond better to your clients if you remember that your clients have hopes, fears, and feelings, just as you do. Clients will also respond better to you if are friendly, courteous, thoughtful, and responsive. Develop a flexible, welcoming, and problem-solving attitude.

Most important, whether you are communicating with the CEO of a large corporation or a division secretary, the language you use should always make clear that you value and respect your audience. If you adopt this perspective, you will soon find yourself surrounded by people who want to do business with you or want to help you.

If you have an interest in learning how to be more social and friendly, read Dale Carnegie's book *How to Win Friends and Influence People*.[1] It is a classic among those preparing to make a career in sales.

Motivation

You cannot motivate clients by impressing them with your educational degrees, your years of experience, or the company you keep. Get beyond yourself and focus on what your products or services mean to your clients.

Motivation is tied to logic and emotion. Ground your approach in how your offering can benefit your clients, Ask the question "What's in it for me?" from your *client's perspective*. What benefits does your proposal offer your client? What needs does your proposal satisfy?

Hierarchy of Needs

Psychologist Abraham Maslow developed a hierarchy of needs which humans seek to fulfill. The hierarchy prioritizes needs from the most basic survival needs to the highest level of emotional, intellectual, and spiritual fulfillment. In general, humans do not seek to fulfill higher needs while lower needs are threatened.

Self-Actualization: emotional and spiritual growth
Esteem: self-respect and respect for others
Social Ties: love, affection, belongingness
Safety: security
Physiological: physical survival

When you are identifying benefits your proposal has for your client, these five broad categories can give you insight into the kinds of needs that corporations and business people address.

Where do your ideas fit into the broader scheme of their objectives?

Resistance

Have you ever tried to make a decision listing all the *pros* and *cons* associated with it? The *cons* side of the list is where *resistance* resides.

Resistance factors into all types of persuasion. Some resistance is tangible and apparent, such as having an inadequate budget or the need to address other priorities. Other types of resistance are intangible, such as a client lacking trust in you or your product or seeing little merit in your proposal.

Attitudes and emotions are often involved. For example, management may fear employee reaction or perhaps decision makers don't want to bother with the kind of work the changes will entail.

- What attitudes or beliefs are involved?
- What behavior do you expect to change? Will the change be difficult?
- What are the costs in terms of money, time, and resources?

To find out what is blocking commitment to your proposal, ask questions and then listen. Consider if the resistance is in response to your approach:

- Are you too eager about your proposal?
- Are you too busy talking to listen?
- Are you too easily discouraged?
- Do you need to adjust your way of thinking?

If your client is resisting for *valid* reasons, do *not* try to talk your client out of his or her position. Forging forward in the presence of valid concerns can create serious, complicated problems. Beyond that, it is unethical and will not lead to long-term, mutually beneficial business relationships.

When a decision maker believes whole-heartedly in a product or idea, nothing can stand in the way from making it happen. In Rome, there is a saying, *Tutto é possibile*: "All things are possible." That's also true in places other than Rome when everyone is committed and passionate.

If your client favors your proposal, you can be direct and start talking about how to implement it. If your client is unfavorable, you need evidence of success and how that success translates to your client: an antidote to resistance is the *benefit* your proposal creates for your client.

Evidence

For evidence, use data, facts, and figures. Evidence is objective and cuts through bias effectively.

- Do you have any formal or informal research to demonstrate that your claims are true?
- Are other clients willing to give testimonials to support your claims?

An example of evidence would be, "when employees take our training course, their average skill improvement is 55 percent." In addition to statistics, comments from other clients are your most convincing and motivating evidence.

Benefits

Evidence relates to facts; *benefits* relate to the *value* your proposal will produce for your client. A benefit is derived from evidence. Break down your idea, product, or service into individual components.

- What is the objective value your proposal will produce?
- What is the subjective value your clients will experience?

Translate evidence into benefits, for example:

> "When employees improve their skills by 55 percent, they will save approximately 2 hours a day due to improved efficiency. They will also reduce errors by about 20 percent resulting in improved customer satisfaction."

Use your words to paint a picture for your clients of how things will look after they adopt your proposal. Visualizing effectiveness can be more persuasive than using words to convince someone about a product's effectiveness.

With the above example, you might say, "Imagine how relieved you will feel when customer complaints are cut by 20 percent due to your employees' improved efficiency. Picture your employees feeling less stress and more satisfaction with their jobs."

Credibility

Credibility equates to believability and leads to trust, which develops over time. You build credibility and trust by being accountable through your words and actions.

Everything that you say and do contributes to your credibility. By providing evidence, demonstrating follow-through, giving examples, and providing referrals, you can expedite the process.

You must establish your credibility *before* you present your proposal. If your client does not find you credible, your product or idea is inconsequential. Trust does not mean that your client will accept your ideas, but lack of trust ensures your ideas or product will not be adopted.

Action Plan

Action comes in stages, and an action plan consists of tasks along with specific due dates.

Before you actually send a persuasive document, you are likely to have a phone conversation, followed by an e-mail or meeting. Define a plan so that you stay in contact with your client:

- Who or what will be involved?
- What is the time frame?
- What costs are involved?
- What steps can I take to network with my client?

By interacting with your client, you will identify the steps to include in your action plan. Use every contact to research your client's needs and identify resistance; use this information to tailor your proposal to your clients and their current circumstances.

Customer Loyalty

Persuasion relates to serving customers so that they become loyal to your company; loyal customers keep a company fiscally strong.

As discussed, persuasion is *not* an event: persuasion is a process. When companies regard persuasion as an event, they spend extraordinary amounts of money and energy to recruit new clients; however, they allow themselves to systematically lose others because of oversights and poor quality.

Think about your own experience. When was the last time you were "rubbed the wrong way" by a business establishment? Was it a restaurant that gave you bad service or food? Was it a phone call that led only to recorded messages with no real person to answer your question? Was it an understaffed store with no one available to assist you with a purchase? Now think about how that experience changed your views and possibly your behavior: *Are you likely to go back? How many people will you tell about your bad experience?*

According to Dr. Paul Timm, author of *Building Customer and Employee Allegiance*, businesses would fare much better if they focused on developing loyalty among their current customers and employees. Instead, many companies rely on marketing or advertising to bring in new business while overlooking ways to keep old business from walking out the door.[2]

Now let's go back to your experience as a consumer. Did that particular business establishment spend massive amounts of money and effort to recruit your business? Probably so, but it's the little things that have a big impact on customers. And it's the little things that make or break a business relationship.

Customer Feedback

One way to develop customer loyalty is through feedback. By giving customers an opportunity to say what is on their minds, you have an opportunity to change lemons into lemon-aide. Rather than avoid the negative, embrace it. Let your customers lead you to effective solutions and better customer relations.

By giving customers an opportunity to give feedback, you may diffuse their negative feelings. By responding effectively to their feedback, you may not only keep them as customers, you may also turn their complaints into a source of growth and change.

Customer feedback will open your eyes to what is turning business away; it will help you retain more of your hard-earned customer base. According to Dr. Timm, here are three simple questions that can give you the insight you need:[3]

1. How satisfied are you?
2. Do you intend to keep doing business with me?
3. Would you recommend us to a friend?

This creates a dialog between you and your customers and establishes an active-listening process. Know what turns customers off and then reduce those things that cause them to feel discounted, mistreated, frustrated, or angry. This approach addresses persuasion but from an often overlooked direction.

Disenfranchised Customers   Customer dissatisfaction often relates to customers not having their expectations met. Once you know that a customer is disappointed, what can you do? The first thing is to act quickly to solve the problem. Here is a three-step process Paul Timm suggests:[4]

1. *Feel empathy for the customer.* Realize the customer is in pain over the situation and say something such as, "I understand how you could feel that way."

2. *Resolve the problem.* Ask the person what he or she thinks you could do to solve the problem (which might be something quite different from options that you were considering).

3. *Offer something that exceeds the customer's expectations.* If you can compensate the customer in some way for time and money lost (such as paying for their parking or throwing in a little extra compensation), you are more likely to regain their business.

Initially, this approach might sound expensive, but consider the long-term effects of losing one customer. If that customer spends $1000 in one year, that's more than $10,000 in ten years. Also consider the damage that one dissatisfied customer can do when he or she tells several friends about poor service or bad products.

Spending funds to build customer loyalty is at least as effective (if not more effective) as spending funds on advertising or marketing.

Once again, it's the little things businesses do to keep their customers feeling important. The human touch brings balance back to even the most difficult situations.

Visual Persuasion

Persuasion involves understanding. Therefore, especially when you write persuasive documents such as proposals, apply the tools and techniques of visual persuasion.

In addition to white space, bullet points and numbering, boldface, and italics, here are *techniques* to incorporate visual persuasion:

- Paragraphing
- Headings and Subheadings
- Subject Lines

Paragraphing   Break information into readable chunks by limiting the number of lines in a paragraph.

Just as a sentence is more readable under 25 words, so is a paragraph easier to read when it takes up fewer lines. For letters, consider limiting paragraph length to 6 lines; for e-mail, keep your paragraphs to 4 lines or under.

Headings and Subheadings   In shorter pieces of writing, such as letters and memos, writers are hesitant to use headings. However, headings highlight key points so that the reader begins to understand the message at first glance. The worst kind of writing is when readers need to struggle just to understand the message!

When writers state their purpose clearly and up front, the reader digests information more easily. When the main point is clear, necessary details add effective support. In contrast, details can be tedious when they build to a main point.

To develop a heading, pull out the main point from the topic sentence of a paragraph. If you turned it into a heading, would it add value for your reader? Does it enable you to cut out other detail in your paragraph, making your message more concise?

Subject Lines   Whether you are writing an e-mail, a memo, or letter, use a *subject line* to enhance reader understanding. A subject line also enables your reader to file your message for future reference.

You need a subject line for memos, but also consider using a subject line for letters, especially letters that you send to clients you don't know well. A subject line enhances understanding for your reader, and readers are more likely to agree with you when they understand what you are saying.

To avoid getting stuck trying to think of a subject line, pull out the main point after you have written your message. *Short, descriptive subject lines are the best.*

Recap

Formal persuasion plays a major role in some positions but a minor role in most careers. Regardless of your position, you will use informal persuasive skills every day with your manager, those you supervise, your customers, and your co-workers.

When you persuade someone to buy your product or service, ensure that it serves your client well. There is a difference between selling a client a product one time and selling your product to the same client over and over again. To achieve repeat business, understand your clients' needs and assist them in solving problems, enhancing efficiency, or improving productivity.

Writing Workshop

The Entrepreneur, Part 1 – An Individual or Team Project

Large Fortune 500 companies employ only a small percentage of the workforce. More people are self-employed or work for small businesses and "mom and pop" operations than they do for the large firms.

You may or may not have the desire or ambition to start your own business, but take a moment to dream: *If you could create any kind of business you wanted, what would it be?* Do you spend your free time on one particular activity because you have a passion for it? What about social or environmental problems? Do you have vision for a different kind of world? If you do, what changes could you make? What do you love enough that you would be willing to do something br ave and bold about?

Here is the first part of this project:

1. Identify a problem and identify your target audience.
2. Develop a product or service.
3. Develop your "company" by defining a vision statement, mission statement, and working motto.

Identify Your Target Audience

Who are the major stakeholders?

What are their needs, interests, likes and dislikes?

Why serve this group?

Develop a Product or Service

What is your product or service?

Who are your competitors?

How will your product or service differentiate itself from competitors?

Build a Brand

What is your company name? Where are you located and why?

What are your company's vision and mission statements?

What is your motto? What is your company logo?

In what other ways can you *brand* your identity?

As Richard J. Leider says, "Each life has a natural built-in reason for being . . . the integration of who we are with what we do is one of the true joys of life."[5]

Editing Workshop

Draft

Instructions: The following letter was sent as a follow-up to a meeting. How can you revise the letter to have more visual appeal and persuasion?

Dear Chuck:

Bob and I enjoyed meeting with you and Marcie and appreciate the time you spent with us so we could learn about your company. You and your staff have done a great job expanding your business.

I'm sure your background and experience lead you to know how important a good banking relationship is for any company. Since we specialize in commercial banking, we would be glad to help you explore banking and financing opportunities that could benefit your company, such as reducing your costs and giving you more liquidity. We can also provide the capital that you need to meet your growth objectives.

Please feel free to call me at any time. The resources of the First Bank network are here for you to use. We wish you continued success in your company ventures.

Sincerely,

Grace

Revision

Notice the use of visual persuasion in the revision below.

> Dear Chuck:
>
> We enjoyed meeting you and Marcie today and learning about your company. You have all done a superb job expanding your business.
>
> You understand the value of a good banking relationship, and we'd like to help you look at banking and financing options to benefit your company. We specialize in serving the commercial banking needs of companies like yours; our products and services can help you:
>
> 1. **Reduce** your costs.
> 2. **Increase** your liquidity.
> 3. **Provide** the capital you need to meet your growth objectives.
>
> I will call you in the next few days to discuss the possibility of our working together. In the meantime, please call me at (630) 555.1212 if you have questions.
>
> We wish you continued success; thank you again for your time.
>
> Sincerely,
>
> Grace

End Notes

1. Dale Carnegie, *How to Win Friends and Influence People*, Simon & Schuster, New York, 1964.
2. Paul Timm, Building Customer and Employee Allegiance, Communication Solutions, Orem, Utah, 2004.
3. Ibid., page 15.
4. Ibid., pages 35-55.
5. Richard J. Leider, The Power of Purpose, Berrett-Kowhler Publishers, Inc., San Francisco, 1997, pages 25, 55.

16

Writing Persuasively

With persuasive writing, you will get the best results when your meaning is accessible and your priorities stand out. That's true whether you are sending a request to a co-worker or a marketing letter to a customer.

Here are the types of persuasive messages that you will review in this chapter:

- Routine Requests and Favors
- Feasibility Memos
- Complaints or Claims
- Apologies
- Sales and Marketing Letters
- Two-Page Letter Proposals

Let's get started working on the more simple and common types of persuasive writing first.

Routine Requests and Favors

By far, the most common kind of persuasive document you will write is an e-mail that makes a routine request of a team member. Routine requests are part of taking care of business, so don't feel inclined to apologize for asking for a colleague's help.

When making routine requests via e-mail, get right to the point and keep your message short.

1. Present requested action and due dates close to the beginning of the message and even in the subject line.

2. Comment on why the request is important or what the request will help you accomplish.
3. Express appreciation and include next steps, if relevant.

In addition to routine requests to co-workers, you will write routine requests to customers. For example, your client may need to fill out papers so that a signature is on file. Other types of requests to clients might request them to consider additional services your company provides.

When writing letters or messages for routine requests, state your purpose and then get to the action at the end.

1. Connect to the reader and state your purpose.
2. Explain the reason for the request.
3. Tell the reader what to do and supply a due date.
4. Show appreciation for action taken, and let the reader know that you are available to answer questions.

When sending correspondence as an attachment to an e-mail, use the e-mail as a "cover letter" for the correspondence that you are attaching. When you are writing to someone within your corporation who is not a team member, take extra care with routine requests. Though you both support a common mission, someone from another department may not immediately understand the relevance of your request. You may want to treat your request more like a *favor*.

A favor goes beyond what would be considered a routine request because you are expecting the reader to do something out of the ordinary. Your favor may take little or great effort, but it is effort that may not benefit the reader directly.

For example, if you ask a co-worker to attend a meeting, that is a *request*. If you ask the same colleague to make a presentation in your place, that is a *favor*. For routine requests, you may include why the request is helpful, but for favors also include how the favor will benefit the person doing it for you.

Figure 16.1 | Routine Request Via E-Mail

> To: George Clone
> Cc: Jan Clark
> Subject: May 5 Presentation
>
> ---
>
> George,
>
> Jan Clark has asked that you and I present at the May 5 client conference.
>
> The presentation should cover all changes that we expect to include in the next policy revision. If we identify how the new procedures will benefit clients, our sales staff will be more motivated to make the changes.
>
> Can you work this into your schedule? If so, when can we meet?
>
> Sandro

Figure 16.2 | E-Mail Requesting a Favor

> To: Alessandro Ferro
> Cc:
> Subject: November 3 HR Presentation
>
> ---
>
> Sandro,
>
> I am scheduled to present HR trends at our department's annual retreat in Kohler, Wisconsin, on November 3. Unfortunately, I suddenly find myself unavailable due to a family emergency.
>
> You know more about human resource trends than anyone I know. Would you consider making the presentation in my place? I would supply you with all of the data along with PowerPoint slides. Also, if you are able to present at the retreat, I will add your name as a major contributor when the report is published in *HR Journal Today*.
>
> Please let me know by Friday if you can grant me this significant favor.
>
> Dina
>
> PS: Our new CFO will be at the meeting, and I'm sure he'll be impressed by your presentation!

Sharing important ideas in writing rather than verbally improves their prospect of being adopted. At times, you may turn your idea into a project by presenting it as a **feasibility memo**.

Because you build friendly relationships with co-workers, you may not consider turning your ideas into informal proposals. However, your team and superiors will give your ideas more credence when you put them in writing. A *feasibility memo* can suggest ways to solve a problem as well as suggest ideas for change: developing a new process or procedure, buying a new product, or revising plans already in progress.

A feasibility report or memo is an abbreviated form of proposal, containing two basic parts:

1. The first part presents the project and gives details about how it would work.
2. The second part urges the project's adoption by outlining its benefits.

As you write, you are able to present your ideas clearly and concisely. More important, you address some of your readers' questions *before* they ask them, removing some of the *devil's advocate* type of challenges. If you give team members a copy of your memo before a meeting, you can incorporate subtle changes and eliminate some concerns before your team discusses the merits of your proposed project.

So remember, if you want others to apply your ideas, consider putting them in writing. No one may officially recognize your memo as a feasibility report. However, your memo improves the likelihood of the group adopting your ideas or turning them into projects.

Figure 16.3 | Feasibility Memo

To: Jake Miller
From: Roberta Edwards
Subject: Enhancing Productivity
Date: January 16, 2011

Our staff is focused and productive. However, we are always looking for ways to improve our bottom line. Here's an idea we might want to discuss at our next team meeting.

In general, each member of our team has excellent writing skills. However, some have been complaining that they are expected to respond to over 100 e-mail daily. This is an extraordinary amount of writing; quite frankly, some of the messages that I receive are long-winded and difficult to respond to because I can't figure out what is needed from me.

By getting some training, specifically, in writing effective e-mail messages, we might be able to help our staff manage their time and their inboxes more effectively.

Let me know what you think and whether we can address this idea at our next team meeting. I will be happy to work out a more detailed proposal or research training options.

Complaints or Claims

Making a complaint can be an emotional experience. Agreements or expectations have been violated, and you may have experienced some harm, financial or otherwise. When you have a legitimate complaint, you are likely to get results by putting your complaint in writing.

In fact, when you take the time to complain, you are actually doing a favor for the ones to whom you are complaining: you are giving them an opportunity to right a wrong. You are also giving insight into a problem that can then be corrected before others experience your pain and inconvenience.

A letter is the most formal response, and generally letters command action; recipients take written communication seriously. In fact, a letter becomes legal documentation, as it demonstrates that all parties have been informed. In addition, writing clarifies the issue and possibly how to resolve it. (You may find that once you have written about your experience, you no longer have strong feelings about the issue; or you may find that you are partly responsible.)

Regardless of your experience, a letter of complaint should never be unprofessional or rude. Most of the time, the person to whom you are writing did not purposely create your problem—in fact, often the person who receives the letter had nothing to do with creating the problem. If you start to point blame, you will lose your reader, who may be the decision maker in how to resolve your claim.

Letters of complaint traditionally follow an indirect pattern. However, indirect does not mean that your letter should be wordy.

Introduction

Connect with the reader as one person to another, being as positive as you can be:

- What is your relationship with the company or product? Are you a loyal customer? If so, for how long?
- What is the problem?

Body

Give details about the product and your experience.

- What expectations were violated?
- How were agreements broken?

Conclusion

State your expectations of how to resolve the complaint.

- How could this situation be resolved?
- What actions do you expect? A refund or an exchange?
- Is it possible to turn the situation into a win-win solution?

Figure 16.4 | Letter of Complaint

Use the Simplified Letter Style when you do not know the name of the person to whom to address the letter. Note: When you space down 3 lines, you leave 2 blank lines between parts.

February 28, 2011

Internet Provider, Inc.
2003 Bell Drive
Twin Oaks, MI 44508 ↓ 3

ATTENTION CUSTOMER SERVICE ↓ 3

For the past six years, I have been a loyal customer of your company, paying my bills regularly and recommending my friends to your service.

However, for several months now, I have been receiving tons of spam to my e-mail account. Your customer service department suggested that I open a special spam account, which would intervene so that I do not receive these bothersome messages. Unfortunately, their remedy has not helped the problem but instead made it worse. I still get as much spam as ever; the only messages the spam account intervenes are from friends and associates.

Unless you resolve this problem within the next two weeks, I will change Internet providers. Please let me know as soon as possible the changes you can make to my account. ↓ 2

Sincerely, ↓ 4

Jennifer J. Reed

As Duke Ellington once said, *a problem is a chance for you to do your best.*

By remaining objective, you will help ensure that the problem is resolved to your satisfaction. Remember, you are dealing with people who have feelings; most people do not make mistakes intentionally.

Your objective is to solve the problem, not to make those involved feel bad. Do not use language that you will feel embarrassed by later; revise your initial emotional response to an objective one:

Emotional: Your bank has really botched up my account, and I would like this mess cleaned up ASAP!

Objective: An inaccurate transaction was posted to my account on June 30, 2010.

Consider using the passive voice when blame is involved.

Emotional: You made a serious mistake in my account.

Objective: A serious mistake has been made in my account.

After you have drafted your letter or e-mail message, wait a day before sending it. The old saying, "You will get more bees with honey than vinegar" applies to complaints. By offering only constructive comments, you will confront less resistance and encourage more corrective action. *Even when you are correct and another is wrong, acting without dignity is never justified.*

When you receive a complaint, your response will determine the future of your business relationship with the customer. It is normal to feel defensive when someone is telling you that you did something wrong. The truth is, mistakes happen. Someone is responsible and at times that may be you. An *honest mistake* is one in which you inadvertently broke an agreement or misread the situation.

When someone complains directly to you, determine whether you need to make a formal apology. Depending on the situation, you may call or write; at times, you may need to do both.

Making an apology acknowledges that you are human. Being able to apologize for your mistake without being defensive is a mature character trait and a quality of emotional intelligence. Before you respond, clarify the complaint and clearly understand the other person's perspective.

Here are some guidelines for acknowledging a mistake and apologizing:

1. Acknowledge the person for letting you know about the problem:

   Poorly worded: I received your letter about the problem in your account.

   Revised: Thank you for taking the time to inform me about the problem in your account.

2. Do not go into great detail about why you made the mistake, which could sound defensive. Focus on the solution, not the problem; assure your client that resolving the issue is important:

   Poorly worded: I usually don't make mistakes like this; I guess I was too busy and just wasn't thinking.

   Revised: I apologize for your inconvenience. Your business is important, and I will work to resolve this issue immediately.

3. Avoid using adjectives and adverbs, such as *truly* and *really*, or you may sound insincere.

   Poorly worded: I am truly sorry that your account was overdrawn and really appreciate your patience.

   Revised: I am sorry that your account was overdrawn and appreciate your understanding and patience.

4. Keep a positive tone and don't make excuses.

   Poorly worded: The mistake should not have happened.
   Poorly worded: I was very busy and not able to meet the deadline.

   Revised: I apologize for the mistake and any inconvenience it has caused you.

5. Remain humble and try to re-establish the relationship, regain trust and respect:

   Poorly worded: I will not let this happen again if you give me another chance.

   Revised: I appreciate your giving me a chance to regain your confidence.

When you are working with someone who is reasonable, most apologies will dissolve bitter feelings. When you are working with someone who is not reasonable, any apology—whether written or spoken—will not suffice. In those situations, acknowledge that you did your best and then dust yourself off and move on.

Use the *direct approach* for letters of apology:

1. Start by stating your apology.
2. Let the reader know that you value the relationship.
3. Solve the problem and compensate the reader, if appropriate.
4. Invite the reader to call you to discuss the issue further.
5. Encourage the reader to let you know if the problem resurfaces.
6. Follow up with a phone call to make sure that the problem is solved.

Figure 16.5 | Letter of Apology

Suppose you wrote the letter in Figure 16.4 to Internet Provider, Inc. Would you be satisfied with this reply? Why or why not?

March 5, 2011

Ms. Jennifer J. Reed
5101 Roosevelt Road
Dearborn, MI 44802

Dear Ms. Reed:

Thank you for letting us know about the problems you are having with your Internet account.

Our customer service department has received similar complaints recently, and we have taken immediate action to block these new types of spam. When we receive information from valuable customers like you, we are able to gain control of the situation quickly.

Management also approved more stringent procedures to combat the unwelcome bombardment of such ads. Thus, we are proud to inform you that we now offer the best protection available, including fire walls, subject line detectors, and methods to ban specific addresses and domains.

Because you are valued customer, we are crediting two months of service to your account. Whenever you have concerns, please contact me directly at 800-555-1212.

Sincerely,

Jack B. Ritter
Customer Service Manager

Sales and Marketing Letters

By learning how to construct a sales letter, you may not only become a better writer, but you may also become a more enlightened consumer.

Unlike other types of persuasive writing, sales and marketing goes beyond logic and primarily taps into the emotions of the reader. To reach emotions, you must present a topic so that it *hooks* your reader. That assumes some sort of pre-existing condition, such as a fear, discomfort, or dissatisfaction. The reader may not realize the pre-existing condition before you present it, but if you tap into something real with the reader, you may provoke the reader to respond.

In general, advertising offers you products and services that make you feel better. Advertising targets specific issues and translates them into problems that you need solve to be happy. In general, advertising isolates a problem and then gives an instant solution: quenching thirst, eliminating odors or bacteria, cleaning stains, saving time, improving productivity, losing weight, gaining stamina, providing security, saving money—and the list goes on.

Marketing letters get at a discordance or imbalance between the way things are for the reader and the way the reader would prefer them to be. These letters target a reader's fear, discomfort, or dissatisfaction and then present the solution. They attempt to build the reader's trust by stating that their solution is the best the most reasonably priced. Finally, they tell the reader what action to take.

Here is breakdown of what you are trying to achieve with your letter:

1. Draw attention to how your product relates to your reader's dilemma.
2. Offer a solution; show how your proposal offers unique benefits to the reader.
3. Build trust and credibility for your product and company.
4. Make it easy for your reader to take action to contact you.

This process is all around you—have you ever seen a TV infomercial that uses this format? This type of advertising targets impulse buying.

> **COACHING TIP**
> **AIDA Model:** The AIDA model provides a traditional approach to developing sales letters.
>
> | | |
> |---|---|
> | *Attention* | Grab the reader's attention with a catchy, flashy claim, question or statement. |
> | *Interest* | Develop the reader's interest by making the claim relevant. |
> | *Desire* | Explain how the change will benefit your readers. |
> | *Action* | Make it easy for your readers to contact you; keep actions simple and convenient. |

When you pose a question, you speak directly to each reader. Questions form connections and activate readers' minds, engaging them. For example, consider starting your letter with a question such as, "When is the last time you left a store angry?" Your question turns the complaint letter from your point of view to your reader's, thus invoking your reader's experiences, emotions, and interest.

Though attention-getters can assist you in getting your message across, do not feel compelled that you must use one: *It is your message that counts.* First spend your energy developing your message effectively and then work on finding the best type of opening.

Writing a Proposal

As a blend of informative and persuasive writing, proposals are important business tools. However, the word *proposal* can intimidate writers. This might be because formal proposals require adherence to rules and protocols or because the word *proposal* implies acceptance as well as *non-acceptance.* Beyond that, some proposals involve inordinate planning and research, which can be the most difficult aspects of writing.

However, the most important elements of proposal writing are the following:

- Establishing that a problem exists and that you are the best one to solve it.
- Knowing who the key stakeholders are what they are seeking.
- Incorporating into your plan solutions tailored to your key stakeholders.

A team may find itself writing a proposal for various reasons: for example, to persuade members of its own organization to make changes or to persuade external organizations to adopt a product. One common type of proposal is to request funds from a not-for-profit foundation or government agency to implement a project.

Define the scope of your proposal:

- What are your client's requirements? Has your client published a formal RFP (request for proposal) that outlines their needs?
- Does your proposal answer each and every question posed in the RFP?
- Can your proposal be a short letter or memo that addresses only a few questions?

Different types of proposals have different types of requirements, some more rigid than others. When you respond to an RFP, the first step is checking the proposal to see if all questions are answered. If not, the proposal may be tossed out without consideration.

Client Relationships

Writing proposals is a form of listening to a client's needs and then customizing a solution. Thus, proposals should extend from your client's actual needs, not from what *you think* the client needs.

In addition, proposals are often part of a larger organizational process that helps the organization fulfill its mission. Proposals need to tailor *every detail* to the targeted audience. Here are steps in developing a base for your proposals:

1. Research the philosophy, culture, and mission of your target audience.
2. Establish an honest dialog with decision makers and key stakeholders.

Obviously some situations will not allow direct contact with a prospective client; but when you can meet with the client, doing so is your most important work. After the client clarifies the problem, that information becomes the foundation for defining purpose, methods, and outcomes.

Cover Letter

Formal proposals include a cover letter that summarizes the main points of the grant.

The cover letter is secondary to the proposal itself. Though the cover letter should be accurate and well written, it does not need to contain *new* information; you can use direct statements from the proposal or executive summary in the letter. By summarizing highlights from the proposal, the letter prepares the reader for the language and ideas that the proposal contains.

Formal Proposals

Formal proposals involve considerable research and development. To be successful, the writer (or writers) must have a command of the problem and its solution as well as the formal structure of how to write the proposal.

In a proposal, you are detailing a problem and showing how you would solve it. However, often you must first appeal to the reader's motivation by showing that the problem needs to be addressed. Then you must demonstrate that the manner you suggest—your plan—is the best way to proceed. Thus, your proposal must convince the reader of the following:

- That a problem exists and needs to be solved.
- That you are the best choice to solve the problem.
- That your approach is the most effective.
- That your costs are competitive and justified.

If an organization has a particular need, they may put out a public announcement in the form of a *request for proposal* or RFP. An RFP establishes the scope of the intended project and alerts interested parties that the company is soliciting competitive bids and formal proposals.

Companies use RFPs so that responding vendors provide information that is uniform and complete. Before submitting—*or even starting*—a formal proposal, learn the organization's requirements for writing the proposal.

State and federal governments along with not-for-profit foundations have the most complicated guidelines for grants and proposals. According to The Foundation Center, here is the format for a formal proposal:

Table 16. 1 | The Foundation Center Format for Formal Proposal[8]

Part	Description	Length
Executive Summary:	A summary of the entire proposal.	1 page
Statement of Need:	A description of why the proposal is necessary.	2 pages
Project Description:	How the program will be implemented and evaluated.	3 pages
Budget:	Financial description of the project and explanation.	1 page
Organization Information:	History and governing structure of the nonprofit; its primary activities, audiences, and services.	1 page
Conclusion	Summary of the proposal's main points	2 paragraphs

An individual or committee may evaluate your proposal along with many other proposals; consistency in format makes it easier to identify if the proposal is complete and compare it with others. In fact, if a proposal does not follow the prescribed format exactly, it may be returned without being read.

Though proposal format varies from organization to organization, here are some questions to get started organizing the basic parts of a proposal:

Statement of Need:

Purpose: Start with a short statement connecting you to your client's needs. Briefly state information about the need to solve the problem; relate confidence in developing a comprehensive or innovative solution.

Background: Give a brief history of the problem; include details that relate to individual objectives the proposal will address.

Include enough information so that the reader becomes motivated to have you solve the problem. *In short, why should they hire you?*

Project Description:

Objectives: State what you will accomplish by writing individual objectives for major parts of the project.

Plan, methods, and schedule:
Discuss the details of how you will achieve your purpose and objectives; identify your methods and the order in which you will use them. State how long the activities will take and give dates, if applicable. For example, "phase one," "phase two," and so on.

Results: Summarize the expected outcomes from implementing your proposal.

Remember, *the devil is in the details* (but only details that your client wants).

Organization Information:

Your company: Your company's history, management structure, clients, and services.

Staffing and Credentials:
The names and credentials for those who will be implementing the proposal. (For letter proposals, present this information in a less formal way.)

Budget:

Include a detailed breakdown of the costs. Justify any costs that may seem extraordinary.

Evaluation:

> Explain how you will measure results. Indicate how you (and your client) will know if you achieve the objectives?

Authorization:

> Formal proposals include an authorization statement for your client along with a signature line. (In short, less formal proposals, the authorization statement is often omitted.)

A formal proposal is a contract, so expect to be held responsible for any service you indicate that you can provide and at the cost that you list. Thus, you may want to indicate the time frame during which the proposal is effective.

For example:
The prices quoted in this proposal are valid until the end of this year.

Proposals represent partnerships. You are linking your skills with others to solve a problem that may affect people you have never met. Hence, early in the process, get to know your client.

Letter Proposals

Many corporations do not require formal proposals. When this is the case, a two-page letter proposal will generally suffice.

The letter proposal contains most of the same information that a longer, formal proposal contains. However, the client is likely to be familiar with the problem and convinced it needs to be addressed. The client may also be familiar with the services and solutions you will offer.

Though all proposals need to be tailored to the specific audience, here are guidelines for a two-page letter proposal:

Statement of Need:

> Start with a short statement connecting your client's needs with your expertise. Once again, *why should they hire you?*
>
> When a letter proposal is written at the client's request, the client may be asking for details in writing to receive approval or finalize authorization.

Description of Project

Objectives:

> State what you will accomplish by writing objectives for major parts of the project.

Plan and schedule:

> Discuss only important details of your plan. Identify each phase of the proposal and give dates for availability, if applicable. If feasible, give your client options.

Results and evaluation:

> State the results your proposal will accomplish and how you will measure them.

Budget:

> Include a detailed breakdown of the costs. If you include options, make sure the costs for each option are clear.

Figure 16.6 | Two-Page Letter Proposal

Young Communication   *Training for Results*

October 16, 2011

Ms. Glenda Borg
LaSalle Bank Corporation
200 West Monroe Street - Suite 660
Chicago, IL 60606

Dear Glenda:

Thank you for inviting me to the 10th Annual Run for Life on Saturday. I had a fabulous time, and I enjoyed talking to you. Even though our conversation had to be cut short, here is the proposal I promised you.

As we discussed, your goal to help your employees write effectively, efficiently, and correctly are commendable.

Training Outcomes

Each of our workshops leads to client-focused, quality writing. Participants improve their skills and learn to use communication to build business relationships.

Participants reduce time on task while improving the quality of their final product. As a result, you can expect your employees to produce more in less time and with increased confidence.

Programs and Time Frame

Each program meets on site; here are the two programs designed to meet your needs:

- **Writing Effective E-Mail, .5 or 1 day**
- **Business Writing Workshop, 1.5 days**

Attached are program descriptions. As you review the programs, please keep in mind that you can customize the training for your employees at no additional cost.

Note: For the second-page heading, include the name, page number, and date. Then space down 3 lines (leaving 2 blank lines) before continuing the body.

Ms. Glenda Borg
Page 2
January 16, 2011

Pricing Options
Each workshop is priced at a day rate $4,000 for groups of 12 or fewer. For larger groups, the per participant rate is $400. If you plan more than four workshops annually, your rate will be reduced by 10 percent.

Evaluation
Participants take a pre- and post-assessment to measure skill gain. You receive a report that shows the aggregate improvement for each group. In addition, you receive quantitative and qualitative feedback based on an instrument that reflects program content.

Follow-Up
Your employees can receive additional assistance through coaching sessions. We can discuss this option as a follow-up to one or both or the trainings proposed.

Young Communication prides itself on having the expertise and experience to meet the writing needs you described. We look forward to working with you to improve your employees' skills and, thus, the credibility of your corporation.

The pricing options in this proposal are flexible; if these programs do not fit your budget or requirements, please let me know. In addition, these prices are valid are for the remainder of this year.

I also look forward to receiving your feedback to see how to further adapt these programs to meet your employees' needs. I will contact you next week to see if you have questions.

Sincerely,

Robert Young
President
Enclosures: The Business Writing Workshop
             Writing Effective E-Mail

Since many proposals are team projects, let take a look at how to organize a team writing project next.

Team Writing

From rough draft to final copy, you can do team writing projects in various ways. Here are a few suggestions:

1. *Map out the various parts or sections.* Start with a *concept map* by identifying each major component of the project, creating a visual so that you can see how the pieces fit together.

    With certain types of documents, such as proposals, standard parts can be identified immediately.

2. *Research and become familiar with the content and topics.* Fill in details as you go along, using post-it notes or any other creative tool you can devise.

3. *Brainstorm ideas together.* Assign a facilitator to lead brainstorming sessions at any phase of the writing venture. (If feasible, use a lap top, flip chart, or white board).

4. *Coordinate writing assignments with task assignments.* In this way, team members and partners write about tasks they complete and about topics they are familiar with.

5. *Map pages and compose together or alone.* Mind map each part and turn mind maps into *page maps*. Then compare notes.

6. *Respect differences in learning styles.* Some team members work better alone than they do in a group; a team can respect that style through individual tasks rather than forced partnerships.

7. *Establish reasonable due dates.* Team members need to have clear expectations; allow room for error as unforeseen circumstances can arise—that means setting *internal due dates* in ample time to meet *external due dates.*

8. *Evaluate and revise your draft together:*
   - Agree up front that every draft will need at least one revision.
   - Allow time for silent reading *before* discussing a section.
   - Give suggestions for improving the document rather than criticizing its current state. (Avoid criticism that points blame without adding anything constructive.)

9. *Bring the parts together for a final editing.* Write your project in a consistent voice even if several team members contribute portions. Early on, your team may identify the member who is the most competent and reserve that individual's time for the final edit.

10. *Recognize each other for effort that results in work well done!*

Of course, every team is unique, developing its own team dynamics. Work on understanding each other's strengths and weaknesses and then work in constructive ways to get the job done.

Break up the project into manageable tasks and then pull it all together; use effective communication skills to ensure a successful group process.

Recap

You write persuasively every day as you communicate with coworkers and clients. A proposal is the most formal type of persuasive writing. When you write a proposal, ask yourself the following:

- Have you connected your proposal to your client's needs?
- How does your proposal benefit and add value to your client?
- Have you established trust with your client?
- Does your client show resistance to any part of your proposal?
- What are the pros and cons of your proposal from your client's point of view?
- Have you used visual persuasion effectively?
- Have you considered ways to enhance customer loyalty?

Writing Workshop

The Entrepreneur, Part 2 – An Individual or Team Project

If you worked on Part 1 of this project, now you can add the finishing pieces by writing a two-page letter proposal.

1. If you have created a not-for-profit organization, you can write a proposal requesting possible funding for your organization or a project.

2. If you have created a for-profit corporation, you can write a proposal selling your products or services.

If time permits, you can also do the following:

- Present your company and product in a PowerPoint presentation.

- Develop a mock up of the home page for a Web site. Include all of the vital information for your project, such as your company *mission statement* and a description of your product or service. You may also want to include tabs for other information.

Editing Workshop
Draft

Instructions: Edit the following letter; look to make changes in the following:

- Formatting, paragraphing, and wording
- Punctuation
- Active voice

    Mrs. Georgia Roberts
    1456 West Maple Avenue
    Manchester, RI 55555

Dear Mrs. Roberts:

It is my pleasure to inform you that your request to add your daughter Alicia Roberts Grey has been honored to your checking and savings accounts to which she now has full privileges as a joint owner with full rights of survivorship. In order for this request to be validated we ask that you and your daughter please sign your names where indicated on the lines below, including the date:

_____	_____
Georgia Roberts	Date
_____	_____
Alicia Roberts Grey	Date

The signed letter should be returned to us in the enclosed, self-addressed envelope or drop it off at the bank. As soon as your signed form is received, we will finalize these changes to your account. If you have questions, please call us at (800) 555-5555 or stop by the bank. Your business is appreciated.

Sincerely,

Martha Steward
Account Specialist

Are you able to use visual persuasion to make the letter more effective?

Revision

October 2, 2011

Mrs. Georgia Roberts
1456 West Maple Avenue
Manchester, RI 55555

Dear Mrs. Roberts:

I am pleased to inform you that we have honored your request to add your daughter Alicia Roberts Grey to your checking and savings accounts. She now has full privileges as a joint owner with full rights of survivorship.

To validate this request, we ask that you and your daughter please:

1. **Sign your names below** where indicated.

   _____   _____
   Georgia Roberts   Date

   _____   _____
   Alicia Roberts Grey   Date

2. **Return the signed letter** to us in the enclosed, self-addressed envelope or drop it off at the bank.

As soon as we receive your signed form, we will finalize these changes to your account. If you have questions, please call us at (800) 555-5555 or stop by the bank.

We value our relationship with you; thank you for this chance to be of service.

Sincerely,

Martha Steward
Account Specialist

End Note

1. The Foundation Center, http://fdncenter.org/learn/shortcourse/prop/.html, accessed February 11, 2004.

17

Best Practices for E-Mail

Has your day ever been ruined because you received an e-mail that seemed accusatory? Or have you ever sent a message that you wish you could have retrieved as soon as you clicked *send*?

Though the benefits of e-mail are too numerous to mention, the fact that e-mail has a dark side merits addressing. Every day, people create major *faux pas* with e-mail, some of whom lose their jobs because they use e-mail or the Internet inappropriately. Others waste hours each day because they are unsure of how to compose an effective message or how to respond to a complicated one.

If you find yourself avoiding someone, e-mail should not be your communication mode of choice. Pick up the phone and call the person or walk over to his or her office and have a brief chat. Seeing someone's face or hearing that person's voice can magically melt tension in a way that e-mail cannot. In fact, e-mail has a tendency to perpetuate problems, if not escalate them.

Once you start down a wrong path with a colleague, assert your better side and work to dissolve the issue. Otherwise, you may find yourself losing energy and credibility with your co-workers. You see, negative energy spreads like a bad virus, and no one is immune.

An underlying purpose of all business communications is to build relationships, and that includes e-mail. This chapter covers guidelines and best practices for using e-mail. As you begin this chapter, realize that you are not alone—everyone has had an e-mail nightmare that would better be left forgotten.

To put e-mail use in perspective, let's start by reviewing some facts about e-mail use, some of which may come as a surprise.

E-Mail Facts

Over time, you might feel as if your co-workers have become like family and that you are a permanent part of your company. That is not the case, so do not let those cozy feelings lead you to let your guard down, even if your father owns the company—here is why:

E-mail messages are official documents and can be used in litigation.

Your messages can become evidence in legal actions. As a result, your e-mail can also become part of the public domain, as the former employees of Enron discovered. Even casual messages to friends became part of the litigation process.

Your computer at work is the property of your organization.

Your company can—and probably does—monitor your use of e-mail, whether you are aware of it or not. Companies have the legal right to review any messages that you create or receive. In fact, you have no legal right to privacy for any type of Internet usage while at work.

Once you click *send*, your message is out of your control forever.

Even *deleted* messages can be restored by experts, should the need arise. In addition, your message can be forwarded to the CEO of your company or even around the world; and you can't stop it, even if you know about it.

Like any sort of communication, your e-mail message can be twisted and read out of context. We live at a time in which people suddenly find themselves scrutinized by the entire world. Most people who become immersed in notoriety do not expect it to happen . . . until suddenly it happens. And then life suddenly feels out of control.

By using technology appropriately, many people could have avoided heartbreaking scenarios—and countless can still be avoided. Do not say or do anything that you would not mind having discussed on the national nightly news or a morning talk show, and you are likely to be safe.

E-Mail Format

Limit each message to one main issue. Start with the most important information and get right to the point. If you need the reader to take action, put that information at the beginning of the message. In fact, if you are up against a deadline, you may consider putting the due date in the subject line, as in the following:

>Subject: Report Due November 18
>Subject: April 18 Meeting Postponed

After you exchange information about the same topic a few times, change the subject line to reflect the evolving information. Keep the first few words of the subject line the same so that the reader can access the group of messages easily, for example:

>Subject: April 18 Meeting Rescheduled for May 10

The first part of any business document should connect with the reader, and the easiest way to connect with a reader is to use his or her name. You will set a cordial, business tone by starting your messages with a salutation and ending with a closing.

Salutations For e-mail, business professionals use the recipient's name as their salutation, commonly preceding it with the word *hi* or *hello*. However, if you do not know your recipient well or prefer to be formal, use the word *dear* in the salutation. Any variations of the following are acceptable business salutations:

Hi Cynthia,	Cynthia,	Cynthia:	Mr. Carter:
Hello Jesse,	Dear Jesse,	Dear Jesse:	Dear Mr. Carter:

When you are addressing a group of people, feel free to use a word such as *team* or *all*, as in "Hi team," or "Hello all." As you exchange a few messages back and forth, take note of your associate's style. If you would feel more confident following your associate's lead, do so: imitation is a form of flattery.

Closings   With formal letters, use *sincerely*. In fact, other than sincerely, most formal closings now seem passé; for example, *yours truly* or *very truly yours* sound overly formal.

With e-mail, no standard protocol guides writers. Therefore, feel free to be more expressive with your closings, for example:

Take care.	Hope your day goes well.
Talk to you later.	Thanks for your help.
Let's talk soon.	All the best,

If a message is formal, use a closing such as "Best regards." If you are writing to a friend, but the relationship is somewhat formal, use "Warm regards" or "Kind regards."

Even if you use an automatic sign-off, key in your first name so that it appears above your sign-off. This may seem redundant, but it gives your e-mail a personal touch, which adds to a friendly tone.

Below is an example of a short message. Notice how the message is formatted, including the white space.

Hi Jane,

Thank you for sending the information on the book so quickly.

Will you be attending the conference in Toronto next week? If so, would you have time for lunch? I'd like for you to meet an associate of mine who is in charge of the London office.

All the best,

Diana

Diana Gatto, Facilitator
WTK Training Corporation
200 North Randolph
Chicago, IL 60611

White Space

Though your software generally sets appropriate margins, you need to control the blank lines, or white space, between the various parts.

As mentioned in previous chapters, white space is critical to the quality and readability of all documents. As well, good use of white space adds to the writer's credibility. Here is what the message to Jane (that appears on the previous page) might look like if no white space were added.

> Hi Jane, thank you for sending the information on the book so quickly. Will you be attending the conference in Toronto next week? If so, would you have time for lunch? I'd like for you to meet an associate of mine who is in charge of the London office. Best,
>
> Diana Gatto, Facilitator
> WTK Training Corporation
> 200 North Randolph
> Chicago, IL 60611

Does the above message seem less appealing than the original? Without even reading the message, can you see a difference? Here are some spacing guidelines for e-mail:

1. Double space (DS) by striking "enter" (aka "return") two times.
2. DS after the salutation, leaving one blank line.
3. DS after each paragraph, opening up the space for your reader.
4. DS before and after a closing, such as "Best regards."
5. DS between your name and your automatic sign off.

By leaving the recommended amount of white space, you will achieve a more professional looking message that is easier to comprehend.

In addition to paragraph breaks and white space, another important visual element is the use of side headings.

E-Mail Guidelines

E-Mail does not have rigid rules as compared other types of business correspondence such as letters, memos, reports, and proposals. Though e-mail use continues to evolve, use the following guidelines to keep communications flowing on a professional level:

1. Start your message with the most important information: put purpose up front and clearly state what you need from the reader at the *beginning* of the message.
2. Respond to e-mail within one or two days, even if you are simply acknowledging that you are working on the request; in turn, give your recipient two days to respond to you before following up.
3. Use an automatic out-of-office response if you will be out of reach for a day or more.
4. Do not Cc people unless they are in the loop. When people are copied unnecessarily, it wastes their time and can send a negative message that creates an awkward situation.
5. Press "reply all" *only* when you are sure that everyone needs to receive your message; when only the sender needs a reply, other recipients may become annoyed because it wastes their time.
6. Include a note at the top of a group message stating that only you should receive a reply. Consider developing group lists: by using the blind copy (Bcc) option, you are able to show names but not e-mail addresses.
7. Forward messages rather than use Bcc when you want to keep people in the loop privately; this approach protects you should the message be forwarded.
8. Use standard capitalization: CAPS connote shouting; use all lower case only if you are a *techie* writing to other *techies*—otherwise, adapt your writing for your audience.
9. Never use text abbreviations in e-mail: *When in doubt, spell it out.*
10. Use an accurate and updated subject line so that your reader can refer to your message and file it easily; include action needed in the subject line.
11. Avoid using *read now* and *urgent*; all messages are urgent; use a subject line that includes action needed to demonstrate urgency.
12. Avoid sending the following types of information via e-mail: confidential, sensitive, or bad news.

13. Use visual persuasion so that you reader can pick up key points at a glance; for example, white space, side headings, bolding, and numbering.
14. Encrypt sensitive information, such as credit card numbers, when you must send it. (If you don't know how to encrypt information, do a search on "sending sensitive information by e-mail.")
15. Use an indirect message style when you must send bad news via e-mail.
16. Number questions and requests so that they stand out.
17. Add a note at the beginning of forwarded messages: explain the action that the reader should take, or let the reader know that the message is only *FYI* (for your information).
18. Leave the history unless you are sure the reader does not need it: at times, the thread is clutter; at other times, it provides the context of the current request. Deleted history can create frustration and time lost.
19. Avoid jargon; however, if you use an acronym or initialism, spell it out the first time, putting the abbreviated form in parentheses.
20. Avoid slang, and do not use sarcasm; refrain from sending jokes or being humorous, and use emoticons sparingly, if at all.
21. Use e-mail at work sparingly for personal messages.
22. Avoid sounding suspicious, as in "Delete this message upon reading."
23. Avoid saying, "No, that's not our policy," and instead state what you *can do* for a client.
24. Do not respond to controversial or emotional messages unless you are confident and objective.

If you need to say *I'm sorry*, say it; but say it tactfully.

Don't Say: Please forgive me for making such a stupid error. You are such a valuable client, and I'm hoping we can mend the fences and get back on track.

Don't Say: Clearly you didn't understand what I was saying or you wouldn't have reacted so strongly.

Say: Thank you for letting me know about this issue. I am sorry that this has caused you an inconvenience, and I have taken immediate steps to correct it.

Unless discussed directly, some issues will not go away. Addressing them in a timely way can keep additional challenges from taking root.

E-Mail Versus Text Messaging

A strong boundary exists between professional e-mail messages and text messaging. Though you may use contractions in e-mail messages, do not use text abbreviations in professional messages.

When in doubt, spell it out.

Never use text abbreviations such as "u" or "ur" in a business e-mail. And be careful *never* to use a lower case "i" in place of the personal pronoun "I," which is a proper noun and is always capitalized.

These kinds of mistakes are blatant, and writers quickly lose credibility by confusing e-mail with text messaging.

Also keep in mind that text messages, along with e-mail, never really go away. In fact, because of its informality, text messaging can easily encourage users to forget boundaries. Stay on the alert. People have ruined their careers and even their lives by the way that they conduct themselves through these communication channels.

Thinking Points

An underlying purpose of all business communications is to nurture business relationships. When communications become stressed, your hard skills, or mechanical skills, are not likely to help you much. Instead, you will need to rely on your soft skills, your people skills.

Use these points to remind yourself that you are one human communicating with another human who has fears and insecurities, just as you do. Respond to challenging messages only when you are clear-headed and objective.

Point 1: *Do not send communications when you are in doubt.*

Your doubt is an important signal that you need to listen to. Why are you doubtful? Is something negative going on? Are you hiding behind e-mail to avoid speaking directly to someone? Are you sure that you are taking the most positive, constructive path to resolving the problem? When in doubt, *do not send it out.*

Point 2: *Explore your options: help your clients save face.*

If you are stuck thinking that you have only one possible response and that response is negative, you are wrong. In other words, you *always* have more than one way to make a point, especially if emotion is involved.

Once you have lost a client's trust, you will feel as if you are stuck in quicksand, being expected to prove that you can accomplish even the ordinary. Or worse, the relationship will disconnect, leaving you "right" but not necessarily happy.

Think outside of the box until you come up with a solution that feels good in your gut, your second brain. Turning communication into a win-win solution is usually possible and always a good choice.

Point 3: *Dance in step with your partner.*

Communication is like a dance. To dance in step with your clients, listen to their needs. Also, look for similarities and mirror their behavior. Common ground enhances good feelings.

When you feel unsure of yourself, follow their lead and model your communications after theirs. However, when things do not seem to be going in a positive direction, take the lead until communications once again become constructive. Everyone has a bad day, so give your clients the benefit of the doubt when you can.

And consider this: when a problem exists, everyone involved shares some of the blame. Dwelling on what the other person did or did not do is much easier than honestly assessing your part.

Do not perpetuate a problem by focusing only on someone else's mistakes. Instead focus on what you can do to take responsibility or change the course to get things back on track, and the dance will flow much more smoothly.

Point 4: *Do not write it if you would not say it face to face.*

Human contact has intangible feedback loops to support communication that technology does not have. When you speak with someone, an immediate interchange of ideas occurs, with tone of voice and body language giving important cues.

In contrast, looking at a computer screen instead of a human face can lead to a temporary sense of power along with lapses in judgment. Especially when emotions run high, do not write anything in a message that you would not say to someone's face.

One college professor who teaches nursing classes online said, "You wouldn't believe the things that students write in an e-mail that they would never say if they were speaking to me. When I receive that kind of an e-mail, I call the student. When they find out who is on the line, there's dead silence. Finally I say, 'What did you expect would happen after you sent an e-mail like that to me?'"

Point 5: *Be aware of your micro-messages.*
What you communicate *between the lines* is just as important as what you say directly. Before you send a message, check to make sure that you are not implying something negative. Make sure that your emotions do not come through, especially under stressful conditions.

Unspoken messages can speak louder than actual words. Revise your message until you are sure that you are saying what you mean, even if you need to wait another day to respond.

Point 6: *Choose to be kind rather than right.*
Though you are keenly aware of the pain and suffering in your own life, you are not aware of what goes in the lives and minds of other people. As Plato said, "Be kind, for everyone you meet is fighting a hard battle."

Being kind not only contributes to keeping your relationships in good standing, but your kindness also benefits your own health and well being.

Point 7: *Do not label people.*
People are not things, and labeling people turns them into objects. Once you label a person, you will not be capable of seeing that person as a fellow human being who has feelings and aspirations, just as you have.

Always remember, you can build good business relationships even with people whom you do not necessarily like, as long as you avoid labeling them. In addition, at some level, all people know when they are being treated differently. Labeling can start a negative cycle that escalates, humiliating the target while simultaneously diminishing the integrity of those perpetuating the label. Rise above the norm by treating everyone with respect.

In business, whether or not you like someone is not exactly relevant. In business, you need to associate with all sorts of people whom you would not necessarily invite over for a holiday dinner.

Point 8: *Do not infer there is a problem, or you may create one.*

If you receive a negative-sounding message and then react with a negative tone, you may get yourself into a dynamic that has serious consequences.

Do not respond to controversial messages until you do the following: draft, save, and edit until you get things on a constructive footing; and you may need to get a good night's rest before your final edit, as stress creates distorted vision.

Do not fight any battle that puts you in a position to lose a war. Also, do not hide behind e-mail: instead of using e-mail, call the person or set up a face-to-face meeting.

Point 9: *Do not play "tug of war."*

The sooner you gain insight into a power play, the better. Most of the time, playing harder will not work—you will just up the ante. Unfortunately, the person with the stronger sense of integrity is more likely to end up with the bigger losses.

When you find yourself involved in a power play, rent *War of the Roses* and then have a good laugh. Lighten up whenever you can.

Point 10: *Answer all questions in a timely manner.*

When you see a question mark, generally the writer is waiting to receive an answer from you. Although this statement should go without saying, many questions go unanswered on a regular basis.

If someone sends you a message posing questions, assume the writer *needs* to receive a response. When questions are not answered, not only does the writer feel disrespected, but the situation itself becomes ripe for misunderstanding and discord.

You see, it is impossible to know exactly what a lack of response means, so it should not be a surprise if a slighted party sits back and assumes the worst—especially if a pattern of shaky communications exists.

On the receiving side, just because someone has not responded to your message does not mean that the other person does not care. The vast majority of the time professionals become so busy that they cannot keep up with their e-messages. The world is moving at warp speed, and clients do not generally create a problem intentionally.

The next time that you do not receive a reply or do not get your questions answered, ask again, but in a polite way when you are feeling confident. If need be, put a due date in the subject line. Due dates are always motivating.

When you have done your best and the situation does not seem to be getting better, walk away for a while. Always remember, tomorrow is another day. A good night's sleep refreshes even the worst situation.

When your energy feels drained, put off making important decisions or writing sensitive messages. Like everyone else, you do your best work when your mind is clear.

Recap

Most people end up sending a message or two that they regret. As a wise philosopher once said, *experience is the best teacher*—so do not be too hard on yourself if you commit a *faux pas*.

➤ Stay aware of the legal ramifications of corporate e-mail.

➤ Send messages only when you are clear headed and objective.

➤ Use text abbreviations in text messages, and professional language in e-mail messages.

If you find that you are struggling over writing an e-mail, instead call the person or set up a time to meet. Focus on making every situation a win-win experience.

Writing Workshop

Topic: Misinterpretations—Miscommunications

Short of telepathy, one person cannot transfer feelings and thoughts to another person in pure form. Something is lost in translation when words are the vehicle of communication.

Describe an experience in which miscommunication occurred because of a *misinterpretation*. What could have been done to avoid the situation? How was the situation rectified?

Editing Workshop

Draft

Instructions: Edit the following message. You will find the revision on the next page.

Nick,

Where are you??? Your phone off??? I'm trying to contact you ….Im waitng on hearing back frm you on the message that i sent you yesterday. I know you have your Blackberry with you so Im confused why you havent answered me yet.

Ill be in the office until 5 today so contact me when you get this message, I know you are busy, but this is a priority for me too.

I'm also waiting for Matteo to answer me on some things so if he's with you ask him if he can call me too. I just got to make sure everythings in place for the meeting on Friday OK?

Ana

Revision

Do you think that Nick might find the following message easier to respond to?

Nick,

Can you let me know by 5 p.m. today if everything is in place for the meeting on Friday?

Once I hear from you and Matteo, things will be set.

Hope your day is going well.

Ana

18

Job Search Tools

Charles Darwin once said, "It is not the strongest of the species that survive, nor the most intelligent, but the ones most responsive to change."

Though you may expect that this chapter is about learning use the Internet to find a job, it isn't: this chapter is actually about helping you define your unique career profile. By creating a career portfolio and a strategy for networking, you will be ready for your online search at sites such as Monster.com, CareerBuilder.com, Dice, and many more.

Regardless of your achievements, looking for a job can make you question everything you have ever achieved. That is because the job-search process is different from other activities and projects. You are not just using your talents to solve a problem: you have become the *central theme* of the project. Finding a job is a full-time job; like it or not, *you* are the focal point, and the job itself is secondary.

You may feel more confident using your skills than talking about them. Verbalizing your job survival skills equates to marketing yourself; to do that, you first need to identify your unique qualities so that you can prepare your résumé and ready yourself for interviewing.

Career Portfolio

All job seekers need to be organized and ready to present their credentials so that employers recognize their skills at a glance.

In fact, the first screening of an applicant lasts only seconds. Today employers are looking to eliminate applicants at the beginning of the process. Something as small as using a comma (instead of a colon) after the salutation in your cover letter can be reason enough for some to toss out your letter and résumé.

However, stay optimistic: if you are good at what you do, there will always be a place for you. You may find, though, that you need to continue to reinvent yourself throughout your career. If you keep your mindset geared toward change, you will succeed.

Here are some suggestions about what to include in your portfolio:

- *Purpose Statement.* To gain clarity and make effective career choices, write a purpose statement that reflects your life's mission.
- *Résumé.* Prepare your traditional and electronic résumés, tailoring your résumé for each job. Keep your résumé to two pages at *most*. For international corporations, prepare a curriculum vitae (CV).
- *Work Samples.* Select a few exhibits of your best work from previous jobs or classes: a letter, a report, a paper, and so on.
- *Reference Letters.* Ask for letters now, before you need them, using the salutation, "To Whom It May Concern."
- *Networking contacts.* Become an expert at networking on site and online. Networking is still the best way to find a job; and, like it or not, e-networking is here to stay.
- *Business Card.* Design your own job-search card with your name, e-mail address, phone number, and vital points about your skills.

Start with a three-ring binder; use tabs to organize the various parts. Keep an electronic file of everything that you collect so that you can transform your hard copy into an *e-portfolio*.

If you have a Facebook page, now is the time to edit it: prospective employers routinely screen applicants' social networking activity and photos. Also, make sure that you have a professional-sounding e-mail address!

The most important part of your job search is being able to verbalize your skills, qualities, and experience. Let's get started.

Skills, Not Titles or Degrees

Has anyone ever asked you, "What do you want to be when you . . . ?"

Most of us fumble with this question until we can answer it with a job title: teacher, accountant, mechanic, doctor, nurse, lawyer, engineer, and so on. However, titles and majors are *labels*, and they do not accurately reflect who you are or what you are capable of doing.

Do not limit yourself in the job market by being too attached to a job title or your college major. Keep your objective flexible—new job titles are created every day as traditional titles are eliminated.

Though a title will not follow you throughout your career, your skills, talents, and achievements will. Identify how your skills transfer to *any* business environment, and you gain a broader understanding of what you can offer.

Transferable Skills

Defining marketable skills is a challenge, especially when you think that you do not have any. By defining what you have achieved, you are able to see the unique qualities that you bring to an employer. Every exercise that you do in this chapter helps ready you for your interview.

Some of your skills have come from interests or hobbies, and you may not even be aware of what you have learned. Let's start to develop your job search profile by exploring these basic areas:

- Working with People
- Identifying Knowledge You Can Apply
- Identifying Personal Qualities

Working with People   *How do you work with people?* Consider formal and informal experiences at school, at your place of worship, with volunteer groups, on part- and full-time jobs, in sports activities, and in associations.

Here are some terms to open up your thinking. As you go through the list, notice your impressions as well as specific experiences that come to mind.

Selling	Giving feedback	Receiving feedback
Working on teams	Supervising	Working independently
Marketing	Expressing humor	Listening actively
Leading	Organizing projects	Organizing events
Delegating	Counseling	Care giving
Advising	Negotiating	Mediating
Entertaining	Serving	Phoning/soliciting
Cleaning	Being Compassion	Fixing
Training	Evaluating	Facilitating

Identify three of the terms listed above that seem to stand out among the others and that describe you. For each term, recall an experience in which you used your people skills successfully, for example:

> *Giving Feedback:* When working on a team project, I gave objective feedback that kept our team focused and on track. I deal well with conflict, so I was able to negotiate communication challenges among team members. As a result, we ended up with a successful project.

> *Serving:* I work part-time at the local diner and take pride in assisting our customers in whatever they need. Sometimes they can't make up their minds, and I'm honest about the best things to order, which develops loyal customers.

For each of the three terms you choose, give an example of how you used your people skills successfully, giving a specific example of an experience that demonstrates it.

Identifying Knowledge You Can Apply *In which areas have you developed knowledge?* In addition to formal learning, consider hobbies and interests. Read through the list below and circle three or more of the items that reflect your abilities:

Writing (composing, editing, revising) / Communication / Languages (speaking, writing, translating, interpreting) / Global Communication / Business Management / Accounting / Math / Statistics / Budgeting / Calculus / Science / Physics / Biology / Medicine / Pharmaceuticals / Music / Instruments / Voice / Theater / Film Making / Art / Archeology / Anthropology / Law / Criminal / Civil / Police Science / Political Science / History / Social Sciences / Psychology / Sociology / Social Work / Counseling / Physical Sciences / Sports / Nutrition / Cosmetology / Physical Therapy / Organizational Development / Human Resource Development / Fundraising / Child Care / Early Child Development Elementary or Secondary Education / Graphic Arts or Design / Interior Design

---

What other subjects or major areas can you identify? If need be, take out your college catalog and list specific classes and assignments that were particularly meaningful.

Can you come up with three or more areas in which you feel especially competent? For example:

> I feel confident with my *writing* skills. I can compose, edit, and revise e-mail messages, letters, and reports.

> I like working with *numbers*. I make a budget, follow it, and balance my checking account online; I also have good *computer skills*.

> *Nutrition* and *sports* have always been major interests. I *coach* my friends when we're at the gym and they've seen good results.

In the spaces below, identify three subjects and for each one write a sentence describing your experience or competence.

1._____

2._____

3._____

Working on Tasks *What kinds of tasks can you perform?* Consider all of the classes that you have taken as well as job experience, paid or volunteer. Also consider your hobbies and interests; these activities are important to employers.

Which tasks can you perform well? Which tasks do you enjoy? (Later in this chapter, you'll list part- and full-time jobs.) Use the list of nouns and verbs below to generate a list of tasks that you do well:

Computers / CAD / Keyboarding / Drafting / PowerPoint / Web Design
Automotives / Machinery / Repair / Design / Paint / Draw / Sketch
Sculpt / Construct / Build / Maintain / Restore / Analyze / Solve Problems
Trouble Shoot / Survey / Landscape / Gather Information / Organize and
File / Spreadsheets / Tables / Graphs / Letters / E-mail / Memos / Agendas
Minutes / Reports / Proposals / Set Goals / Canvass / Meet Quotas / Read
Write / Edit / Work with Children / Counsel / Wait Tables / Caddy Greet
and Receive / Clean Houses, Cars, or Offices / Play Music / Compose
Cashier / Style Hair / Drive / Walk Dogs / Care for Children / Coach
Groom Horses / Manage / Supervise

Though some of these tasks may not seem relevant to your ultimate career goal, every task you do well contributes to your unique career profile.

Give examples of successful experiences, for example:

> During my free time, I enjoy walking dogs. I posted an announcement in my neighborhood, and now I get several jobs a month. The dogs are fun to work with and their owners are grateful that I can help them out in a bind.
>
> My mother is a member of an organization that helps raise funds for the disease lupus. I helped the director by taking minutes at one of their meetings and then organized and filed papers in their office. I even made some calls to solicit money for fundraising. Every part of it was fun because I was helping people.
>
> My phone work is good. I enjoy making follow-up calls to tell people about a meeting or to let them know what we did at a meeting that they missed.

What tasks do you do well and enjoy? Give at least one detailed example below:

_____

_____

_____

In addition to the specific tasks that you performed, also describe what you learned about yourself and others from performing these tasks, for example:

> When I volunteered at the lupus organization, I acted friendly and confident, even though I didn't feel secure at first. I was also patient with clients on the phone. When I made a mistake, I took responsibility for it and corrected it quickly.
>
> When I posted the sign for my dog-walking business, I showed initiative and courage. I didn't know if I'd get any business and was very excited when people started to call.

This exercise is difficult because most people are used to doing a task rather than analyzing what they learned from it. Select three of your tasks or work experiences and record what you learned about your skills and attitudes.

The unfamiliar is challenging for everyone—until it becomes *familiar*. Reviewing tasks you do well builds your confidence, reminds you of your competence, and puts your job search into perspective.

Identifying Personal Qualities   You are unique whether or not you realize it. *What are your personal qualities that shape you into who you are? Which of the following qualities describe you?*

reliable	dependable	motivated	self-starter
persistent	optimistic	self-reliant	strong
independent	capable	fast learner	supportive
eager	focused	purposeful	task oriented
disciplined	friendly	persuasive	artistic
committed	easy going	encouraging	flexible
balanced	open minded	accepting	prompt
courteous	patient	dedicated	supportive
loyal	adaptable	credible	ethical
competent	kind	helpful	determined
confident	decisive	creative	enthusiastic
honest	responsible	self-learner	passionate

Close your eyes and reflect for a moment. *What adjectives come to mind when you think of yourself?*

_____

284 *A Guide for Business Writing*

Next, write three of your positive qualities below, and give examples of times when you displayed them to get a job done or help someone.

1. _____
   _____

2. _____
   _____

3. _____
   _____

Now that you have established several good qualities, list an area or two that you wish to improve; call them your *growing edges* if you wish.

Prospective employers do not expect you to be perfect, and they will ask about your weaknesses. By responding effectively, you have the perfect opportunity to show that your self-awareness leads to self-growth.

Because they interview hundreds of applicants, human resource (HR) professionals can see through insincere answers. By being honest yet optimistic about your weaknesses, you will actually score points. State your weakness in a constructive way. For example:

Don't Say: I'm late getting my work done sometimes, and I need to get control of my schedule.

Say: Sometimes I get so involved in solving a problem that I lose track of time. I'm working on time management so that my schedule is more balanced. Overall, it feels as if I have more time and more control over my time.

Don't Say: I feel frustrated working on a team, especially when others don't hold their weight. Sometimes I'm very critical.

Say: I prefer working independently than working on a team because I have more control over a project, but I am becoming more patient as well as learning how to give constructive feedback to move a project along.

Chapter 18: Job Search Tools **285**

Asking for Feedback   When you are on a job interview, one of the questions that you may be asked is "How do others perceive you?"

To prepare, ask three people who know you well to describe your skills and attitudes. Choose people who are positive and supportive. Let them know that you are doing research for your job search profile. If they are willing, ask if you could receive your feedback in writing via a short note or e-mail so that you can refer to it later.

Here are some questions you can ask:

- What are three adjectives that you would use to describe me?
- What are some tasks that you have seen me do well?
- In your eyes, what achievements have I made?
- Do you consider me a team player? A leader? A self-starter?
- What do you think are my growing edges or areas in which I can improve?

You may be surprised at how positively others perceive you. If you feel uncomfortable when you hear good things about yourself, simply say *thank you* and move on. The same advice is true if you hear negative things. Keep an open mind, and use the feedback to develop objectives for self-growth.

Take a few moments to reflect on the input that you received and record it, especially if it is all verbal.

Work Experience

Make a list of all paid or volunteer jobs you have had; for each, specify how long you had the job. Instead of giving start and end dates, you can just list the months and years and then quantify the time. For example:

Market Store, Part-time Cashier	January to March, 2010	7 weeks
	July to August, 2010	6 weeks
	December, 2010	3 weeks
	Total	about 4 months

Though you are concerned with dates, you also want to have an idea of the amount of time on the job. Quantify your experiences in terms of years and months or even weeks.

After you tally the specifics, you can list your experience as follows:

> Market Store, Part-time Cashier
>
> January to December, 2010   4 months

Now take a moment to record the jobs you have held and tally your job experience in months and years.

For each position, write a sentence or two that demonstrates the skills that you applied. Write active sentences using strong verbs, and avoid filler verbs and phrases, such as "I learned how to" or "I gained experience doing," as shown in the examples that follow.

Don't Say: While working as a cashier at Market Store, *I learned how to communicate* with all types of clients.

Say: While working as a cashier at Market Store, *I communicated* effectively with all of our clients.

Don't Say: While I volunteered at Benevolent Hospital, *I gained experience from assisting some of the* nurses distribute medication.

Say: While volunteering on the children's ward at Benevolent Hospital, *I assisted* nurses distribute medicine to children.

Don't Say: As an apprentice at the Car Exchange, *I was able to learn how* to make minor repairs.

Say: As an apprentice at the Car Exchange, *I assisted* in minor repairs such as changing oil, changing brake fluid, and assessing transmissions.

> **COACHING TIP**
>
> **What is your track record?**
>
> When you go on an interview, be prepared with an example to demonstrate one of your achievements.
>
> For example, perhaps you are the first person in your family to graduate from college or maybe you recently won an award. These types of notable experiences give prospective employers insight into your personality and interests as well as how you apply your skills.
>
> Of course, use discretion in choosing which achievements to cite. A prospective employer does not want to hear about personal milestones such as engagements or weddings; and no matter how cute your children are, save those stories for your friends and relatives.

Business Cards

Especially if you are new to the job market, create a business card. Select a few accomplishments and list them as bullet points on your card:

James B. Franklin   312.555.1212
                                                jbf@email.com

B.A., Journalism, Philadelphia College

- Three years of editorial experience
- Creative, Focused, and Motivated
- Excellent GPA and References

Your new business card is a useful tool for networking, providing your contact information and reminding associates of your skills.

Networking

Networking is the best way to secure a job. For example, you have a better chance of getting an interview by contacting someone you know at a company than by contacting human resources.

Networking has changed dramatically in recent years; the sooner you become networking savvy, the better. In her book *Graduate to LinkedIn: Jumpstart Your Career Network Now*, author Melissa Giovagnoli adds science to the art of networking, coining the term *networlding*.[1]

Professional networking groups give you a steady stream of new contacts. By doing a search of "online professional networking," you will discover many groups in which you can use your social skills to build your reputation and credibility within your field.

- *Connect with people who have similar goals and values.* Stay active and involved on site and online.

- *Build your network before you need it.* Start now and network on an ongoing basis so that you make contacts, remain visible, and get the support you need.

- *View networking as a communication exchange, not a one-sided dialog.* Before you call on someone to network, articulate why the meeting would be *mutually* beneficial. Look for common interests, experiences, or shared acquaintances.

- *Reciprocate favors: when you ask people for help, also ask what you can do for them in return.* You may find that an opportunity that did not work out for you is perfect for someone else.

- *View organizations within your field as career opportunities.* Through professional organizations, you will meet new people and have experiences that enhance your leadership skills.

- *Continue to network within your organization.* By networking within your organization, you build relationships as you promote your visibility and flexibility.

Volunteer to serve on committees, participate in focus groups, and attend company activities. Find new friends in the company cafeteria. Treat everyone at your organization with respect, including the support staff such as mailroom and cleaning personnel.

Job-Search Letters

Letters are important tools for initiating, developing, and following up with contacts and job prospects. Even though everyone seems to be using e-mail for everything, a hard-copy letter still makes a strong impression. Here are two types of letters that are part of the job search process:

1. Cover Letter
2. Thank-You Letter

Tailor every letter that you write to the specific position that you are going after and the company that you are sending it to. In addition, some companies prefer that all application letters and résumés be submitted online; other companies prefer to receive hard copies. Check each company's preference as you engage in your job search.

Let's review how to customize your letter.

Cover Letters

Send a cover letter with your résumé; or a *cover message*, if you send your résumé online. State why you would be the best person for the job and highlight your accomplishments. While your letter—or message—may not get you the job, a poorly written one will keep you from getting in the door to apply. Here are some guidelines that relate to job-search letters.

- *Know the name and title of the person to whom you are writing.* Do *not* address a letter to "Dear Sir" or "Dear Madam." Go to the company Web site or call to find out the addressee's name and its correct spelling.

- *Find out whether the company preference for receiving résumés is online or through the mail.* If you submit an application letter and résumé online, e-mail it to yourself first and print out your file to make sure it looks professional.

- *Stress what you can offer the organization.* Rather than focus on what you are looking for in a position, instead stress how your skills can benefit the organization.

- *Develop a plan for follow-up.* Take charge: do not expect others to contact you after they receive your information.

- *Aim for perfection:* your written communication creates a strong first impression. A letter of application presents high stakes. Write in the active voice, use the *you viewpoint,* and be concise.

A strong cover letter has an opening to capture the reader's attention but also identifies the job for which you are applying.

Example: The opportunity listed with CareerBuilder for a marketing associate is a great fit with my background and qualifications; my résumé is enclosed.

Example: Our mutual colleague Jennifer Lopez suggested that I have the talent and qualifications that you are looking for in a marketing associate. My enclosed résumé highlights some of that experience.

In the next paragraph, explain your special skills by listing some of your major accomplishments or qualifications that are relevant to the position you are seeking.

Example: As a recent college graduate, I have knowledge of the latest computer systems and accounting software. My degree in marketing includes a three-month internship. As an intern, I supported three vice presidents who trusted me with clients and managing their portfolios.

In the last part of your cover letter, request an interview. State that you will call within a specific time frame to find a mutually agreeable time to meet.

Example: I'd appreciate the opportunity to meet with you to discuss how my background can benefit your corporation. I will contact you the week of June 12 to see if we can meet.

Thus, the first paragraph identifies the job, the second paragraph explains your special skills, and the third paragraph is the call to action.

Be sure to follow up with your commitment to call. If the party is not available, ask if there is another time that would be convenient for you to call back. Leave your name and number, but do not feel slighted if you do not get a callback: the responsibility for communication is on your shoulders.

Follow-Up Letters and Thank-You Notes

Two of the most powerful tools in your job search toolkit are a follow-up e-mail and a handwritten thank-you note.

Your note will make a new networking associate or potential employer feel good for finding the time to meet with you or for making a call or two on your behalf.

If you choose to write a formal thank-you letter, you have another opportunity to sell yourself. Your letter allows you to restate your skills and accomplishments. Write a letter that is simple, friendly, and genuine. Do not use a boiler-plate, *one size fits all* message. Customize each letter, e-mail message, and handwritten note by specifically referring to something you discussed.

Get a business card from each of your contacts so that sending a note or e-mail takes less effort. Surprisingly, no matter how good the results are when letters are sent, few thank-you letters are actually written.

Dear Elaine:

Looking for a job in today's job market is extremely stressful, but meeting helpful individuals like you makes the journey easier.

I have contacted Joe, as you suggested, and will keep you informed on my progress. If I can assist you in any way, do not hesitate to contact me. I would be pleased to put my strong computer skills to use on your behalf!

Again, thank you for your valuable time and advice.

Sincerely,

Sophie

---

292 *A Guide for Business Writing*

Figure 18.1 | Sample Cover Letter

Keep your cover letter short, and a prospective employer is more likely to read it. Write your letter so the reader can pick up key information from a glance.

Rosalie D. Lindsey
1212 Arquilla Lane
Winter Haven, FL 35319

January 6, 2011

Ms. Jane Fleming
Human Resource Manager
The Writer's Toolkit, Inc.
8007 Nashville Boulevard
Tallahassee, FL 35316

Dear Ms. Fleming:

Thank you for the time that you spent discussing opportunities at The Writer's Toolkit.

My résumé is enclosed. As you can see, I've worn a number of hats in the publishing field—writing, editing and managing—almost all in the areas of marketing and advertising.

I will follow up with you soon to find out if there is a convenient time for us to meet.

Sincerely,

Rosalie D. Lindsey
Enclosures

The Résumé

Human resource executives and hiring managers receive hundreds of résumés for every job opening. What will make your résumé stand out among others?

Brevity is critical: highlight your experience effectively on one page; at any rate, do not exceed two pages.

Do not use flamboyant fonts or fancy paper: use conservative fonts such as Times New Roman and Arial (use one font for the body and another for headings) and crisp, white heavy-weight bond paper. Customize your résumé for the specific job that you are applying for.

Chronological Formatting

The *chronological format* lists your education, work experience, and accomplishments in order, starting with the most recent and working backward in order of occurrence.

Because this format is the more traditional, readers find it easy to evaluate your background quickly and to see a history of steady promotions or increased responsibility. To produce a clean, crisp résumé, do the following:

- Use *career focus* or *summary* rather than *objective*; however, make sure that prospective employer understands at a glance the job or job category for which you are applying.
- Be specific about your accomplishments; quantify your achievements when possible.
- Apply parallel structure (represent words in a consistent form).
- Keep your résumé to one page if you can, two pages if you cannot.

Write your résumé to answer questions *before* they arise. On your cover letter, fill in gaps of unemployment that might appear on your résumé. Employers assume you are telling the truth until they find out otherwise. When employers check specific details, they usually do so only after they have already decided to hire you.

Figure 18.2 | Sample Chronological Résumé

In her book, Happy About My Resume, *Barbara Safani gives cutting-edge tips on building an effective résumé, including how to use formatting to set your résumé apart from the crowd.*[2]

PAT VINCENT

109 Hillcrest Avenue
Downers Grove, IL 60515
(630) 555-1212 (H) • (630) 555-1212 (C)
pv@email.com

CAREER FOCUS

Dedicated **administrative professional** with extensive experience in office and facilities management, meeting planning, and computer applications. Good organizer who can lead, train, and motivate.

EXPERIENCE

Professional Doctors, Chicago, Illinois   June 2008 to Present
Executive Assistant

- Scheduling calendar, appointments, files, and travel.
- Contacting attorneys, doctors, and patients.
- Renewing state and federal licenses.
- Coordinating building issues, such as furniture and office moves.
- Ordering office supplies.
- Composing correspondence and completing monthly reports.

EDUCATION

B.A., Business Management, Best College
A.A., Communications, Ivy Tech

SKILLS

Word, Excel, PowerPoint, WordPerfect, Lotus Notes, Harvard Graphics, AIM, Calendar Creator Plus, Pegasus, Outlook E-mail, Internet (Orbitz & Expedia)

Electronic Formatting (E-Résumés)

An electronic résumé (e-résumé) provides the same information as a traditional résumé.[1]

Here are tips for your e-résumé:

- Use a maximum of 65 characters per line.
- Omit italics and underlines.
- Include a key-word summary at the top of the page.
- Adhere to parallel structure and end verbs in their *ing* form, for example, "answering phone and e-mail messages."

Send your electronic résumé through e-mail, attached as part of online applications or posted on the Internet within personal Web pages. On your electronic résumé, include a *key word summary*.

Place a *key word summary* that consists of 20 to 30 words at the top of the page after your name and contact information:

- Use words and phrases that highlight your education and experience.
- Customize your summary with words used in the description of the job for which you are applying.

On a traditional résumé, you describe your work experience in verb phrases that begin with strong action verbs (such as managed, supervised, processed). Instead, on an e-résumé, key word summaries consist of noun and adjective phrases, such as "fluent in Spanish," "team-oriented," or "strong communication skills." Emphasize your knowledge, experience, and skills that are likely to attract prospective employers.

Employers report receiving thousands of résumés for jobs listed online. Unless the job advertisement calls for "apply by e-mail only," the best approach is to respond with a traditional résumé and cover letter. At one time you would have gotten noticed in a good way by dropping off your résumé in person; however, that is not the case in the current job market.

Figure 18.3 | Sample E-Résumé

Customize your key word summary for each position for which you apply.

PAT VINCENT
109 Hillcrest Avenue, Downers Grove, IL 60615
E-mail: pv@email.com
630-555-1212

KEYWORDS

leadership and management ability, communication and writing skills, graphic arts, digital arts, Office 2010, Flash MX, Dreamweaver MX, JavaScript, analytic, willing to travel, college graduate

OBJECTIVE

A position in which I can use my management, communication, and leadership skills to grow within an organization that has an environmental mission.

EDUCATION

BA, Business Management, Best College

AA, Communications, Ivy Tech

Related courses: psychology, journalism, political science

Diploma, South Side High School, Downers Grove, Illinois
Graduated 2006

WORK EXPERIENCE

Professional Doctors, Chicago, Illinois, 2008 to present

Scheduling and maintaining calendar, appointments, files, and travel; contacting attorneys, doctors, and patients; renewing State and Federal licenses; composing correspondence and completing monthly reports.

SKILLS

Word, Excel, PowerPoint, WordPerfect, Lotus Notes, Harvard Graphics, AIM, Calendar Creator Plus, Pegasus, Outlook E-mail, Internet (Orbitz & Expedia)

Though traditional résumés contain tabs and bolding for headers such as *Education* and *Experience*, e-résumés lack tabs and highlighting. E-mail programs usually have difficulty reading tabs and highlighting, so remove both to ensure your recipient receives your résumé in tact.

Here's how to change your traditional résumé into an electronic one:

1. Remove all highlighting: bolding, underlining, and italics.
2. Eliminate bullets, and replace them with dashes, small o's, or asterisks.
3. Move all your text to the left.
4. Remove returns except for those separating major sections.
5. Use all capitals for headers.
6. Provide an additional line or two of spacing between sections.
7. Save the file in ASCII or Rich-Text Format.

To send your electronic résumé, start with a *subject line* that states the title of the job for which you are applying, such as "Graphic Arts Applicant." Then copy and paste your cover letter followed by your résumé within an e-mail.

Check first before sending your traditionally-formatted résumé as an attachment. Employers are reluctant to open attachments from applicants whom they do not know. In your cover letter, refer to the résumé that follows. Then copy and paste your letter into the e-mail first and follow it with your résumé.

Quick Skills Pitch

By developing a quick pitch of your skills, you will be ready for any networking event or even the impromptu meeting of a potential employer.

Think of the quick pitch as an *elevator speech: a short monologue that provides vital information*, keeping the listener's attention and peaking their interest. Create an actual script that you memorize—but be sure to sound natural when you use it.

Here is an example of a quick skills pitch:

> Hi. My name is Reggie Jones, and I have a degree in communications. As well as specializing in effective communication systems, I am a good team player with strong leadership qualities. Would you be interested in receiving my résumé, or do you have any positions that I might apply for?

Your elevator speech should take no more than *ten seconds*. Give the listener enough honest information that highlights key reasons how you could contribute to his or her company.

Before you end your conversation, get contact information and find out how you should send your information: electronic copy or hard copy.

Recap

Finding a job is itself a job. Commit to preparing your career portfolio as well as preparing your mindset toward success.

You have worked hard to build your skills. Though searching for a job might feel daunting, the best response is to take action and stay active until you achieve your dreams. As Leonardo daVinci is credited for saying,

> "Inaction weakens the vigors of the mind . . . action strengthens the essence of creation."

Take action: *Do the work, and you will see the results.*

Job-Search Checklist:

_____ Write your career objective or personal mission statement.

_____ Create a personal business card.

_____ Collect samples of your written work.

_____ Compose a sample cover letter.

_____ Prepare your résumés: chronological and electronic format.

_____ Ask two to three contacts for a letter of reference.

_____ Prepare a list of networking opportunities.

_____ Buy heavy-weight bond paper and envelopes for résumés and letters.

Writing Workshop
Topic A: Writing a Self-Appraisal

Instructions: Write an honest self-appraisal.

- What are your strengths? Your best qualities?
- What are some of your recent accomplishments?
- What are your growing edges?

As part of this activity, write two or three goals, identify specific steps to achieve them, and include a time frame for each step. By including a time frame, you are creating an *action plan*.

Finally, write yourself a letter of recommendation identifying your best qualities and highlighting your skills and abilities. Give yourself the same kinds of words of encouragement that you would give your best friend. Keep your letter and refer to it periodically.

Topic B: Writing a Thank-You Letter

Thank-you letters are important job-search tools. Who would you like to recognize for assisting you? *A networking contact? An interviewer? A friend or family member?*

By taking the time to send a thank-you note, you are setting yourself apart from the crowd.

Résumé Worksheet

Career Focus

_____

_____

Summary

_____

_____

Education

School/College   **Degree to Be Conferred**

_____   _____

Major: _____   **Minor:** _____

School/College   **Degree Conferred**

_____   _____

Major: _____   **Minor:** _____

Skills and Training

_____

_____

Clubs and Extra-Curricular Activities

_____

_____

Job Experience Summary

For each position, list several job duties or tasks that you performed. Start each with a strong verb and maintain parallel structure.

Position	Job Duties or Tasks
1._____	_____
From ____ to ____	_____
	_____
Total time: ____	_____
2._____	_____
From ____ to ____	_____
	_____
Total time: ____	_____
3._____	_____
From ____ to ____	_____
	_____
Total time: ____	_____

End Notes

1. Melissa Giovagnoli-Wilson, *Graduate to LinkedIn*, Networlding Publishing, 2010.
2. Barbara Safani, *Happy About My Resume: 50 Tips for Building a Better Document to Secure a Better Future*, Happy About, 2008.

More Mechanics

Part 1: Capitalization and Number Usage
Part 2: Quotation Marks, Apostrophes, and Hyphens
Part 3: Similar Words and Spelling Tips

Though you have already covered the critical elements of mechanics, many little details still linger. Since you are well on your way to becoming an incurable editor, these final details will turn you into an expert editor.

Capitalization and number usage may give you headaches, but learning only a few simple rules helps clear up the confusion. Then there are quotation marks, apostrophes, and hyphens. Memorizing how to use these marks is unrealistic, so instead go over them with the goal of becoming familiar with them. You know where to find the rules when you need them.

Improving your vocabulary improves your critical thinking skills as much as it improves the quality of your writing. Go over the similar words, such as *affect/effect* and *loan/lend*; in this chapter, some surprises await you. Develop a plan to improve your vocabulary, whether by working with the Greek and Latin roots or by subscribing to a daily e-newsletter. Use each new word in context, so it becomes part of your thinking. Repetition is a key to learning language arts.

Grammar and mechanics are trivial compared to the critical thinking behind the writing: your ability to use writing to solve problems is key to a successful career. However, knowing the grammar and mechanics of writing gives you more confidence and credibility.

Now go have some fun with the mechanics of writing!

Part 1

Capitalization and Number Usage

Capitalization decisions can be confusing. Some words and titles sound official, so they simply *must* be capitalized, right? However, you may be surprised to learn that most of the time those official-sounding words and titles are not capitalized: they are not proper nouns. Instead of wasting time and energy guessing, this chapter gives you the information that you need to make most capitalization decisions.

Then there is number usage. When you stop to decide whether to spell out a number in words or to use numerals, you waste time. Knowing a few basic number rules makes a big difference in how you use numbers in your writing.

Let's start with capitalization and then work on number usage.

CAPITALIZATION

Many writers are naïve about capitalization. Instead of respecting the basics and staying safe, they capitalize words almost randomly. However, capitalization becomes easy by learning a few simple rules. Let's start with the following:

> When in doubt, do *not* capitalize.

Unless you know for sure that a word should be capitalized, leave the word in lower case. Here are the two major categories of words that should be capitalized:

- Proper nouns
- First words of sentences, poems, displayed lists, and so on

The challenge then becomes knowing which words are proper nouns and which are common nouns. Let's start by taking a look at the difference between the two and then identifying some of the most common types of capitalization errors.

Proper Nouns and Common Nouns

To avoid capitalizing common nouns, you must first learn the difference between common nouns and proper nouns. The chart below helps illuminate some of the differences:

Proper Noun	Common Noun
John Wilson	name, person, friend, business associate
Wilson Corporation	company, corporation, business
Southlake Mall	shopping, stores, shops
New York	state, city
Italy	country

Words derived from proper nouns become proper adjectives and are also capitalized:

Proper Noun	Derivative or Proper Adjective
England	English language
Spain	Spanish 101
Italy	Italian cookware
French	French class

Names are proper nouns, and that includes the names of people as well as the names of places and things, such as the following:[2]

Titles of literary and artistic works	Chicago Tribune, the Bible
Periods of time and historical events	Great Depression
Imaginative names and nicknames	Big Apple
Brand and trade names	IBM, 3M, Xerox copier

Points of the compass	the North, the South, the Southwest *(when they refer to specific geographic regions)*
Place names	Coliseum, Eiffel Tower
Organization names	National Business Education Association
Words derived from proper nouns	English, South American
Days of the week, months, and holidays	Thanksgiving, Christmas, Chanukah

Articles, Conjunctions, and Prepositions

Not every word of a title is capitalized, and the types words in question are articles, conjunctions, and prepositions. Here's what to look for:

Articles:	the, a, an
Conjunctions:	and, but, or, for, nor
Prepositions:	between, to, at, among, from, over, *and so on*

Here are rules about capitalizing articles, conjunctions, and prepositions:

1. Capitalize any of these words when it is the first word of a title or subtitle.

2. Capitalize prepositions only when they are the first or last word of a title or subtitle. (However, this preference varies among sources, with some sources saying to capitalize prepositions when they consist of four letters; others, when they consist of five or more letters.)

Here are some examples that display prepositions and conjunctions:

> The University of Chicago
> *Pride and Prejudice*
> *Writing from the Core*

First Words

As you have already seen, the *first word* is given special designation. Make sure that you capitalize the first word of each of the following:[3]

> Sentences
>
> Poems
>
> Direct quotations that are complete sentences
>
> Independent questions within a sentence
>
> Items displayed in a list or an outline
>
> Salutations and closings

Also capitalize the first word of a complete sentence that follows a word of caution or instruction, such as *Note* or *Caution*.

Hyphenated Terms

At times, you will need to determine how to capitalize hyphenated words, such as e-mail, long-term, up-to-date, and so on. Here are some guidelines:

- Capitalize parts of the hyphenated word that are proper nouns:

    If I receive your information by mid-December, you will qualify for the training.

- Capitalize the first word of a hyphenated word when it is the first word of the sentence, for example:

    E-mail is the preferred mode of communication.

    Mid-January is when the quarterly reports are expected.

- Capitalize each word of a hyphenated term used in a title (except short prepositions and conjunctions, as previously noted), for example:

Up-to-Date Reports	Mid-July Conference
E-Mail Guidelines	Long-Term Outlook

Let's look at titles and terms associated with organizations, for which capitalization decisions can also be challenging.

Organizational Titles and Terms

Most people believe that their job title is a proper noun, but professional titles are *not* proper nouns.

Here are some rules to follow:

- Capitalize a professional title when it precedes the name.
- Do not capitalize a professional title when it follows the name.
- Capitalize organizational terms, such as the names of departments and committees, in your own company (but not necessarily other companies).

Here are some examples:

Incorrect: John Smith, Vice President, will be meeting with the Finance Department.

Corrected: John Smith, vice president, will be meeting with the Finance Department.

Corrected: Vice President John Smith will be meeting with the Finance Department.

You may capitalize organizational terms from other companies to show special importance. In addition, the titles of high government officials are capitalized, for example:

The President had a meeting in the West Wing of the White House.

Two Common Capitalization Errors

You will have improved your skills significantly if you stop capitalizing words randomly and follow the rules discussed above. However, the two common types of errors discussed here are in a class of their own.

Error No. 1: Leaving the pronoun *I* in lower case.

The personal pronoun *I* is a proper noun: *always* represent it in upper case. Partly due to text messaging, the problem of leaving the personal pronoun *I* in lower case has escalated, for example:

Incorrect: A friend asked me if i could help, so i said that i would.
Corrected: A friend asked if I could help, so I said that I would.

Whenever you use the pronoun *I*, capitalize it; and that includes its use in e-mail messages.

Error No. 2: Using all UPPER CASE or all lower case.

Another type of error that occurs, especially with e-mail, is typing in either all lower case or all upper case. Neither version is correct, using all upper case has earned the reputation that the writer is shouting. The truth is, the writer is not necessarily shouting. Most of the time, when writers use all caps, it is because they are unsure about writing decisions; putting the message in all caps (inaccurately) seems to be an easy way out.

When writers use all lower case, it often reflects a tradition within certain professional niches. For example, some computer professionals communicate primarily with other technical professionals, and they write to each other almost exclusively in lower case.

When communicating to professionals outside of their inner circle, these technical professionals sometimes continue to leave their words in lower case. For these professionals, adjusting to their audience is the key: Distinguish who is within your circle and who is not and then adapt accordingly.

Global Communication and the Rules

Most professional communication is now global communication: global communication involves English is a second language (ESL) speakers and writers.

Global communication makes following the rules, such as the ones discussed throughout this book, critical for clear communication. That is because ESL speakers find it difficult to understand deviations from the rules. Using a second language according to the standard rules is hard enough, and adapting to the idiosyncrasies that result from misuse of language adds another layer of confusion.

The rules create standards so that everyone can understand the meaning of the message, reducing confusion and misunderstanding among all readers. Following the rules is an important element of adapting to your audience. In addition, by writing correctly, you enhance your ability to communicate across borders and continents.

PRACTICE PART 1.1

Capitalization

Instructions: In the following paragraph, correct errors in capitalization.

Next year the President of my Company will provide a Financial Incentive for all employees, and i plan to participate in it. Jack Edwards, Vice President of Finance, will administer the plan. Everyone in my Department is looking forward to having the opportunity to save more. A Pamphlet entitled, "Financial Incentives For Long-term Savings" will describe the plan and be distributed next Week. If the Pamphlet has not arrived by friday, i will check with the Vice President's office to find out the details.

Note: See page 369 for the key to the above exercise.

NUMBER USAGE

Many writers, unaware of number rules, do not even stop to consider how to represent numbers. Other writers, aware of the rules but unsure of the details, seek every possible way to represent numbers, thinking that they will be right at least some of the time.

The only way to break the confusion is to learn the rules; however, the rules can seem complex at times. For example, the first number rule states the following:

> Write numbers under ten as words,
> but write numbers above ten as figures.

After this basic rule, every additional rule is some form of exception to it. In fact, *The Gregg Reference Manual* states that, when the writer wants the numbers to stand out, all numbers can be represented as figures—including those under ten.

The number rules are not that difficult to learn, and your only other option is to guess, which creates more confusion for you than it creates for your readers. However, when you do guess, at least represent numbers consistently—do not go back and forth, representing a number as a word in one place and then as a numeral in the next. Let's get started with the basics.

Ten Basic Number Rules

The following list of ten basic number rules provides a foundation for making most decisions about how to display numbers.[2]

Rule 1: Numbers 1 through 10

Spell out numbers 1 through 10 within written text (unless displaying the numbers for quick reference); use numerals for numbers above 10.

For example: I have ten reports to complete.

Our department recognized 12 employees for providing excellent client service.

Rule 2: Numbers Beginning a Sentence

Spell out numbers beginning a sentence (however, avoid starting a sentence with a number whenever possible). If you start a sentence with a number, all numbers in that sentence must be spelled out.

For example: Sixteen new chairs and twelve new desks have arrived for offices on the fourth floor.

Rule 3: Related Numbers

Use the same form for related numbers within a sentence, with figures trumping words. In other words, if some numbers should be written in words (numbers under 10) and they are mixed with numbers that are above 10, write all numbers in figures.

For example: Bob Anderson brought 12 new individual clients as well as 5 new corporate accounts to our firm.

Rule 4: Unrelated Numbers

When two unrelated numbers come together, write the shorter number in words and the longer number in figures.

For example: Order 7 two-piece organizational units for the employees my department.

Rule 5: Indefinite Numbers

Write indefinite numbers, such as thousands or hundreds, in words.

For example: You say that you have hundreds of problems.
Thousands of people support you.

Rule 6: Ordinal Numbers

Write ordinal numbers such as *first*, *second*, or *third*, and so on, in words.

For example: Lorraine lives on the fourteenth floor at 900 North Lake Shore Drive.

Rule 7: Large Numbers

Numbers in the millions or higher can be written as a combination of figures and words if the number can be expressed as a whole number or as a whole number plus a simple fraction or a decimal amount.

For example: Our company extended their $1.5 million loan until April.

Rule 8. Fractions and Mixed Numbers

Write fractions as words with a hyphen between the numerator and denominator; write mixed numbers as figures.

For example: Mix one-half of the dry ingredients before adding any liquid.

Increase the amount of tomatoes to 2½ cups.

Rule 9. Percentages

Use figures for percentages and spell out the word *percent* unless the percentage is part of a table or technical material. Use the word *percentage* rather than *percent* when no number appears with it.

For example: Chicago had a 10 percent decrease in crime last year.

That lower percentage pleased the mayor.

Rule 10. Weights and Measures

Use figures for weights, measures, and other types of dimensions.

For example: If you can lose 10 pounds, you are a better person than I am.

The new room needs a carpet that is 10 feet by 15 feet.

In addition to these ten basic rules, dates and time have special guidelines, which we will look at next.

Dates and Time

Dates and time are commonly used in e-mail messages as well as other formal types of communication. Here are some basic guidelines:

- Use figures for dates and time on everything except formal invitations.
- Use the abbreviations *a.m.* and *p.m.* or the word *o'clock*, but not both.
- Spell out the names of days and months: do not abbreviate.
- For time on the hour, you may omit the :00 (unless you want to emphasize time on the hour).
- Use the ordinal ending for dates only when the day *precedes* the month.

Here are some examples:

Incorrect: The meeting is scheduled for Sept. 17th at 5 PM.
Corrected: The meeting is scheduled for September 17 at 5 p.m.

Incorrect: Will you be available at 8:30 AM on the sixteenth of this month?
Corrected: Will you be available at 8:30 a.m. on the 16th of this month?

Now let's review how to represent addresses and phone numbers.

Addresses and Phone Numbers

As with dates, parts of addresses should not be abbreviated. So before reviewing the rules for addresses and phone numbers, here is a guideline:

> When in doubt, spell it out.

Abbreviate parts of addresses when space is tight or when you are following a specific system of addressing. However, do not abbreviate simply for the convenience of it.

Here are some rules for displaying addresses:

- Spell out parts of addresses: Do not abbreviate points of the compass such as *North* or *South* or words such as *avenue, street,* or *apartment*.
- Spell out street names *One* through *Ten*.
- Use figures for all house numbers except the number *One*.
- Add ordinal endings only when points of the compass (North, South, East, and West) are not included, for example: 1400 59th Street.
- Use two-letter state abbreviations.
- Leave one or two spaces between the two-letter state abbreviation and the zip code.

Here are some examples:

Mr. Alistair Cromby
One West Washington Avenue
St. Clair, MN 56080

Dr. Michael Jules
1214 79th Place, Suite 290
Chesterton, IN 46383

Ms. Lionel Hershey
141 Meadow Lane South
Seattle, WA 92026

Ms. Lorel Lindsey
Associate Director
The Fine Arts Studio
500 North State Street, Suite 311
Chicago, IL 60611-6043

In general, the broadest part of an address is on the last line (the name of the country or the name of the city and state), as shown above and below.

Mr. Lucas M. Matthews
72 O'Manda Road
Lake Olivia, VIC 3709
AUSTRALIA

Pierluigi e Sylvia D'Amici
Via Davide No. 1
00151 ROMA
I T A L I A

On the next page, you will find a list of two-letter state abbreviations.

Two-Letter State Abbreviations

Alabama	AL	Montana	MT
Alaska	AK	Nebraska	NE
Arizona	AZ	Nevada	NV
Arkansas	AR	New Hampshire	NH
California	CA	New Jersey	NJ
Colorado	CO	New Mexico	NM
Connecticut	CT	New York	NY
Delaware	DE	North Carolina	NC
District of		North Dakota	ND
Columbia	DC	Ohio	OH
Florida	FL	Oklahoma	OK
Georgia	GA	Oregon	OR
Guam	GU	Pennsylvania	PA
Hawaii	HI	Puerto Rico	PR
Idaho	ID	Rhode Island	RI
Illinois	IL	South Carolina	SC
Indiana	IN	South Dakota	SD
Iowa	IA	Tennessee	TN
Kansas	KS	Texas	TX
Kentucky	KY	Utah	UT
Louisiana	LA	Vermont	VT
Maine	ME	Virgin Islands	VI
Maryland	MD	Virginia	VA
Massachusetts	MA	Washington	WA
Michigan	MI	West Virginia	WV
Minnesota	MN	Wisconsin	WI
Mississippi	MS	Wyoming	WY
Missouri	MO		

Display phone numbers by using a hyphen or period between parts, for example:

> You can reach me at 312-555-1212.
>
> I left the message at 502.555.1212.

PRACTICE PART 1.2
Numbers

Instructions: Make corrections to the way numbers are displayed in the following sentences.

Incorrect: Reggie sent 10 copies of the report, but I received only 5.
Corrected: Reggie sent ten copies of the report, but I received only five.

1. We r meeting on Jan. 5 at 10 AM at our offices on Lake St.
2. Call me on Mon. at (407) 555-1212.
3. Alex lists his address as 407 S. Maple St., Hobart, Ind. 46368.
4. We received 100s of calls about the job opening but only five résumés.
5. Purchase 12 laptops but only seven new printers for our department.

Note: See page 369 for the key to the above exercise.

Recap

Below is a summary of the rules and guidelines that you have learned in this chapter.

Capitalize the following:

- The personal pronoun *I*.
- Proper nouns and their derivatives, such as *England* and *English*.
- The first words of sentences, poems, displayed lists, and so on.
- Titles that precede a name, such as *President Gerry Smith*.
- The names of departments within your own organization.

Represent numbers as follows:

- Spell out numbers 1 through 10; use numbers if you want them to stand out.
- Use figures for numbers above 10.
- If numbers above and below 10 are in a sentence, use figures.
- Use numbers with the word *percent*, as in 25 percent.
- Use the word *percentage* (rather than *percent*) when used without a number.

Display dates, time, and addresses as follows:

- Do not abbreviate: *When in doubt, spell it out.*
- Omit the :00 for time on the hour.
- Use a.m. and p.m. or o'clock, but do not use both.
- Use two-letter state abbreviations.

Writing Workshop

Topic: What Is Listening?

Steven Covey's advice on listening is "Seek first to understand, then to be understood."

What does this advice mean to you? How can you become a more effective listener? How can becoming a more effective listener enhance your life and relationships?

You may have found that writing is itself a listening tool. As you put your insights and feelings on the page, you connect with a deeper part of yourself. When you pause to listen to your innermost thoughts, you are giving yourself a valuable gift.

Editing Workshop
Draft

Instructions: Correct the errors in the following e-mail message. You will find a variety of errors, including errors in capitalization and number usage as well as punctuation.

Dear Victoria;

THANK YOU for asking for more information about my work history. For 5 yrs. i worked for Rapid Communications as an Associate Manager in the Customer Service Dept. Here's info about how to contact my former boss Jake Roberts, Human Resources Director:

Mr Jake Roberts
Human Resources Dir.
Rapid Com.
14 N. Ogden Rd.
Burlington Iowa   52601
Jake.roberts@rc.com
(209-555-3465)

I look forward to hearing from u. You can reach me at (209) 555-1212 anytime between 9:00 AM and 5 o'clock PM Mon. thru Fri. until the end of Aug.
Best Regards,

Sylvia Marina

Revision

Dear Victoria,

Thank you for asking for more information about my work history.

For five years, I have worked for Rapid Communications as an associate manager in the Customer Service Department. Feel free to contact my former manager, Jake Roberts, human resources director. Here's his contact information:

Mr. Jake Roberts
Human Resources Director
Rapid Communications
14 North Ogden Road
Burlington, IA 52601

jake.roberts@rc.com
209-555-3465

You can reach me at 209-555-1212 between 9 a.m. and 5 p.m., Monday through Friday, until the end of August. I look forward to hearing from you.

Best regards,

Sylvia Marina

Endnotes

1. William A. Sabin, *The Gregg Reference Manual*, Tenth Edition, McGraw-Hill/Irwin, 2005.
2. Dona Young, *Business English: Writing for the Global Workplace*, McGraw-Hill Higher Education, Burr Ridge, 2008, page 208.
3. *Ibid.*, pages 212-213.

Part 2

Quotation Marks, Apostrophes, and Hyphens

Quotation marks, apostrophes, and hyphens are minor marks of punctuation, but they occur frequently: using them correctly improves the quality of writing and enhances its credibility.

QUOTATION MARKS

The primary reasons for using quotation marks are as follows:[1]

1. Inserting a direct quote of three or fewer lines within the body of a document.
2. Identifying technical terms or coined expressions that may be unfamiliar.
3. Using words humorously or ironically.
4. Showing a slang expression or an intentionally misused word.

However, do not use quotation marks to make a word stand out, for example:

>That is a really "good" idea.

In the above example, your reader will assume that you really do not mean the idea is *good* because the reader may assume you were being sarcastic. To avoid overuse of quotation marks, follow this motto:

>When in doubt, leave quotations out.

Quotation Marks with Periods and Commas

One of the reasons that quotation marks confuse writers is that there are two basic ways to display them: the **closed style** and the **open style**. Here is the major difference between the two:

- *Closed style:* Place quotation marks on the outside of commas and periods.
- *Open style:* Place quotation marks on the inside of commas and periods.

Here are a few examples:

Closed: Bill's exact words were, "That dog can't hunt."

The president said that he wanted "the data," but which data?

Open: Reginald described the situation as "grim but not hopeless".

Terry instructed me to put the package in the "boot of the car", so I did.

If you live in the United States, use the *closed style*; if you live in Great Britain, use the open style. (This book applies the *closed style*.)

Quotation Marks with Semicolons and Colons

For semicolons and colons, *always* place the quotation marks on the inside of the semicolon or colon, for example:

Senior management wants us to "go the extra mile"; however, everyone seems to be burnt out already.

Bryan said, "George's bid is overpriced": Is that correct?

According to policy, "Distribution of funds can be made only before the 15th of the month"; therefore, your funds will be sent in 10 days.

Quotation Marks with Questions and Exclamations

When using quotation marks with a question mark or an exclamation point, determine whether the question or exclamation is part of the quote or the entire sentence, for example:

> Did Iva say, "Rose is getting married next month"?
>
> Fred asked, "How do you know?"
>
> Iva said, "Rose is getting married next month!"
>
> I just won "the grand prize"!

Short Quotes and Long Quotes

Display short quotations (three lines or fewer) with quotation marks, leaving the quote in the body of the paragraph. However, for quotations four lines or longer, do not use quotation marks; instead set off the quote from the body of your writing by indenting it by five spaces on each side.

Here is an example of a short quote:

> According to Campbell, "Protein, the most sacred of all nutrients, is a vital component of our bodies and there are hundreds of thousands of different kinds."[2] Different kinds of proteins play different roles in health and nutrition, and some of these are discussed.

Quotation within a Quotation

When you need to display a quotation within a quotation, use the single quotation mark (') for the inner quotation and the double quotation mark (") for the outer quotation, for example:

> Bob said, "I'm not going to 'insult' George by inviting him to the meeting."

Complete the following exercise using the closed quotation style.

PRACTICE PART 2.1

Quotation Marks

Instructions: Place closed quotation marks where needed below.

Incorrect: Beth's exact words were, "I'll be in Boston next week".

Corrected: Beth's exact words were, "I'll be in Boston next week."

1. My answer to your request is an enthusiastic "yes".
2. If you think that's a "good idea", the so do I!.
3. The code was "307A", not "370A".
4. All he wrote was, "Our dog can hunt".
5. If you call that "good timing", I don't know how to respond.

Note: See page 369 for the key to the exercise below.

APOSTROPHES

The apostrophe (') is used for contractions and possessives. Since possessives are a bit more complicated than contractions, let's review possessives first.

Possessives

When a noun shows possession of another noun, use the apostrophe to show ownership. Regular nouns are made possessive as follows:

- For a singular possessive noun, place the apostrophe before the s ('s).
- For a plural possessive noun, place the apostrophe after the s (s').
- If a noun ends in an s, add an apostrophe and s ('s) or simply an apostrophe (').

Singular Possessive	**Plural Possessive**
the cat's whiskers	the cats' toys
the dog's scarf	the dogs' bones
Mary's books	my friends' books

326   *A Guide for Business Writing*

Here are a few examples of names and other nouns ending in *s* and showing possession:

> Francis' new job *or* Francis's new job
> Mr. Jones' office *or* Mr. Jones's office

When pronunciation would sound awkward with the extra syllable, do not add the *s* after the apostrophe, as follows:

> Los Angeles' weather
> the witnesses' replies

Irregular nouns are a bit tricky: place the apostrophe before the s ('s) for both singular and plural possession:

Singular Possessive	**Plural Possessive**
the child's coat	the children's toys
the woman's comment	the women's association
a man's advice	the men's sporting event

The easiest way to work with plural possessives—whether regular or irregular—is to make the noun plural first and then show the possession.

To show joint possession, place the apostrophe after the second name, for example:

> Janet and Bob's car

To show individual possession, place the apostrophe after each name, for example:

> Janet's and Bob's cars

Next, let's look at a category of possessives that often goes unnoticed, inanimate possessives.

Inanimate Possessives

Possessives are easier to spot when a person possesses an object, such as *Bob's car*. However, an inanimate object, such as *wind* or *newspaper* can also show possession, for example:

    the wind's force   the newspaper's headline

To know if a word shows possession, flip the phrase around. If you need to use the word *of*, in all likelihood the word shows possession, for example:

    the force of the wind   the headline of the newspaper

Here are more examples:

    the ending of the play   the play's ending
    the work of the day   the day's work
    the cover of the book   the book's cover
    the fender of the car   the car's fender

Now let's look at another common use of apostrophes: contractions.

Contractions

Some words, primarily verbs, can be shortened by omitting a few letters and using the apostrophe in their place, for example:

Verb	**Contraction**
will not	won't
cannot	can't
did not	didn't
should not	shouldn't

Contractions are acceptable for e-mail; however, avoid using contractions for formal or academic writing. The contraction "it's" creates problems for writers. *It's* is the contraction for *it is* or *it has*. The possessive pronoun *its* has no apostrophe.

PRACTICE PART 2.2

Apostrophes: Possessives and Contractions

Instructions: Make corrections where needed in the following sentences.

Incorrect: Its all in a days work.
Corrected: It's all in a day's work.

1. My supervisors report wont be ready until next week.
2. The weather report says its going to rain later, but I dont believe it.
3. Though its Junes responsibility, its in Jacks best interest to do that task.
4. Dr. Jones office isnt located down the hall; its next to Dr. Raines.
5. If you tell me its Tess project, i'll adjust my expectations.

Note: See page 369 or the key to the above exercise.

HYPHENS

Here are some of the primary uses of hyphens:

1. To divide words.
2. To form group modifiers.
3. To display fractions and numbers above twenty-one.
4. To form certain prefixes and suffixes.

Let's take a look at using hyphens for each of these uses.

Word Division

Computers have eliminated the need to divide words at the end of lines. However, when you need to divide a word, make sure that you divide it only between syllables.

If you are unsure of a word's syllabication, look it up: *When in doubt, check it out.* However, avoid dividing words whenever possible.

Compound Modifiers

When two or more words come together as a unit to modify a noun, place a hyphen between them. When the modifiers follow the noun, the hyphen is needed only if a modifier remains as a unit.

Modifiers Following a Noun	**Group Modifier Preceding a Noun**
The news is up to the minute.	up-to-the-minute news
The items are out of stock.	out-of-stock items
The report is two pages in length	the two-page report
The meeting is for one or two days.	the one- or two-day meeting

Writers often mistakenly omit the hyphen in compound modifiers, so here are a few more examples:

> long-term project   two-word modifiers
> first-quarter report   short-term earnings
> second-class service   first-class accommodations

When two or more compound modifiers occur in sequence, use a suspension hyphen at the end of the first modifier followed with a space:

> The short- and long-term prognoses are both excellent.
> The 30- and 60-day rates are available.

In fact, some modifier combinations have become so common that they no longer need to be hyphenated, for example:

> data processing (procedures)   high school (diploma)
> life insurance (policy)   income tax (returns)

Now let's take a look at compound numbers.

Numbers

Compound numbers from twenty-one to ninety-nine are hyphenated:

> thirty-three   forty-nine   seventy-three

Also display fractions standing alone as words, and use a hyphen:

    one-half   two-thirds   one-quarter

A hyphen is needed with some prefixes; so let's take a brief look.

Prefixes

Rules about prefixes can be complicated, but here are a few points about common uses of hyphens with prefixes:

- Use a hyphen after the prefix *self*, for example:

        self-confidence   self-esteem   self-employed

- Use a hyphen after the prefix *re* when the same spelling could be confused with another word of the same spelling but with a different meaning: [2]

I re-sent the papers.	I resent your comment.
He will re-sign the contract.	I will resign immediately.
Sue will re-lease her car.	Sue will release her car.

- Use a hyphen after a prefix that is attached to a proper noun:

ex-President Carter	trans-Atlantic flight
pro-American policy	pre-Roman period

Work on the practice below, applying the principles you have just learned.

PRACTICE PART 2.3

Hyphens

Instructions: Make corrections as needed in the following sentences to show correct use of hyphens.

Incorrect: The short term progress is good.
Corrected: The short-term progress is good.

1. Your first class treatment has impressed all of us.
2. The finance department approved one half of our budget.
3. The short and long term outlooks are quite different.
4. Twenty five people attended the conference.
5. Do you have funding for your 30 and 60 day payment schedules?

(*Note*: See page 370 for the key to the above exercise.)

Recap

Below is a summary how to use quotation marks, apostrophes, and hyphens.

➢ Use quotation marks with closed punctuation as follows:
- Place periods and commas inside of quotation marks.
- Place semicolons and colons outside of quotation marks.
- Place question marks and exclamation marks based on the meaning of the sentence.

➢ Use the apostrophe to show possession:
- With singular nouns, use an apostrophe plus *s*: *cat's meow*.
- With plural nouns, use an apostrophe after the *s*: *dogs' bones*.
- With inanimate objects, use an apostrophe, as in the *wind's force*.
- For joint ownership, place the apostrophe after the second noun: *Reggie and Grey's vacation*.
- To show individual ownership, place the apostrophe after each noun: *Janet Sue's and Toni's cars*.

➢ Use hyphens as follows:
- In group modifiers, such as *first-quarter report*.
- With numbers *twenty-one* through *ninety-nine*.
- For certain prefixes, such as *self-confident*.
- For words that would otherwise be confused, such as *re-sent*.

Writing Workshop

Topic: Measuring Your Skill Gain

To take another skills assessment, go to www.commasrule.com.

Compare your results with the pretest you took when you started your process. In what areas did you make your biggest skill gains? What areas do you still need to work on? Do you feel more confident with your writing skills?

Editing Workshop

Draft

Instructions: Edit and revise the paragraph below. Look for all types of errors and feel free to cut!

Trusts a important element of friendship. If you cant trust friends then whats really the point of being around them. Friends are they're to support you in everything that you do. They can tell you that they dont agree, but should always support you. Loyal and trustworthy friends are with you to the end and they should be treated just like family. If you learn and grow with someone, someone that you allow your feelings to open up and you can trust and beginning to share and enjoy things with. They are there threw the good times but they are there for the bad times also. A real friend understands what your going through even before you even tell them. A good friendship lasts for a very long time sometimes a life time.

Revision

> Trust is an important element of friendship. Friends support you in everything that you do. Though they may not always agree with you, they should always support you.
>
> Loyal and trustworthy friends are with you to the end, so treat them like family. If you grow with your friends and allow your feelings to open up, they will enrich your life.
>
> Real friends understand what you are going through even before you tell them. A good friendship lasts for a long time—sometimes a lifetime.

Endnotes

1. Dona Young, *Business English: Writing for the Global Workplace*, McGraw-Hill Higher Education, Burr Ridge, 2008, p. 327.
2. T. Colin Campbell and Thomas M. Campbell II, *The China Study*, Bendella Books, Dallas, 2004, p. 29.
3. William A. Sabin, *The Gregg Reference Manual*, Tenth Edition, McGraw-Hill/Irwin, Burr Ridge, 2005, p. 2

Part 3

Similar Words and Spelling Tips

Are you ready for some surprises? In all likelihood, you have been using some words incorrectly without any clue they were wrong. For example, did you know that *alright* is not a Standard English spelling? Or when was the last time you *loaned* someone something or drove *thru* the car wash?

The English language has many common words that confuse writers. These are the words that sound alike but are spelled differently and have different meanings, such as *its* and *it's* or *affect* and *effect*. These kinds of words are called *similar words* or *homophones*.

Like any skill, the only way to build your vocabulary is through practice and repetition. Use new words in context, and you are more likely to remember them. Also, practice new words until you reach a comfort zone using them.

Plan time into your daily or weekly routine to build your vocabulary, targeting ten new words at a time. Also, keep a running list of words that you are likely to misuse or misspell.

To get started, take the pretest that follows to identify the words that give you problems.

Part 3 Pretest: Similar Words

Instructions: In the sentences below, cross out any words that are used incorrectly, and write in the correct word above it or to the right of the sentence. (For the posttest, see page 356.)

1. Will that decision effect you in a positive way?
2. The principle on my loan is due on the 1st of the month.
3. My advise is for you to get a job before you buy that new car.
4. Please ensure my manager that I will return in one-half hour.
5. Its been a challenging day, but things are getting better.
6. Their are a few issues that we need to discuss.
7. The agency gave are report a new title.
8. Pat lives further from work than I do.
9. You can have a meeting everyday, if you prefer.
10. Whose going to the ballgame?
11. I enjoy movies more then I enjoy plays.
12. Megan assured that the project would be successful
13. It's alright for you to contact the manager directly.
14. I didn't mean to infer that you were late on purpose.
15. Try and be on time for the next meeting.

Note: See page 370 for the answer key to this pretest.

Spelling Tips

Only about 40 percent of English words are spelled according to phonetics, which is how they sound. For example, about 60 percent of English words are written with silent letters or other non-phonetic qualities, thereby requiring them to be memorized. These statistics help explain why learning to read and write English can be so challenging.

Here are some suggestions that you can use to improve your spelling and vocabulary usage:

- *Make a running list of words that you find challenging.*

  The way you use language is unique. Your reading, writing, and spelling skills have different strengths and weaknesses from everyone else. Become stronger by learning the specific words that challenge you. As you read, circle words that you do not understand, and take the time to look them up.

- *Subscribe to online vocabulary-building newsletters.*

  For example, Merriam-Webster (www.merriam-webster.com) has a "word of the day" as does Wordsmith (www.wordsmith.org).

- *Use new words in context: write two or three sentences with each new word.*

  To learn a new word, you must practice it in context. By writing two or three sentences, you are applying the new word in a way that will make it easier to remember and use correctly.

- *As you learn a new word, check the correct pronunciation.*

  Break up the new word into syllables and use the dictionary guidelines for pronunciation. Ask a friend to pronounce the word for you; say the word out loud several times until you feel comfortable.

- *Use spelling rules that are easy to remember.*

  Use spelling rules that you find helpful. For example, the rule "use *i* before *e* except after *c* or when the sound is like *a* as in *neighbor*" is easy to remember and helpful. However, learning complex spelling rules that have a lot of exceptions may not be as helpful. Go to the

Internet and Google "spelling rules." Glean what you need, and then move on.

- *Learn some of the Latin and Greek roots of words as well as prefixes and suffixes.*

    Learning roots, prefixes, and suffixes will help you figure out new words and gain a deeper understanding of the words you already know. A few are listed below.

A Sampling of Roots, Prefixes, and Suffixes

Root	**Meaning**	**Origin**
anthrop	man	Greek
biblio	book	Greek
cent	one hundred	Latin
equ	equal, fair	Latin
geo	earth	Greek
hydro	water	Greek
ortho	straight	Greek
psych	mind, soul, spirit	Greek
sci	to know	Latin
techn	art, skill	Greek
viv, vit	life	Latin

Prefix	**Meaning**	**Example**
a- or *an-*	not, without	amoral, apolitical
ab-	away from	abduction
ambi-	both	ambidextrous
anti-	against	antisocial
bene-	good	beneficial
bi-	two	biannual
contra-	against	contradict

de-	not	derail
dis-	not	disengage
ex-	out from	exhale
hyper-	over	hypertension, hyperactive
il-, im-, in-	not	illegal, impossible, indivisible
inter-	between	interstate
ir-	not	irreversible
macro-	large	macrocosm
micro-	small	microcosm
mis-	not	misconduct, misplace
mono-	one	monologue
post-	after	postpone
pre-	before	pretest
pseudo-	false	pseudonym
re-	again	repeat
semi-	half	semiannual
sub-	under	subversive
trans-	across	transport
un-	not	unable

Suffix	**Meaning**	**Example**
-able	able to	durable
-age	result of action	courage
-er	doer of	teacher
	more	greater
-ectomy	cutting	appendectomy
-ful	full of	peaceful
-ic, -tic, -ical	having to do with	dramatic, Biblical
-ism	the belief in	mysticism
-logy	the study of	psychology, biology

-ly or -y	like	friendly
-ment	state of	judgment
-ness	quality	kindness
-phobia	fear	claustrophobia
-ship	condition, status	ownership
-ous	full of	ridiculous

PRACTICE

Instructions: Select five Greek or Latin roots. For each root, identify two words that were developed from it.

Recap

Improving your vocabulary improves your critical thinking skills as well as your writing skills. Practice new words in context: write two or three sentences with each new word so that you can use it with confidence.

Quick Reference to Similar Words

This part contains some of the most common similar word combos. Write two or three sentences for each word that you are serious about mastering.

The part of speech for each word is indicated by the following key:

> **adj** = **adjective**
> **adv** = **adverb**
> **n** = **noun**
> **p** = **pronoun**
> **prep** = **preposition**
> **v** = **verb**

a lot   adj: much (sometimes considered colloquial)
alot   not a Standard English spelling

We have *a lot* of issues with that company.

accept   v: to receive or approve of
except   v: to exclude

Can you *accept* my apology?
Everyone *except* me attended the meeting.

access   v: to have admittance
excess   n: a surplus; adj: extra

You can gain *access* to the funds next week.
We have *excess* cheese and nowhere to put it.

adverse	adj: unfavorable, bad
averse	adj: reluctant, unenthusiastic

If you have an *adverse* reaction, get help immediately.
If you are *averse* to going to dinner, don't go.

advice	n: a recommendation (advice rhymes with "ice")
advise	v: to give advice or to make a recommendation

Please give me some *advice* about my paper.
I *advise* you to trust the writing process.

affect	v: to influence
	n: feelings
effect	n: result
	v: to bring about

When you cannot figure out which word fits, substitute its definition:

How will this *affect* (influence) you?
The *effect* (result) is good.

As a noun, *affect* refers to emotions and is used primarily within the field of psychology; as a verb, *effect* means "to cause to happen" or "to bring about," for example:

Celia was diagnosed with an *affective* (emotional) disorder.
The new law will *effect* (bring about) changes in hiring practice.
When in doubt, use *affect* as a verb and *effect* as a noun.

all right	adv: satisfactorily, very well, certainly
	adj: satisfactory, acceptable
alright	not a Standard English spelling

Everything is *all right*, so we can take a short break.
More specifically, something is either "all right" or "all wrong."

342 *A Guide for Business Writing*

altogether	adv: completely, entirely, wholly
all together	adv: a group that acts or is acted upon collectively

These are *altogether* mine.
The members were *all together* in the board room.

among	prep: together with, along with (more than two)
between	prep: among, together with (when only two are involved)

Between the two of us, who has more time?
Among the three of us, Gerry has more time.

amount	n: quantity, sum, total that cannot be counted individually
number	n: amount or quantity that can be counted individually

A large *number* of people are in the lobby making a huge *amount* of noise.

appraise	v: to assess
apprise	v: to inform

Before you *appraise* the situation, speak to Denise.
She will *apprise* you of the latest developments.

are	v: part of the verb *to be* (is, are, was, were)
hour	n: an amount of time
our	p: possessive pronoun for *we*

What *are our* options? We have an *hour* to decide.

assure	v: to give someone confidence (the object is a person)
ensure	v: to make certain (the object would be a "thing")
insure	v: to protect against loss

I *assure* you (give you confidence) that nothing is wrong.
I want to *ensure* (make certain) that nothing goes wrong.
I need to *insure* (protect against loss) this ring.

brake   n: a stopping device
break   v: to split apart

Put the *brakes* on that deal, or it will *break* up our company.

breath   n: lungful of air
breathe   v: to take in breaths

I need a *breath* of fresh air.
When I *breathe* fresh air, I feel much better.

bridal   adj: pertaining to brides
bridle   v: control, rein in, restrain

The *bridal* shower is on Sunday.
We need to *bridle* our spending.

broach   v: to raise a subject
brooch   n: a piece of jewelry

The president *broached* the subject rather gingerly.
Your *brooch* complements your jacket beautifully.

buy   v: to purchase
by   prep: near
bye   interjection: farewell as in "good bye"

Buy the outfit over there *by* the sale items.
I need to tell you *bye* until next week.

cannon   n: a gun
canon   n: body of law

The Civil War *cannon* was on display.
That *canon* explains how to solve my problem.

canvas	n: a type of rough cloth
canvass	v: to examine thoroughly

I made a *canvas* table cloth.
We need to *canvass* the area to determine potential clients.

capital	n: assets, money
	adj: most important
capitol	n: center of government

Our corporation is making a *capital* investment in stocks.
Obtaining financing is the *capital* step to advance the project.
When I visit our *capitol*, I intend to go to the Smithsonian.

censor	v: to cut, edit, or suppress "unacceptable" parts
censure	v: to criticize, show disapproval, or find fault

Parts of the movie were *censored* for young viewers.
Sonny *censured* his department for not following policy.

coarse	adj: rough
course	n: path of travel

Use *coarse* pepper for this recipe.
I'm not sure what *course* we will follow.

complacent	adj: self-satisfied
complaisant	adj: willingness to please

Micha had a *complacent* look after the deal.
Silvia's *complaisant* attitude is perfect for this job.

complement	n: something that completes
compliment	n: praise, flattering remark
	v: to flatter

Your scarf *complements* your outfit.
She *complimented* him on his suit and tie.

continual	adj: happening frequently with intervals between
continuous	adj: without interruption

The buses run on a *continual* basis throughout the night.
The woman's *continuous* talking annoyed everyone.

core	n: center, nucleus, focal point
corps	n: body, group, unit

Integrity is at the *core* of our values.
The Marine *Corps* has a code of honor.

could of	These spellings are based on colloquial pronunciation.
should of	Use *could have* and *should have*.

council	n: a group of leaders
	n: advice, guidance
counsel	n: advisor, such as an attorney
	v: advise, guide

The student *council* has authority over the dress code.
Seek professional *counsel* so that you reduce liability.

desert	n: arid region
	v: abandon
dessert	n: after dinner treat

The *desert* blooms in wintertime.
Don't *desert* your values when tempted to do wrong.
Pass up *dessert* whenever you have the will.

device	n: tool, gadget, method
devise	v: plan, develop, create

Your *device* should be patented.
When you *devise* a plan, let me know.

doesn't	v: does not (contraction); third person singular; –s form
don't	v: do not (contraction)

Speakers mistakenly use *don't* for third person singular subjects when the correct choice would be *doesn't*.

She *doesn't* have a care in the world.
    Not: She *don't* have a care in the world.

Bob *doesn't* go to school here anymore
    Not: Bob *don't* go to school here no more.

elicit	v: to draw out
illicit	adj: unlawful

We can *elicit* a response by offering them a contract.
Illicit behavior in the workplace can lead to a lawsuit.

elude	v: to escape from
illude	v: to deceive; to mock; to raise hopes and then disappoint.

The answer *eluded* me for some time.
A "bait and switch" tactic can *illude* even astute buyers.

everyday	adj: ordinary or daily
every day	each day: *every* modifies *day*; if you can insert "single" between every and day, it is two words.

That is an *everyday* routine.
We do that procedure *every (single) day*.

farther	adv: to a greater distance that can be measured: tangible distance
further	adv: to a greater degree or extent: intangible degree

She lives *farther* from work than you do.
Let's discuss this proposal *further*.

faux	adj: fake (pronounced "foe")
foe	n: enemy

In some ways, even *faux* fur hurts animal rights.
Recognize your *foe* early so you do not lose ground.

fewer than	Use *fewer* with items that you can count.
less than	Use *less* with non-count nouns.

I have 5 fewer cookies than you do.
However, you have less cake than I do.

gaff	n: a barbed spear
gaffe	n: a mistake

In the Medieval re-enactment, the soldier carried a *gaff*.
Everyone noticed the speaker's *gaffe*.

has	v. third person singular of *to have*
have	v. present tense of *to have* for all persons except third person singular

The boy *has* a cute haircut.
The boys *have* to get their hair cut.

A *block* of rooms *has* been reserved.
 Not: A block (of rooms) *have* been reserved.
The car *has* a few dents on its fender.
 Not: The car *have* a few dents on its fender.

heal	v: to cure
heel	n: the hind part of foot

To *heal* from your injury, you must rest.
The *heel* of my foot was hurt badly and was bleeding.

hoard	v: to save, stockpile, collect, or squirrel away
horde	n: a crowd, mass, or large group

Many people begin to *hoard* without realizing the consequences.
A *horde* of people awaited the verdict.

imply	v: to express or state indirectly
infer	v: to deduce, conclude, or assume

From Jim's statement, I *inferred* that I was invited to the meeting; do you think that is what he meant to *imply*?

its	p: possessive pronoun of *it*
it's	p/v: the contraction for *it is* or *it has*
its'	This form does not exist.

The building lost *its* appeal after the crime.
The dog chased *its* tail.

It's a good idea to plan for the future.
It's been a productive day for all of us.

Writing Tip

By spelling out "it is" instead of using the contraction "it's," you will make fewer spelling errors. So until you have these words mastered, do not use "it's."

lacks	v: deficient in, short of
lax	adj: loose discipline

The young girl *lacks* nothing but wants everything.
Her behavior might be a result of *lax* parenting.

lend	v: to give someone a loan
loan	n: temporary provision of money

The bank will *lend* you the money.
When you get a *loan*, expect to pay high interest.

For example, *loan* is a noun, not an action; the past tense of *lend* is *lent* (not "loaned").

loose	adj: not tight
lose	v: to misplace or to be defeated

You will feel more comfortable wearing *loose* clothing.
Did you *lose* the game?

may be	v: to suggest possibility
maybe	adv: perhaps

He *may be* the next mayor.
Maybe it will rain tomorrow.
    Not: I *maybe* able to help you.

miner	n: one who mines
minor	adj: small

Both of my grandfathers were *miners*.
That problem is *minor* compared to others.

passed   v: past tense of *to pass*: approved, accepted

past   n: earlier period, previous

adj: earlier, bygone

adv: passing or going beyond something

Jon jogged *past* the diner. As he *passed* it, he saw his friend.
In the *past*, he wouldn't have stopped.

personal   adj: individual, private

personnel   n: employees; an administrative division of an organization.

adj: relating to employees

Try not to let *personal* problems affect your work.
All *personnel* are required to attend the meeting.
There are many *personnel* issues to discuss at our meeting.

principal   n: the original amount of a debt; leader, first in command

principle   n: theory or rule of conduct

The school has a new *principal*.
What is the *principal* on your loan?
I would rather pay my *principal* than my interest.
Good *principles* will serve you well.

rain   n: precipitation, rainfall

reign   n: time in power, sovereignty

v: to have control, rule, or influence

rein   v: to curb, restrain, or control

The sound of *rain* is relaxing.
The CEO *reigns* like a king, but his *reign* will soon be over.
If he would *rein* in his power, everyone would be happier.

review   n: a critical report

v: to examine, appraise

revue   n: theatrical sketches

Be prepared for your annual *review* next week.
John's boss reviews drafts of his proposals.
When in New York, we went to a comedy *revue*.

saw   v. past tense of to see (do not use *saw* with a helper)

seen   v. past participle of to see (use *seen* with a helper)

We all *saw* Tasha enter the conference room.
   Not: We all *seen* Tasha enter the conference room.
We had *seen* that movie twice already.
   Not: We had *saw* that movie twice already.

sight   n: vision, mental perception

site   n: a location

cite   v: to quote, to name

Her *sight* was impaired due to the accident.
My Web *site* is under construction.
I *cited* the article in *Business Week* in my report.

sometime   adj/adv: an unspecified time

some time   a period of time: *some* modifies *time*; to check if it should be written as one word or two words, remove "some." If your sentence still makes sense, represent it as two words.

He said he would call me *sometime* next week.
We plan to spend *some time* on this before it is complete.
Check: We plan to spend *time* on this before it is complete.

stationary   adj: not moving

stationery   n: writing paper

A *stationary* bicycle is a good type of exercise equipment.

Our company needs new *stationery* because our logo has changed.

supposed to   v: meant to; intended to

used to   v: to express a "habit in the past"

In speech, the –ed ending of *supposed* and *used* is often left off erroneously.

You *are supposed* to attend that class.
I *used* to go to that school.
    Not: You are *suppose* to assist in the lab.

than   a conjunction used in comparisons

then   adv: referring to time, as in "after that" or "next"

I would rather get up early *than* sleep late.
When you agree, *then* I will have more time.

To help remember, use *then* when it has to do with a "when."

their   p: possessive form of *they* (*their* will be followed by a noun)

there   adv: in or at "that" place

p: an anticipating subject

they're   the contracted form of *they are*

Their apartment is next to mine.
Put the binders over *there*, next to the paper clips.
There are a lot of people in the lobby.
They're standing next to the reception desk.

themselves p: the reflexive form of *they*
theirselves not a Standard English form

They put *themselves* in a *precarious* position.

threw v: past participle of *throw*
through prep: by means of; from beginning to end; because of
thorough adj: carried through to completion
thru not a Standard English spelling; use only with "drive-*thru*"

Walk *through* the room quietly.
Jenkins *threw* the paper at the judge.
We all did a *thorough* job on the report.

to prep: toward, in the direction of
too adv: also, besides, very, or excessively
two n: a number (between one and three)

If you go *to* the club, call me *to* tell me what transpired.
We have *too* much information and *too* little time.
I will go to the meeting *too*.
We prepared *two* versions of the presentation.

try to v: attempt to
try and incorrect use of *try to*

Try to arrive before the meeting starts.

vain adj: ineffective, hopeless, worthless
vane n: weather vane
vein n: blood vessel

In my *vain* attempt to help, I created a bigger problem.
The weather *vane* on my house creaks.
The nurse looked for a good *vein* in *vain*.

354 *A Guide for Business Writing*

ware	n: merchandise
wear	v: to be dressed in
where	adv: a place

The vendor's *wares* were out of date.
If you *wear* your best, you will feel confident.
Where did you say you were going?

were	v: past tense form of *to be*
we're	contraction for *we are*

Were you aware of the issue?
We're going to address it at our next meeting.

who's	who is
whose	possessive pronoun of *who*

Who's going to the party?
Whose book is on the table?

you	p: subjective pronoun; *you* is singular or plural.
yous	In some areas, the word *yous* is used as a local language plural form of *you*, as in "yous guys."
y'all:	In southern and southwestern portions of the U.S., the equivalent to *yous* is *y'all*, with *all y'all* being used with larger groups. An additional form is *you'uns* or *you'ins*.

You all should go to the game this Friday.
While *yous* is considered colloquial in the United States, *yous* is an acceptable pronoun in Ireland.

you're	you are
your	possessive pronoun of *you*

You are more capable than you realize.
You're the best at what you do.
Your way of thinking brightens the room.

Part 3 Posttest: Similar Words

Instructions: Correct the words below that are used incorrectly.

1. The affect of that decision is not yet known.
2. When you know principle on your loan, let me know.
3. Her advise was that you take the other part-time job.
4. Can you assure the quality of your work?
5. The dog chased it's tail, amusing several children.
6. They are a few issues that we need to discuss.
7. Is that are new computer?
8. You are farther along on the project than I am.
9. We meet everyday at 3 p.m.
10. Who's book is that?
11. Sue was taller then Mary last year.
12. Melanie ensured me that we would be finished by Friday
13. Its alright for you to contact the manager directly.
14. I'm not trying to infer that you were late on purpose.

Note: See page 371 for the key to the above exercise.

Keys to Practice Exercises

CHAPTER 2

Practice 2.1

Sentence Core: The verb in each sentence is underlined twice; the subject, once.

1. The <u>order</u> <u>contained</u> too many unnecessary products.
2. <u>I</u> <u>thanked</u> the new engineer for fixing the electrical problem.
3. (<u>I</u>) <u>Thank</u> you for asking that question.
4. Our new <u>program</u> <u>will begin</u> in one month.
5. (<u>You</u>) <u>Examine</u> the order carefully before sending it out.

Practice 2.2

Redundant Subjects: The redundant subject has a strikethrough; the remaining subject is underlined once and the verb, twice.

1. My ~~friends and~~ <u>associates</u> <u>tell</u> me now is a good time to buy gold.
2. The <u>details</u> ~~and specifies~~ about the project <u>were</u> fascinating.
3. ~~Visitors and~~ <u>guests</u> <u>should sign in</u> at the front desk.
4. My <u>goals</u> ~~and objectives~~ <u>reveal</u> my dreams.
5. The <u>results</u> ~~and outcomes~~ <u>reflect</u> our success.

Practice 2.3

Redundant Verbs: The redundant verb has a strikethrough; the remaining verb is underlined twice and the subject, once.

1. Milton's <u>decision</u> ~~uncovers and~~ <u>reveals</u> his true motives.
2. Mark's <u>actions</u> ~~surprised me and~~ <u>caught</u> me off guard.
3. <u>We</u> ~~started the project and~~ <u>worked</u> on ~~it~~ **the project** for two hours.
4. <u>I</u> ~~understand and~~ <u>appreciate</u> your commitment to our mission.
5. <u>Melanie</u> ~~greeted us and~~ <u>welcomed</u> us to the banquet.

Practice 2.4

Parallel Lists

List 1:	Infinitives:	Gerunds:
1.	Order office supplies	Ordering office supplies
2.	Schedule appointments	Scheduling appointments
3.	Renew certificate	Renewing certificates

List 2: Infinitives: Gerunds:
  1. Coordinate schedules   Coordinating schedules
  2. Distribute supplies   Distributing supplies
  3. Follow up with clients   Following up with clients
     Or: Call   Calling clients

List 3: Infinitives: Gerunds:
  1. Train staff   Training staff
  2. Develop policy   Developing policy
  3. Reconcile profit and loss   Reconciling profit and loss

Practice 2.5

Real Subjects and Strong Verbs
1. Customer service needs to fill five orders.
2. An electrical problem on the fifth floor caused the outage.
3. Randy will revise the document today.
4. A new report arrived earlier today.
5. Decide tomorrow.

CHAPTER 3

Practice 3.1

Conjunctions

Answers may vary.

The construction for the 9th floor conference room was extended two more weeks, *but* we were not informed until Friday. *Therefore*, our meetings for the following week needed to be reassigned to different rooms. *However*, none were available. *Fortunately*, Jane Simmons agreed to let us use her office. *As a result*, several serious conflicts were avoided.

Practice 3.2

From Fragments to Complete Sentences

Answers may vary.
1. *I made* the right decision at the right time and *felt* good about it.
2. ~~Because~~ *He* finished the project much earlier than anyone expected.
3. ~~After~~ I made the decision to reclaim my initial investment in the stock.
4. To show interest in a project that no longer had merit *is not wise*.
5. ~~Going~~ *We went* slower than planned but ~~staying~~ *stayed* under budget.

CHAPTER 4

Practice 4.1

Rule 2: Conjunction (CONJ)

1. <u>Mary O'Rourke</u> <u>is</u> the new district manager, and <u>she</u> <u>starts</u> on Monday. CONJ
2. <u>Mary</u> <u>will be</u> an inspiration to our staff and an excellent spokesperson for our product. (no commas)
3. <u>You</u> <u>can leave</u> her a message, but <u>she</u> <u>will</u> not <u>be</u> able to reply until next week. CONJ
4. The <u>office</u> in St. Louis also <u>has</u> a new manager, and his <u>name</u> <u>is</u> Alessio Rivera. CONJ
5. <u>You</u> <u>can mail</u> your information now and <u>receive</u> a reply next week. (no commas)

Practice 4.2

Rule 3: Series (SER)

1. <u>We</u> <u>were assigned</u> Conference Rooms A and B on the first floor. (no commas)
2. <u>(You)</u> <u>Make</u> sure that you bring your laptop, phone, and client list to the meeting. SER
3. <u>You</u> <u>should call</u> your manager, arrange the meeting, and submit your proposal. SER
4. <u>Mitchell,</u> <u>Helen,</u> and <u>Sally</u> <u>conducted</u> the workshop on culinary science. SER
5. <u>They</u> <u>gave</u> a workshop for Elaine, Arlene, Donald, and Joanne on preparing, cutting, and storing vegetables. SER

Practice 4.3

Rule 4: Introductory (INTRO)

1. Because the <u>letter</u> <u>arrived</u> late, <u>we</u> <u>were</u> not <u>able</u> to respond on time. INTRO
2. However, <u>we</u> <u>were given</u> an extension. INTRO
3. Although the extra <u>time</u> <u>came</u> in handy, <u>we</u> still <u>felt</u> pressured for time. INTRO
4. To get another extension, <u>George</u> <u>called</u> their office. INTRO
5. Fortunately, the office <u>manager</u> <u>was</u> agreeable to our request. INTRO

Practice 4.4

Rule 5: Nonrestrictive (NR)

1. Our <u>manager</u> *who specializes in project grants* <u>will assist</u> you with this issue. (restrictive: no commas)
2. <u>Tomas Phillips,</u> *who works only on weekends,* <u>will call</u> you soon. NR
3. The <u>paralegal</u> *who researched this lawsuit* <u>is</u> not available. (restrictive: no commas)
4. <u>Nick Richards,</u> *who is in a meeting until 3 p.m.,* <u>can answer</u> your question. NR
5. Your new <u>contract,</u> *which we mailed yesterday,* <u>should arrive</u> by Friday. NR

Practice 4.5

Rule 6: Parenthetical (PAR)

1. <u>Customer service</u>, I believe, <u>can</u> best <u>assist</u> you with this issue. PAR
2. <u>T. J.</u>, therefore, <u>will work</u> this weekend in my place. PAR
3. Our <u>invoice</u>, unfortunately, <u>was submitted</u> incorrectly. PAR
4. The new <u>contract</u>, in my opinion, <u>meets</u> specifications. PAR
5. <u>Brown Company</u>, of course, <u>recommended</u> us to a vendor. PAR

Practice 4.6

Rule 7: Direct Address (DA)

1. (<u>You</u>) <u>Give</u> your report to the auditor by Friday, Marcel. DA
2. Jason, <u>do you have</u> tickets for the game? DA
3. Doctor, <u>I would like</u> to know the results of my tests. DA
4. <u>Would you like</u> to attend the banquet, Alice? DA
5. (I) <u>Thank</u> you for inviting me, George. DA

Practice 4.7

Rule 8: Appositive (AP)

1. <u>Jacob Seinfeld</u>, our associate director, <u>decided</u> to hire Williams. AP
2. <u>Janet Sparacio</u>, my best friend, <u>applied</u> for a job here. AP
3. <u>Jim Martinez</u>, the registrar, <u>approved</u> your request. AP
4. The <u>department chair</u>, Dr. George Schmidt, <u>received</u> your transcript. AP
5. The <u>director</u> <u>asked</u> Claire, my sister, to join us for dinner. AP

Practice 4.8

Rule 9: Addresses and Dates (AD)

1. (<u>You</u>) <u>Send</u> in your application by Friday, December 15, to be considered. AD
2. <u>San Antonio</u>, Texas, <u>has</u> a River Walk and Conference Center. AD
3. <u>Would</u> <u>you</u> <u>prefer</u> to meet in Myrtle, Minnesota, or Des Moines, Iowa? AD
4. <u>Springfield</u>, Massachusetts, <u>continues</u> to be my selection. AD
5. <u>We</u> <u>arrived</u> in Chicago, Illinois, on May 22, 2008, to prepare for the event. AD

Practice 4.9

Rule 10: Words Omitted (WO)

1. The <u>president</u> <u>shared</u> two intriguing, confidential reports. WO
2. The <u>photo shoot</u> <u>is</u> on Tuesday at 5 p.m., Wednesday at 6 p.m. WO
3. The <u>problem</u> <u>is</u>, some of the results are not yet known. WO

4. (You) <u>Leave</u> the materials with Alicia at Westin, with Sue at the Hilton. WO
5. Silvana <u>presented</u> a short, exciting PowerPoint on Italy. WO

Practice 4.10
Rule 11: Direct Quotation (DQ)
1. Patrick shouted "Get back!" before debris fell on us.
2. As Tyler stated, "All children can learn if they can find an interest."
3. My father warned me, "When you choose an insurance company, find one with good customer service."
4. As I started the race, Sharon yelled "Go for the gold."
5. Lenny said to me, "Keep your confidence, and you will do well."

Practice 4.11
Rule 12: Contrasting Expression or Afterthought (CEA)
1. You <u>will find</u> the manuscript in John's office, not in Bob's. CEA
2. Marcus <u>secured</u> the contract, but only after negotiating for hours. CEA
3. (You) <u>Chair</u> the budget committee, if you prefer. CEA
4. <u>Lester</u>, rather than Dan, <u>received</u> the award. CEA
5. (You) <u>Work</u> to achieve your dreams, not to run away from your fears. CEA

CHAPTER 5
Practice 5.1
Rule 1: Semicolon No Conjunction (NC)
1. <u>Miller</u> <u>will</u> not <u>approve</u> our expense account; <u>she</u> <u>needs</u> more documentation.
2. (You) <u>Ask</u> Bryan for the report; <u>he</u> <u>said</u> that it was completed yesterday.
3. (You) <u>Arrive</u> on time to tomorrow's meeting; (<u>you</u>) <u>bring</u> both of your reports.
4. A <u>laptop</u> <u>was</u> <u>left</u> in the conference room; <u>Jason</u> <u>claimed</u> it as his.
5. (You) <u>Recognize</u> your mistakes; (<u>you</u>) <u>offer</u> apologies as needed.

Practice 5.2
Rule 2: Semicolon Transition (TRANS)
1. <u>Carol</u> <u>suggested</u> the topic; fortunately, <u>Carlos</u> <u>agreed</u>.
2. The project management <u>team</u> <u>offered</u> assistance; however, their <u>time</u> <u>was</u> limited.
3. <u>Ken</u> <u>compiled</u> the data; therefore, <u>Mary</u> <u>crunched</u> it.
4. The <u>numbers</u> <u>turned out</u>* well; as a result, our new <u>budget</u> <u>was</u> <u>accepted</u>.
5. <u>Roger</u> <u>ran</u> in the marathon; unfortunately, <u>he</u> <u>was</u> unable to finish.

* "Turned out" is a verb phrase.

Practice 5.3

Rule 3: Semicolon Because of Commas (BC)

1. (You) Please include Rupert Adams, CEO; Madeline Story, COO; and Mark Coleman, executive president.
2. By next week I will have traveled to St. Louis, Missouri; Chicago, Illinois; and Burlington, Iowa.
3. Mike applied for jobs in Honolulu, Hawaii; Sacramento, California; and Santa Fe, New Mexico.
4. Your application arrived today; but when I reviewed it, information was missing.
5. You can resubmit your application today; and since my office will review it, you can call me tomorrow for the results.

CHAPTER 6

Practice 6.1

Regular Verbs in Past Time

1. The coach **misplaced** the roster before the game began.
2. My counselor **suggested** that I submit my resume.
3. Bart **received** the award for most valuable player.
4. Last week, no one on our team **wanted** the schedule to change.
5. When Jonika **suggested** that we meet after school, everyone was pleased.

Practice 6.2

Irregular Verbs in Past Time

1. We **saw** George the other day.
2. He **has done** a great job helping the local food bank.
3. The town council **wrote** (or **has written**) a complimentary letter about him.
4. They **brought** up a good point.
5. Even though his budget **was frozen**, George **lent** them the resources they needed.

Practice 6.3

The –S Form

1. The coach **says** that we need to practice for one more hour.
2. Our team **finishes** in first place every year.
3. Taylor **chooses** the players for both teams.
4. The coach **has** enough good players already.
5. If the group **listens** carefully, they will learn the information.

Practice 6.4

Subjunctive Mood

1. The president insisted that Melba **attend** the reception.
2. Jacob wishes he **were** on this year's team.
3. If Dan **were** your team captain, would you support him?
4. The instructions require that the package **be** sent via UPS.
5. If I **were** you, I would run for office.

CHAPTER 7

Practice 7.1

Changing Passive Voice to Active Voice

1. Sean's manager asked him to lead the diversity team.
2. Phelps' coach gave him another chance to swim in the relay.
3. Our department hosted the holiday event last year.
4. Our president implemented a new policy on reimbursement for travel expenses.
5. The mayor cancelled the program due to lack of interest.

Practice 7.2

Changing Passive Voice to Active Voice/Tactful Preference?

1. Meyers made an error in invoicing the Blackburn Account last week.
   For a tactful response, leave the sentence in the in the passive voice and take out "Meyers," the "doer" of the action.
   An error in invoicing was made last week on the Blackburn Account.
2. If you wanted to avoid an overdraft, you should have deposited your check before 4 p.m.
   Tactful response: leave in the passive voice
3. For us to issue a refund, you should have enclosed your receipt with your return item.
   Tactful response: leave in the passive voice
4. We sent your order to the wrong address; we apologize for our mistake.
5. You needed to pay your invoice by the first of the month to avoid penalties.
   Tactful response: leave in the passive voice

Practice 7.3

Changing Nominals to Active Verbs

1. Management (officially) implemented the dress policy in August.
2. Jane suggested that all new hires start on the first day of the month.
3. Our broker gave us information about that stock.
4. We discussed the new account at our last team meeting.
5. Our president announced the merger before the deal was final.

Keys to Practice Exercises 363

CHAPTER 8

Practice 8.1

Parallel Construction with Gerunds and Infinitives

Infinitives:
- Create High Performance Teams
- Develop Effective Communication Skills
- Coach for Effective Job Performance
- Resolve Conflict
- Recruit and Retain Managers
- Value Personality Differences in the Workplace
- Assess Climate in Change Efforts

Gerunds:
- Creating High Performance Teams
- Developing Effective Communication Skills
- Coaching (for) Effective Job Performance
- Resolving Conflict
- Recruiting and Retaining Managers
- Valuing Personality Differences in the Workplace
- Assessing Climate in Change Efforts

Practice 8.2

Parallel Structure

1. My manager asked me to attend the annual meeting and required that I arrive early on Friday.
2. My family will join me in Florida, and my assistant will make reservations for them.
3. Everyone is excited about the trip, but I have little free time to join them in sight-seeing activities.
4. If I can adjust my schedule, I will join them in some fun activities.
5. My boss approved the extra time, so now I (or my assistant) must change my travel arrangements.

Practice 8.3

Tense Consistency

1. The message was not clear and needed to be changed.
2. My boss said that their account was closed for some time now.
3. The new computers arrived today, so then I had to install them.
4. Yesterday my co-worker told me that was supposed to attend the budget meeting.
5. First Mary said that she wanted the position then she *said that she* didn't.

Practice 8.4

Parallel Structure

1. My boss asked me not only to complete the report but also to present it at the meeting.
2. I plan both to visit Rome and (to) see the ancient ruins.
3. Our team focused neither on winning the game nor on showing good team spirit.
4. Your motivation will help you to achieve success and to get what you want in life.
5. I have not only received the new jerseys, but now I must also pass them out.

CHAPTER 9

Practice 9.1

Pronouns

1. If you can't reach the office, feel free to call me.
2. The attendant asked Claudia and me to move to the back.
3. Fred and he collected for the local charity drive.
4. She and her manager have two more reports to complete.
5. That committee is co-chaired by Jim and me.

Practice 9.2

Pronouns

1. Mark said to split the data sheets between you and **me**.
2. The problem has nothing to do with me—it's between you and **him**.
3. The decision is between Bob and **you**.
4. You can split the work between Margaret and **me** so that it gets done on time.
5. Between Bob and **me**, we have our work cut out for us.

Practice 9.3

Pronouns

1. Willow has more time than **I do**.
2. The other team has more resources than **we do**.
3. Bob has a nicer car than **I have**.
4. Massimo should get the job if he is more competent than **I am**.
5. I'm taller than **he is**.

Practice 9.4

Who/ Whom

1. **Who** wrote the monthly report?
2. **Whom** are you going to the meeting with?
3. Is Alleso the person **who** spoke with you?
4. The doctor **who** saw you yesterday is not available.
5. Every person **who** arrives late will be turned away.

Practice 9.5

Indefinite Pronouns

1. Neither of the proposals **is** ready to send out.
2. None of our stores **open** early on Saturday.
3. Everyone should make **his or her** own reservations.
4. Some of the papers **list** the correct date.
5. All of our assignment **has** been completed on time.

CHAPTER 10

Practice 10.1

Pronoun-Antecedent Agreement

1. When employees call in sick, they should give a reason for their decision.
2. When servers do not relate well to their clients, they need more training.
3. Nurses go beyond their job description when they assist a patient's guests.
4. Flight controllers' jobs are challenging because they work long hours under difficult conditions.
5. When customers do not have a receipt, they not should necessarily expect to return items easily.

Practice 10.2

Pronoun Consistency

    I enjoy working on team projects because **I** learn so much from **my** teammates. **Team members need** to be helpful because they never know when they will need assistance from **their** colleagues. ~~When you are on a team, every~~ All members need to carry their weight. That is, teammates who do not do **their** share of the work can be a burden to the entire team and jeopardize their project.

    Team members who stay motivated are more valuable to the team. I always strive to do my best because **I** never know when **I** will need to count on **my** team members.

Note: Answers may vary.

CHAPTER 11

Practice 11.1

Editing for empty information, redundancy, and outdated expressions

1. We hope ~~and trust~~ that as a valued customer you find our services helpful ~~and worthwhile~~.
2. Our new ~~breakthrough in~~ design makes our laptop even more ~~perfect~~ effective than it was before.
3. The ~~final~~ outcome of this project depends on each ~~individual~~ employee doing his or her best.
4. Before you finish this step ~~to go on to the next step in the process~~, please review ~~and examine all~~ the items in your shopping cart.
5. We want you to be ~~absolutely~~ certain that you have not ordered multiple items that are ~~exactly~~ alike.

Practice 11.2

Redundancy and Outdated Expressions

1. Attached ~~please find~~ are the papers that you requested.
2. You have our ~~complete and absolute~~ confidence, and we ~~appreciate and~~ value our business alliance.
3. As ~~per our discussion~~ we discussed, the new policy should be ~~received and~~ reviewed this week.
4. You can ~~completely~~ eliminate any questions ~~or problems~~ by sending your agenda ~~early~~ in advance of the meeting.
5. ~~I would like to~~ Thank you ~~in advance~~ for your ~~cooperation,~~ support~~, and assistance.~~ (or assistance).

Practice 11.3

Simplifying

1. We ~~are utilizing~~ use that product, and the marketing department ~~is cognizant of~~ knows about our choice.
2. ~~Subsequent to~~ After the merger, we have ~~endeavored~~ tried to compromise as much as possible.
3. As ~~per your~~ requested, ~~the inclusion of~~ we are including that information in the report.
4. If the merger ~~is contingent~~ depends upon our ~~utilization of~~ using their facilities, we should ~~endeavor~~ try to change locations.
5. If you are ~~cognizant~~ aware of their objections, ~~endeavor to~~ make ~~respective~~ changes.

Practice 11.4

Misplaced Modifiers

1. While Joanie gave her report, a phone began to ring in her briefcase.
2. In my opinion, you should feel certain about facts before you sign the contract.
3. Can you confirm that they might back out of their agreement?
4. Speak to my friend from college who specializes in energy conservation.
5. I suggest that you speak to the person who knows about this topic.

CHAPTER 12

Practice 12.1

Tone and *You* Viewpoint

1. Would you like for me to assist you with the Baker project?
2. Please complete and return the enclosed paperwork by Friday so that you are officially on our payroll.
3. Your dedication to the project is exemplary.
4. What do you think about the merger?
5. Does this project interest you?

Practice 12.2

Writing in the Affirmative

1. We can change your health insurance after you make your request in writing.
2. When you do respond positively, everyone else does too.
3. By asking the question, you have a chance of getting an answer.
4. If you plan to apply for the job, turn in your application now.
5. The sooner you act, the more likely you will be considered for the job.

CHAPTER 13

Practice 13.1

Information Flow

1. One of the reasons that our economy has shifted is a change in consumer spending patterns.
2. A topic that you might consider for your next paper is outsourcing jobs to third-world countries.
3. The department's new assistant is the applicant who graduated from Indiana University Northwest.

4. The topic of today's meeting is a budget revision that needs to be completed by next week.
5. As you complete your report, please consider the cost as well as the time required to make the revisions.

PART 1

Practice Part 1.1: Capitalization

Next year the president of my company will provide a financial incentive for all employees, and I plan to participate in it. Jack Edwards, vice president of finance, will administer the plan. Everyone in my department is looking forward to having the opportunity to save more. A pamphlet entitled, "Financial Incentives for Long-term Savings," will describe the plan and be distributed next week. If the pamphlet has not arrived by Friday, I will check with the vice president's office to find out the details.

Practice Part 1.2: Numbers

1. We are meeting on January 5 at 10 a.m. at our offices on Lake Street.
2. Call me on Monday at 407-555-1212.
3. Alex lists his address as 407 South Maple Street, Hobart, IN 46368.
4. We received hundreds of calls about the job opening but only five résumés.
5. Purchase 12 laptops but only 7 new printers for our department.

PART 2

Practice Part 2.1: Quotation Marks

1. My answer to your request is an enthusiastic "yes."
2. If you think that's a "good idea," so do I.
3. The code was "307A," not "370A."
4. All he wrote was, "Our dog can hunt."
5. If you call that "good timing," I don't know how to respond.

Practice Part 2.2: Apostrophes: Possessives and Contractions

1. My supervisor's report won't be ready until next week.
2. The weather report says it's going to rain later, but I don't believe it.
3. Though it's June's responsibility, it's in Jack's best interest to complete the task.
4. Dr. Jones's (or Dr. Jones') office isn't located down the hall; it's to Dr. Raines' (office).
5. If you tell me it's Tess's (Tess') project, I'll adjust my expectations.

Practice Part 2.3: Hyphens

1. Your first-class treatment has impressed all of us.
2. The finance department approved one-half of our budget.
3. The short- and long-term outlooks are quite different.
4. Twenty-five people attended the conference.
5. Do you have sufficient funding for your 30- and 60-day payment schedules?

PART 3 PRETEST: SIMILAR WORDS

1. Will that decision **affect** you in a positive way?
2. The **principal** on my loan is due on the 1st of the month.
3. My **advice** is for you to get a job before you buy that new car.
4. Please **assure** my manager that I will return in one-half hour.
5. **It's** been a challenging day, but things are getting better.
6. **There** are a few issues that we need to discuss.
7. The agency gave **our** report a new title.
8. Pat lives **farther** from work than I do.
9. You can have a meeting **every day**, if you prefer.
10. **Who's** going to the ballgame?
11. I enjoy movies more **than** I enjoy plays.
12. Megan **ensured** that the project would be successful
13. It's **all right** for you to contact the manager directly.
14. I didn't mean to **imply** you were late on purpose.
15. Try **to** be on time for the next meeting.

PART 3 POSTTEST: SIMILAR WORDS

1. The **effect** of that decision is not yet known.
2. When you know **principal** on your loan, let me know.
3. Her **advice** was that you take the other part-time job.
4. Can you **ensure** the quality of your work?
5. The dog chased **its** tail, amusing several children.
6. **There** are a few issues that we need to discuss.
7. Is that **our** new computer?
8. You are **further** along on the project than I am.
9. We meet **every day** at 3 p.m.
10. **Whose** book is that?
11. Sue was taller **than** Mary last year.
12. Melanie **assured** me that we would be finished by Friday
13. **It's all right** for you to contact the manager directly.
14. I'm not trying to **imply** that you were late on purpose.

PRE-ASSESSMENT KEYS

Pretest 1: Grammar Skills

1. The issue should remain between Jim and yourself.
2. If you want the promotion, take their recommendations more serious.
3. Your department did very good on last week's report.
4. The funds in our department will be froze until next quarter.
5. Thank you for inviting Charles and I to the discussion.
6. The customer should of enclosed the check with the application.
7. Her and her manager will achieve their goals by working together.
8. They gave us the project at the most busiest time of the month.
9. Mr. Brown asked you and I to design the workshop.
10. My supervisor has spoke about that policy many times.
11. Everyone in the marketing department felt badly about the problem.
12. The new accounts should be divided between Bill and I.
13. Seth is the person that made the referral.
14. If you have more experience than myself, you be the project director.
15. If Tim was available, he would accept the challenge.
16. The manager has not yet given the information to no one.
17. When you need assistance, call Joe or myself.
18. We would have been pleased if the pilot project had went better.
19. Don't Ms. Becker need to approve the proposal before we accept it?
20. Ed, along with his team, are going to the conference.

1. you
2. seriously
3. well
4. frozen
5. me
6. have
7. She
8. ~~most~~ or busy
9. me
10. spoken
11. bad
12. me
13. who
14. I do
15. were
16. anyone
17. me
18. gone
19. Doesn't
20. is

Pretest 2: Punctuation Skills

1. If you are unable to attend the meeting, find a replacement immediately.
2. Should, Bob, Jesse and Marlene discuss these issues with you?
3. As soon as we receive your application, we will process your account.
4. Your new checks were shipped last month; therefore, you should have received them.
5. Will you be attending the seminar in Dallas, Texas, later this year?
6. Fortunately, my manager values my efforts and believes in my ability.
7. Mr. Anderson, when you have time, please review this contract for me.
8. We received his portfolio on May 15, and we promptly developed a new strategy.
9. Ali brought her report to the meeting; however, it was not complete.
10. Ms. Suarez sent a letter to my supervisor; the letter was very complimentary.
11. The merger, however, required that each corporation learn to trust the other.
12. Thank you, Mrs. Dodd, for supporting our quality assurance efforts.
13. I am not sure about the costs, but I recommend we consider this proposal.
14. You must file your application by July 15, 2012, to meet all requirements.

Pretest 3: Word Usage Skills

1.	The policy changes will effect every department in the company.	1. affect
2.	The total amount reflects your principle and interest.	2. principal
3.	He ensured his manager that the project would be completed by June.	3. assured
4.	T he title of the report did not accurately reflect it's content.	4. its
5.	Our assets may not be sufficient for the bank to loan us the capital we need.	5. lend
6.	The finance department has to many policies to consider before the merger.	6. too
7.	There interests are not being taken into consideration.	7. Their
8.	What references do you plan to site?	8. cite
9.	You can reach me this Wednesday some time in the afternoon.	9. sometime
10.	We ensure the quality of all items we carry.	10. assure

Pretest 4: Editing Skills

1. Bob was the right person for the job because he is the most qualified.

   Verb tense: Bob was the right person for the job because he was the most qualified.

   Or: Bob is the right person . . . he is . . .

2. The supervisor asks that every manager report their findings by the 15th of the month.

   Pronoun consistency: The supervisor asks the every manager report his or her . . .

   Or: The supervisor asks that all managers report their . . .

3. Improving writing skills promotes critical thinking, ~~will~~ *enhances* career opportunities, and *develops* confidence.

   Parallel structure: Improving writing skills promotes critical thinking, enhances career opportunities, and develops confidence.

4. Working right up to the deadline, Marie's presentation was finally completed.

   Dangling modifier: Working right up to the deadline, Marie finally completed her presentation. Or: As she worked right up to the deadline, Marie's presentation . . .

5. The contract was negotiated by the attorney and corporate representatives for hours.

   Active voice: The attorney and corporate representatives negotiated for hours.

6. Concerned managers asked for changes in company policies, are appealing recent decisions, and will plan to schedule a meeting to discuss their recommendations.

   Parallel structure: Concerned managers *asked* for changes in company policies, *appealed* recent decisions, and *scheduled* a meeting to discuss their recommendations.

7. Management will begin the implementation of the new policies in June.

   Nominalization: Management will implement the new policies in June. (Or "begin to implement")

8. Account managers purchased new software from a reliable source that cost only $2,000.

   Misplaced Modifier: Account managers purchased new software that cost only $2000 from a reliable source.

9. It is Gerald's recommendation that the executive committee take into consideration the proposal.

   Weak sentence core: Gerald recommended that the executive committee consider the proposal.

10. Per our discussion, the corrected form is being sent to you by our customer service department.

    Outdated phrases/active voice: As we discussed, our customer service department is sending you the correct form.

INDEX

A

abbreviations, 185, 208, 268, 270, 316
   a.m. and p.m., 315
   clear, accurate language, 185
   text, 270, 274
   two-letter state, 317
action plan, 229
a lot/alot, 341
all, 143
and (see coordinating conjunctions)
   comma conjunction, 53
accept/except, 341
access/excess, 341
action plan, 229
action verbs (chart), 92
active voice, 109-114
addresses and dates (commas), 66
adverbial conjunctions, 41, 44-45
adverse/averse, 342
advice/advise, 342
affect/effect, 342
AIDA Model, 249
all right/alright, 342
all together/altogether, 343
although, 43
among/between, 343
amount/number, 343
another, 143
anybody, 143
anyone, 143
apologizing, 186-188
apology, 246-247
   apologies necessary, 186-188
   letter of, 247
   direct approach, 246
apostrophes, 326-328
   contractions, 328
   inanimate possessives, 328
   possessives (singular and plural), 326-328
appositive (commas), 64
   nonrestrictive, 64-65
   restrictive, 65
apprise/appraise, 343
are/hour/our, 343
articles (capitalization), 261
attached please find, 164
as soon as, 43
assure/ensure/insure, 343
audience, 3, 5, 152, 182, 185, 310
   and voice, 11-12
   global communications, 311
   managers and peers, 12
   persuasive communication, 219, 225-226, 234
   proposals, 250, 255
   reader expectations, 10

B

background thinking, 7, 170, 179
bad/badly, 99
bad news messages, 188-190
   e-mail, 268
   indirect message, 214, 215
base form (verb), 27, 33, 93, 125
because, 43
because of comma (semicolon), 76, 80
benefit of the doubt, 10, 176, 180, 271
blame, 242, 271
   blame game, 10, 176
   team writing, 259
blocked letter format, 209
bold typeface, 193, 200, 202, 254
Boomers, 178-179, 185
both, 143
brake/break, 344
branding, 234
breath/breathe, 344
bridal/bridle, 344
broach/brooch, 344
Buckingham, Marcus, 172

Index 375

bullet points and numbering, 201
but (see coordinating conjunctions)
buy/by/bye, 344
Byron, Katie, 14, 102

C

cannon/canon, 344
canvas/canvass, 345
career portfolio, 277-278
cohesive, coherent paragraphs, 194-196
contractions, 282
capital/capitol, 345
capitalization, 224, 268, 305-310
   all caps, 200
   after a colon, 82
   after *note* or *caution*, 262
   articles, 307
   common nouns, 306
   conjunctions, 307
   e-mail, 268
   first words, 308
   hyphenated terms, 308
   organizational titles, 309
   prepositions, 307
   proper adjectives, 306
   proper nouns, 306-307
   titles, 309
Carnegie, Dale, 226
caps, 200
censor/censure, 345
claims, 241-244
clause, 22-24
   dependent, 22
   independent, 22
   that, 101
   who, 59
client relationships, ix, 176-177, 190, 224, 250
   diversity, 177-182
   micro-messages, 9-10
   persuasive writing, 224
   proposal writing, 250

   trust, 176, 227
closings (letters), 208, 266
coarse/course, 345
colon, 81-83
   after salutations, 82
   sentences (following), 82
   illustrating lists or words, 82
comma conjunction, 53
comma rules, 52-71
   addresses and dates, 66
   appositives, 64
   conjunction, 53
   contrasting information or afterthought, 70
   direct address, 63
   direct quotation, 68-69
   introductory, 57
   nonrestrictive, 58-59
   parenthetical, 60
   sentence core rules, 52
   series, 55
   words omitted, 67
comma rules (chart), 71
communication,
   client relationships, 176-182
   and diversity, 177-182
   face-to-face, 10, 32, 271
   trust, 176, 227
complacent/complaisant, 345
complaints, 241-244
complement/compliment, 345
complete subject, 25
composing, 1
   composing vs. editing, 2
   planning tools, 3-4
compound sentence, 32
compound numbers, 330
computer settings (for letters), 207
conciseness, 157-171
   background thinking, 179
   eliminate the obvious, 163
   legalese, 165

opinions and beliefs, 170
outdated phrases, 163-164
redundant modifiers, 160-161
redundant pairings, 159
simple language, 166
vague nouns, 162
verb add ons, 160
conjunction (comma), 53
Conjunction Junction (Sesame Street), 41
conjunctions, 41-45
    adverbial, 44-45
    coordinating, 42
    correlative, 129
    importance of, 41-42
    subordinating, 42-44
consequently, 44
continual/continuous, 346
contractions, 270, 328
contrasting information (comma), 70
coordinating conjunctions, 41, 42
    comma conjunction, 53
copy notations, 208
core/corps, 346
correlative conjunctions, 129, 130
could of/should of, 346
council/counsel, 346
cover letter
    proposals, 249
creative process, 2-6
credibility, 228
critic/criticism, 13-15
    fear of, 14
culture/cultural diversity, 180
    high context, 180
    low context, 180
Curry, Jane, 218
customer loyalty, 230
    customer feedback, 230
    disenfranchised customers, 231

D

Da Vinci, Leonardo, 117, 166, 191

dangling modifier, 169
Darwin, Charles, 277
dash, 83-84
    em dash, 83
    en dash, 84
dependent clause, 22, 46
    comma, 57
    fragment, 46
desert/dessert, 346
device/devise, 346
Dewey, John, xi
diversity, 177-182
    analytic /global learners, 182
    cultural, 180
    generational, 178-179
    micro-messages, 177
    personal, 180-181
    and reader expectations, 10
direct address (comma), 63
direct quotation (commas), 68
don't/doesn't, 347
due to the fact that, 164

E

e-mail, 199, 210-211, 263-274
    abbreviations (using), 315
    capitalization, 310
    closings, 266
    contractions, 328
    facts, 264
    formatting, 210-211, 265
    guidelines, 268-269
    hyphenated, 308
    paragraphing, 199
    salutations, 265
    text messaging, 270
    thinking points, 270-274
    white space, 267
each, 143
Edited English, 91, 95, 100
editing, 2, 158
    voice, 11-13

Editor's Block Type A, 1-2
Editor's Block Type B, 1-2
Einstein, Albert, 110
elevator speech, 298
elicit/illicit, 347
Ellington, Duke, 244
ellipses (ellipsis marks), 84-85
    quotations, 85
    spacing, 84-85
elude/illude, 347
em dash, 83
emphatics, 167-168
empty information, 197
en dash, 84
enclosure notation, 208
enclosed please find, 164
every day/everyday, 347
exclamation point, 69, 82, 84, 279

F

face-to-face communication, 10, 32, 271
farther/further, 347
faux/foe, 348
favors, 237-239
fax cover sheet, 212
fear of criticism, 14
feasibility memo, 240-241
feedback, 14, 196,
    asking for feedback, 286
    criticism, 14
    customer feedback, 230
feel (bad), 99
feelers/thinkers, 181-182
few (see plural indefinite pronouns)
fewer than/less than, 348
fishbone diagramming, 4-5
focused writing, 4
for example (see adverbial
    conjunctions)
formal persuasion, 224
formatting, 199-201, 205-212
    all caps, 200

bold, 200
bullet points, 201
computer settings, 207
e-mail, 210-211
fax, 212
italics, 200
features and marks, 200-201
letters, 207, 208-209
numbering, 201
parentheses, 200
quotation marks, 69, 200
underscore, 200
fragment, 46
    correcting, 46-47
Frankl, Victor, 90
freewriting, 4

G

gaff/gaffe, 348
generational diversity, 178-179
    Boomers, 178-179, 185
    GenXers, 179
    Nexters, 179
    Veterans, 178
gerund, 27
    gerund phrase, 33, 34, 46-47
Giovagnoli, Melissa, 288
Golden Rule, 10, 176
good/well, 99
Google, 115
Gordon, Karen, 24
Greek roots, 338
Greenbaum, Sidney, 40
grammatical subject, 25, 110

H

has/have, 348
heal/heel, 348
hedges, 167-168
Hemingway, Ernest, 15
hence (see adverbial conjunctions)
Hierarchy of Needs (Maslow's), 226

hoard/horde, 349
however, 44
Hudson, Frederick, 38
hypercorrect, 133
hyphens, 329-331
    compound modifiers, 330
    numbers, 330
    prefixes, 331
    suspension hyphen, 330
    word division, 329

I

I (personal pronoun), 134
I understood subject, 25-26
I viewpoint, 152-153, 183, 196
    and paragraphing, 196
    and tone, 183
if, 43
imperative mood, 99
implied subject, 25
imply/infer, 349
inanimate possessives, 282
indefinite pronouns, 143-144
independent clause, 22
indicative mood, 99
indirect quotation (and comma), 68
indirect message (bad news), 214-215
informal persuasion, 220-223
intensive case pronouns, 134
infinitive, 27
    infinitive phrase, 33, 34, 46-47
information flow, 197-198
    empty information, 197
    old to new information, 197-198
inside address, 208
introduction/body/conclusion, 242
introductory (comma), 57
irregular verbs, 96-96, 104-106
    chart, 106
    irregular verb inventory, 104-105
    irregular verb chart, 106
    past time, 95

standard verb tenses, 107
italics, 200
its/it's, 349

J

jargon, 185
job search tools, 277-298
    business cards, 288
    cover letters, 290
    job-search letters, 290
    networking, 289
    quick skills pitch, 298
    thank-you letters, 292
    transferrable skills, 279-285
    résumé (chronological), 294-295
    résumé (electronic), 296-297
journal, vi, 12
    joy journal, 202
    memoir, 18
    sample journal, 18
journaling, 17
    freewriting, 4
journalist's questions, 5

K

King, Dr. Martin Luther, 123

L

lacks/lax, 350
Latin roots, 338
learning gaps, 15
legalese, 165
Leider, Richard J., 234
lend/loan, 350
letterhead, 208
letters (business), 207-209
    bad news (indirect), 188-190, 214-215
    basic parts/business letter, 208
    basic structure (CTA), 213
    blocked letter style, 208-209
    connect-tell-act, 213

cover letter, 251, 290
direct message, 214
follow-up letter, 292
indirect message, 214
simplified letter style, 244
standard business letter, 208-209
thank-you letter, 292
white space and balance, 206
linking verbs, 98-99
local language, 91, 95, 100
loose/lose, 350

M

main clause, 22
many, 143
marketing letters, 248
Maslow, Abraham, 226
Maslow's Hierarchy of Needs, 226
may be/maybe, 350
McLean, Pamela D. , 38
Meister Eckhart, 202
memoir, 18
micro-messages, 9-10, 170
    benefit of the doubt, 10
    trust, 10
mind mapping, 3
miner/minor, 350
misplaced modifiers, 167-169
modifiers, 33, 98,
    dangling, 169
    emphatics, 168
    hedges, 168
    redundant modifiers, 160-161
modify correctly, 170
modify sparingly, 168
mood (verbs), 99

N

neither, 143
new information, 197
networking, 278, 289
    business card, 288

follow-up letters, 292
    online, 278, 289
Nexters, 179
no conjunction (semicolon), 76, 77
no one (see indefinite pronouns)
nominals, 114-117
nominalization, 114
none, 143
nonrestrictive information, 58-59
    commas, 58-59
nor (see coordinating conjunctions)
notwithstanding, 165
noun, 22, 24, 33
    common, 306
    nominals, 114-117
    parallel structure, 124-125
    possessive, 2326-328
    proper, 306-307
    vague, 162
number usage, 312-317
    addresses, 315
    basic number rules, 312-314
    dates and times, 315
    phone numbers, 315
    two-letter state abbreviations, 317
numbering (and bullet points), 201
numbers (hyphenated), 330

O

objective case pronouns, 134
old information, 197
opinions (leave out), 170
or (see coordinating conjunctions)
organizational titles (capitalization), 309
others, 143
outdated phrases, 163-164

P

page mapping, 4
paragraphing, 193-199
    cohesive, 194
    coherent, 194, 196

parallel structure, 34, 123-130
   adjectives, 126
   clauses, 127
   correlative conjunctions, 129
   infinitives, 124-125
   gerunds, 124-125
   nouns, 124-125
   phrases, 126-127
   verb tense, 128
   verbs, 123
parenthetical (comma), 60
parenthetical expression, 60
   and writing style, 62
parentheses, 200
passed/past, 351
passive voice, 111-117
   full passive, 113-114
   nominals, 114-117
   truncated passive, 113-114
   tact, 113-114
   tone, 113-114
past subjunctive, 100
per, 12, 164
   our discussion, 164
perfect tense, 107
perfect progressive tense, 107
perfect writing, 15
personal/personnel, 351
personal diversity, 180-181
   feelers, 181
   thinkers, 181
persuasion (formal), 224
   action plan, 229
   audience 225
   benefits, 228
   credibility, 229
   evidence, 228
   motivation, 226
   purpose, 225
   resistance, 227
persuasion (informal), 219, 220-224
   guidelines for, 221-224

persuasive communication, 219-233
   process of persuasion, 220
   informal persuasion and trust, 220
   guidelines for informal persuasion, 221
persuasive writing, 237-259
phrase, 33-34
   gerund, 33
   infinitive, 33
   prepositional, 33
planning tools, 3
   mind mapping, 3
   fishbone diagramming, 4
   freewriting, 4
   focused writing, 4
   journalist's questions, 4
   page mapping, 4
Platinum Rule, 10, 176
plural indefinite pronouns, 143
point of view (pronouns), 147-153
   and antecedent agreement, 148-150
   and consistency, 150-153
   and voice, 152
positive focus, 184, 190
possessive pronouns, 134
possessives, 326-327
   inanimate, 327
   singular, 326-327
   plural, 326-327
Powell, Colin, 15
predicate, 27
   simple, 27
   complete, 27
prefixes, 329, 331, 337-339
prepositions, 33, 134, 307
   capitalization of, 307-308
prepositional phrase, 33
present subjunctive, 100, 101
pre-writing, 2
principal/principle, 351
prior to, 164
problem statement, 5
progressive tense, 107

pronouns, 133-134
    antecedent agreement, 148-152
    consistency, 150-152
    cases, 134
    following *between*, 138
    following *than*, 139-140
    hypercorrect, 133
    indefinite, 143
    intensive, 134
    objective, 134
    personal, 134
    possessive, 134
    subjective, 134
    subjects vs. objects, 135-137
    reflexive, 134
    viewpoint, 150-154, 183, 196
    who, whom, that, 141-142
proposal writing, 249-257
proposals (formal), 251-254
    letter proposals, 254-257
punctuation
    conjunctions, 41
    comma rules, 51-70
    dashes, 83
    ellipses, 84
    and flow, 85
    semicolon rules, 76-80
    open style, 278
    closed style, 278
    and style, 62, 85-86
purpose, 1, 6-9, 17, 158
    bad news messages, 188, 190
    business communications, 9, 176
    communication, 176,
    creates context, 6
    e-mail, 238, 268
    letters, 213-214
    micro-messages, 9
    and process, 6-8
    persuasive communication, 225
    proposals, 252
    purpose statement, 216, 401
    put purpose first, 6, 7, 158, 232, 238
    as vague noun, 162

Q

quantum learning, 15-16
quotations, 68-69
    direct, 68
    indirect, 68
    punctuation with, 68-69
quotation marks, 69, 200, 323-325
    colons, 69, 278
    commas with, 69, 324
    direct quote (DQ) comma, 68
    exclamations, 325
    periods, 69, 324
    questions, 69, 325
    quotation within quotation, 325
    long quotes, 325
    semicolons, 69, 324
    short quotationss, 69, 325

R

rain/reign/rein, 351
reader expectations, 10
real subject, 26, 110
redundant modifiers, 160-161
redundant pairings, 159
reflexive case pronouns, 134
resistance, 227
restrictive information, 58-59
restricted appositive, 65
résumés, 294-297
    chronological, 294-295
    electronic (e-résumés), 296-297
review/revue, 352
request for proposal (RFP), 223, 250, 251
routine requests, 237-239

S

Sabin, William A., 90

Safani, Barbara, 295
sales letters, 248
salutations, 208, 265
sarcasm, 185, 269
saw/seen, 95, 352
self-criticism, 14
self-talk, 102
semicolon, 75-80
semicolon rules, 76
   because of comma, 79-80
   no conjunction, 76-77
   transition, 76, 78-79
semicolon rules (chart), 87
sentence, 21-22
   compound sentence, 32
   definition of, 22
   sentence structure, 21-37
sentence core, 21-24, 35
   importance of, 35-36
   and punctuation, 52
   sentence core rules, 52
sentence length, 13
series (comma), 55
several, 143
side headings, 199
simple tense 107
simplified Letter Style, 244
sight/site/cite, 306
similar words, 335, 341-356
simple language, 166
simple subject, 25
singular indefinite pronouns, 143
slang, 12, 185, 268
   and quotation marks, 323
some, 143
some time/sometime, 352
spacing after a period, 202
state abbreviations (two-letter), 317
state of being verbs, 29, 98-99
   feel (bad), 99
   linking verbs, 98-99
stationary/stationery, 353

style, 85, 118, 119,
   analytic and global learners, 182
   communication styles, 178-182
   complicated style, 146
   concise, 2
   and conjunctions, 41
   cultural diversity, 180
   generational diversity, 178
   and grammar, 22
   and formatting, 205
   and punctuation, 52, 85
   and process, 119
   tone and meaning, 118
   voice and audience, 11
subject lines, 233
subjects, 24-27
   complete subject, 25
   compound subject, 30
   grammatical subject, 25
   implied subject, 25-26
   simple subject, 25
   understood subject, 25-26
   real subject, 26
subjective case pronouns, 134
subjunctive mood, 99-101
   past subjunctive, 100
   present subjunctive, 101
subordinating conjunctions, 41, 42
supposed to/used to, 353

T

team writing, 258-259
text messaging, 270, 310
   capitalization errors, 309
   and e-mail, 185, 270
   Nexters, 179
than/then, 353
thank you again, 164
thank you in advance, 164
thank you notes, 292
that clause,
that/who/whom , 141-142

their/there/they're, 353
themselves/theirselves, 354
therefore, 44
thinkers/feelers, 180-181
through/threw/thorough/thru, 354
trust, 9, 176-177, 220
Timm, Paul, 230-233
tone, 175-190
    client relationships, 176
    diversity, 177-182
    micro-messages, 177
    Platinum Rule, 176
    trust, 176
to/too/two, 354
try to/try and, 307
topic sentence, 194
topic string, 194-195
truncated passive, 113-114
trust, 10, 176, 271
    benefit of the doubt, 10
    micro-messages, 9-10
two-letter state abbreviations, 317
Twain, Mark, 145, 157
Tyler, Ralph W., xi, 145

U

understood subject, 25-26
underscore, 200
utilization, 12, 166

V

vague nouns, 162
vain/vane/vein, 354
values (core), 38
verb add ons, 160
verbs, 27-29, 91-107
    action verbs (chart) 92
    base form, 27
    compound verbs, 31
    imperative mood, 99
    indicative mood, 99
    infinitive, 27

irregular verb chart, 106
irregular verb inventory, 103
linking verbs, 98-99
past participle, 93
past subjunctive, 100
past tense, 93
past time, 93-96
perfect tense, 107
perfect progressive tense, 107
present subjunctive, 101
progressive tense, 107
regular verbs, 93
-s form, 97
simple tense, 107
state of being verbs, 98-99
strong verbs, 33-34, 91, 92, 243
subjunctive mood, 99-101
tenses, 107
verb charts, 92, 106, 107
verb tenses, 107
    simple tense, 107
    perfect tense, 107
    perfect progressive tense, 107
    progressive tense, 107
Veterans, 178-179
viewpoint (pronoun), 147-153
    consistency, 150
    I,/you/ we, 152
    voice, 152
visual persuasion, 205-213, 232
    business letters, 208-209
    e-mail messages, 210-211
    headings and subheadings, 232
    paragraphing, 232
    subject lines, 233
    white space and balance, 206, 267
voice, 11
    active/passive, 109-117
    critical, 14

W

ware/wear/where, 355

well/good, 99
we viewpoint, 152
were/we're, 309
while, 43
white space, 1, 8-9, 49, 206, 223
    balance, 206
    computer settings, 207
    e-mail, 267
    headings and subheadings, 232
    letters, 208-209
    side headings, 199
William of Ockham, 163
Williams, Joseph M., 122
who/whom/that, 141-142
who's/whose, 355
Wilde, Oscar, ix, 51
words omitted (comma), 67
writing process, 2
    style and process, 119
writing style, 85
    punctuation and flow, 85
    style, tone, and meaning, 117

Y

yet (see coordinating conjunctions)
you viewpoint, 152, 183
    passive voice, 153
you/yous/y'all, 355
you're/your, 355
You understood subject, 25-26

Made in the USA
Charleston, SC
14 October 2012